W9-BNU-604

Pastry 2010
in europe

index

Meditations 5
Profile Yves Thuries 6
Restaurant Oaxen Krog 14
Restaurant L'Arnsbourg 18
Avant Garde RED 22
Mol d'Art 34
City Profile: Vienna 38
Frescati 48
Jelly Gums 52
City Profile Copenhagen 58
Restaurant Bourglinster 70
Restaurant Maison Pic 76
Koppert Cress 84
Spices in pâtisserie 88
Liers Vlaaike 92
City Profile Berlin 96
Marshmallows 110
Irish Soda Bread 114
Chocolate and Spices 118
Dobla 122
Restaurant Maison Troisgros 126
City Profile Florence 129
Meringues 136
Gâteau Battu 140
Wedding Cakes 144
Avant Garde Yogurt 150
Sausage roll 156
City Profile Zürich 160
Puff Pastry 172
Soft Friandises 180
Italian Bread 186
Avant Garde Coffee 194
Profile Zeeland 200
Confitures 214
Macrons d'Amiens 218
Christmas Pudding 222
Hostellerie de L'Illberg 226
Restaurant Vendôme 228
Restaurant Lameloise 232
Chicory 236
Wine Vin de Paille 242
Granité 246
Wine Monbazillac 248
PIE Around the World 252
Map of Europe 254

Colofon

Pastry in Europe is an annual edition
of Culibooks Inc. bvba
Picardielaan 22, B-2970 Schilde – Belgium
phone +32 33 80 17 00
fax +32 33 80 17 10
www.PastryInEurope.com
info@pastryineurope.com

Directors
Norbert Koreman, Carine Van Steen,
Joost van Roosmalen

Publisher/Chief Editor
Norbert Koreman

Assistant Chief Editor
Joost van Roosmalen

Edting Team
Danny Jansen, Philippe Schroeven,
Hans Heiloo

Photography
Norbert Koreman, Dirk Kerstens, Peter Staes

Administrator
Carine Van Steen

Design
Geert Dijkers

Translations
Elly Driessen, Don Genova

Pastry in Europe has been carefully edited and accumulated. Neither the publisher nor editors are responsible for the complete accuracy of information, which is only meant to give explanation. Therefore they will not accept any liability whatsoever, derived from the reader's interpretation and actions or decisions, based on the given information.

The required ingredients in this book will not always be available worldwide. The law in certain countries might even restrict some ingredients, materials, equipment and techniques. Therefore we advise you to strictly abide by the rules and regulations in your country.

Metric system
The recipes given are based on the metric system, which is used all over the European continent. Please refer to the conversion table on our website: www.pastryineurope.com.

meditations of the chief-editor

Our previous edition of Pastry in Europe 2009 has been introduced worldwide. We have been on the European market for fifteen years with our famous magazines Culinaire Saisonnier and Pâtisserie & Desserts, so we know Europe inside out. However we didn't know how PIE 2009 would be received in the rest of the world. When the book was printed and shipped to North America we didn't know what to expect, but it became a very impressive year for us as the book was sold in 70 different countries. We had great help from different blogs that gave us fantastic reviews on our book. We also got lots of support from famous gourmands like Joël Robuchon, Ferran Adrià, Heston Blumenthal, Myrtle Allen, Grant Achatz, Nobuyuki Matsuhisa (Nobu) and many others who showed our pink book. When it was announced that we had received the award as Best Dessert Book of Belgium, at the Gourmand World Cookbook Awards, it was the icing on the cake. PIE 2009 is now nominated for the world finale in Paris. As Pastry in Europe 2010 went into print we didn't know the results, but we are waiting with great anticipation. I like to thank everyone who has been part of this success.

Our Pastry in Europe book will show you new developments of Europe on an annual basis, from super classic to ultra modern. What makes Europe so interesting? The old world consists of dozens of countries where many languages are spoken. Almost every country can be divided in smaller regions. Europe has hundreds of large and smaller cultures. Take for example the Netherlands. Here we have people from the provinces of North and South Holland, Brabant, Limburg, Friesland and Zeeland, each with its own culture and background. In an even smaller country like Belgium three different languages are spoken! In France it is a sin to compare the Alsace with Bretagne, the same in northern Italy that is totally different than Sicily.

Our editors are always traveling to these countries and regions to discover the traditions, but also to get to know the top chefs of these countries. We have a fascinating profession and are happy to share our adventures with you.

Norbert Koreman
Publisher

Yves Thuriès

There are many famous names in the French Pâtisserie world. From Carème to Lenôtre, numerous people have contributed to the recognition of French pastry. However, there is one name that stands out among the others. It is someone who wears many hats: pâtissier, cook, chocolatier and publisher.

His life story starts in 1938 in the region of Tarn in the south of France, when Yves is born at the family bakery. He grew up in the bakery and when he was 14 years old he started the famous learning process, "Tour de France". He apprenticed in many French cities until he was drafted into the military. As a soldier he experienced the war of Algeria but after 30 months he continued his "Tour de France". Yves went to Toulouse to learn sugar work and then moved on to Paris and Strasbourg to continue his pastry education. In 1968 he started working for Monsieur Jantou, who owned a small pastry shop in Gaillac. Yves buys this business and his adventure starts.

Sharing

Proof that Yves is a skilled professional comes in 1976 when he achieved something that never happened. He received the highest national title: Meilleur ouvrier de France (best craftsman in France as pâtissier and as chocolatier-icecream maker). At that time he starts to write his first book and even does his own photography. Years later this book became a 12-volume series and was translated in several languages with a distribution of 200,000 copies. This book series was the foundation and is now a collector's item for which people pay very high prices. What is his secret? "In those days chefs and pâtissiers would never reveal their

recipes. I was the first one who did that. It is important that you share your knowledge with others. I am somebody who likes sharing ideas with other people." While he is working on his book series, he moves to Cordes-sur-Ciel, the village he still calls his home. When he arrived there, this village was deserted and dilapidated, but Yves revives it. In his village he buys hotel-restaurant Le Grand Écuyer that introduces him to the warm kitchen. In the meantime he has started shops in Africa and the United States, but that is not where the adventures stop. In 1988 his first Thuriès Gastronomic Magazine hits the market and is still referenced in culinary circles. It's another way to share his passion with others.

We would need a full page to mention all the prizes and honorable awards Yves Thuriès has received. What we really like about him is that he has stayed a humble and kind individual. He is not pretentious and most important to him is genuine professionalism and passion for top presentations in every way. In 1989 he opened a museum in Cordes-sur-Ciel with sugar as the theme. "The profession of working with sugar had almost disappeared and I wanted to give it a push."

Another passion is chocolate. For that we drive with him to Marssac. We were almost in shock seeing what he calls his chocolaterie: a building of 4000 square metres! "Here we create our own mixes. Chocolate is like wine, it's about terroir and mélanges." All the chocolate products that are made in Marssac are sold in their own stores. In France alone he owns 40 stores.

Philosophy

We continue our conversation with Yves in a small café in Marssac. We want to know more about his philosophy in life. This man has achieved so much that cannot just be luck. What is it? Yves: "It's not about winning everything. You have to be there at the right time, not too early and not too late. I know what I want and I have never started something I was not sure about. But I have always worked hard with the opportunities I had. It is important to work hard, it keeps you healthy."

After a glass of good beer Yves suggests that we continue our discussion in the intimacy of his private home in Cordes-sur-Ciel. It is a castle-like building at the very top of the village. Yves has made an atelier in the castle tower. That's where he paints. The house is full of art from the old masters to avant-garde. This man hasn't just a passion for his profession, he has a broad horizon. "If you do something you should enjoy it, but to be successful you need good people around you. How you deal with people is the key to your success." With two hotel-restaurants, a chocolate factory, over 50 stores, a museum and a publishing company for magazines, Yves has an entourage of more than thousand people. Wherever we go we see smiling faces and hard workers. At an age where most people are retired, Yves starts with new initiatives. He has associated himself with Alain Ducasse to start a school of pâtisserie: the École Nationale Supérieure de la Pâtisserie d'Yssingeaux.

How does the old master see the future of this profession? "Pâtisserie has evolved very well in the last 40 years. Contrary to the warm kitchen, this is a stable profession with security. The warm kitchen has been evolved world wide, but the pâtisserie will always remain French." There is no-one in pâtisserie comparable to him. We can think only of one honorable award: Thuriès is the Paul Bocuse of pâtisserie.

Chocolate Mousse

***Ingredients:* 8 egg whites, 125 g sugar, 4 egg yolks, 200 g chocolate, 30 g butter.**

Beat egg whites and sugar with a whisk and add egg yolks. Melt chocolate au bain-marie and add the butter. Carefully mix beaten egg whites with the chocolate, put in piping bag and fill glasses. Cool for three hours in the fridge.

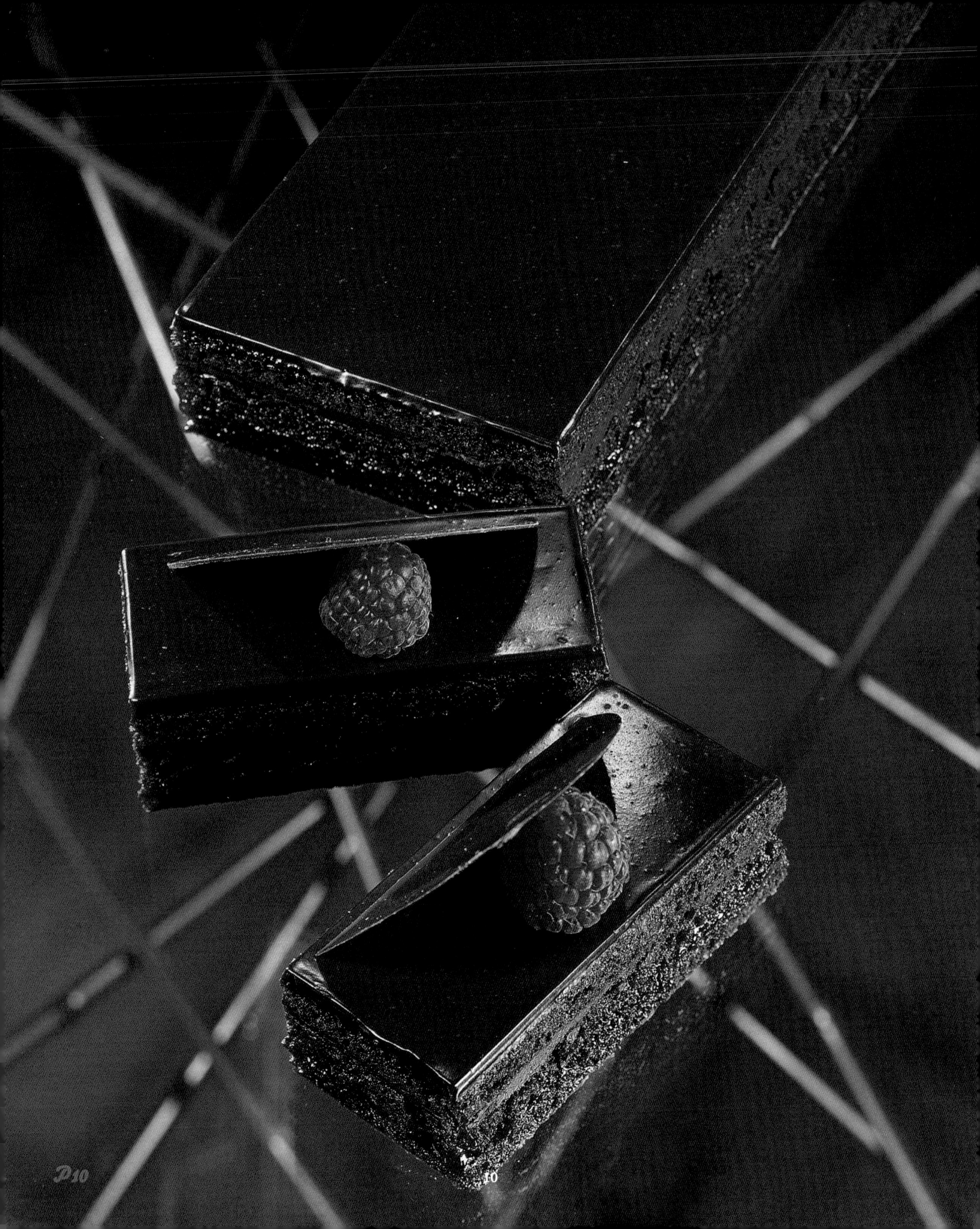

Sacher

Ingredients: **750 g raspberry jam, dark chocolate, chocolate frosting, fresh raspberries, chocolate garnish.**
For the cake biscuit: **800 g raw almond paste, 300 g icing sugar, 6 eggs, 25 egg yolks, 120 g cocoa powder, 10 egg whites, 200 g sugar, 850 g flour.**
For the ganache: **500 g dark chocolate, 600 g cream, 60 g glucose, 60 g butter.**
For the syrup: **1 litre syrup of 30° Baumé(1 litre water with 1.250 kg sugar) 250 g rum.**

For the cake, mix almond paste and icing sugar in a KitchenAid together with eggs and egg yolks. Carefully add the sifted flour and cocoa powder. Beat egg whites and sugar and add to the almond paste mixture. Add melted butter. Weigh dough in portions of 700 grams, put on a sheet of parchment paper (60 x 40 cm) and repeat. Bake in the oven at 220°C/430°F. For the ganache, melt chocolate and slightly heat the cream. Pour glucose on the melted chocolate; add the warm cream and cut up butter. Process quickly. Heat syrup a little bit and add the rum. Take a slice of cake and cover with a thin layer of chocolate. Put in a frame of 60 x 40 x 5 cm. Drench with 500 g syrup and spread raspberry jam on top. Put 250 g syrup on the next slice of cake. Place this on the previous slice and drench again with 250 g syrup. Put a layer of 700 g ganache on top and let rest for a few minutes. Put another slice of cake, drenched with 250 g syrup, on top of the ganache. Cover with the rest of the ganache and put in the fridge. Cover the entire surface with chocolate frosting, remove from frame and cut in small tarts with a warm knife. Decorate with raspberries and chocolate garnish.

Chocolate truffle

Ingredients: **700 g cream, 100 g glucose, 50 g trimoline, 800 g chocolate 70%, 180 g butter, cocoa powder**

Cook cream with glucose. Chop chocolate in small pieces and pour trimoline on top. Add the glucose-cream and reduce the temperature to 35°C/95°F, mix well and add the butter. Using a piping bag, make a roll of 1 cm in diameter and cut pieces of 1.5 cm long. Pull through melted chocolate and roll in cocoa powder.

Plate no 6

Small warm tart, runny heart of Equator chocolate and crunchy brownies

For ten people:
For the heart: **190 g chocolate couverture 72% (Equator), 120 g cream, 60 g dried brownies.**
For the small tart: **280 g chocolate couverture 67% (Equator), 275 g butter, 9 eggs, 320 g sugar, 120 g flour.**

For the heart, melt chocolate with cream, add dried brownies, mix well, pour in small silicon molds and freeze. For the tarts, melt chocolate au bain-marie together with butter. Beat egg yolks with sugar and add to the chocolate. Add sifted flour and let rest for 6 hours in the fridge. Butter small forms and sprinkle with sugar. Pour some cake batter on the bottom, place a heart in the center and cover with batter. Put in freezer. Bake tarts in oven for 6.5 minutes at 195°C/385°F. Sprinkle with icing sugar and dried brownie crumbs. Serve immediately

Caramelized apple tatin with apple caramel cinnamon ice cream

For 10 people:
***For the caramelized apple:* 6 Golden Delicious apples, 300 g sugar, 50 g butter, 10 g rum, 250 g puff pastry.**
***For the ice cream:* 300 g apple caramel cinnamon coulis, 90 g milk, 190 g water, 30 g Grand Marnier.**
***For the caramel with salted butter:* 180 g sugar, 100 g cream, 80 g butter, fleur de sel.**

Core and peel apples and cut in 8 parts. Make caramel with sugar. Fry apple pieces in butter until golden. Pour caramel on it, deglaze with rum and cook for a few more minutes. Pack apple pieces in silicon molds of 12 x 3 cm and bake in the oven for 10 minutes at 150°C/300°F. Press apple firmly and freeze. Roll puff pastry to 2 mm thick and bake between two baking sheets for a few minutes at 210°C/410°F. Cut in rectangles of 12 x 3 cm.
For the ice cream, heat coulis with milk, water, and Grand Marnier. Pour in a Frix or Paco beaker and freeze. For the caramel cook sugar until it is dry, deglaze with cream, then add butter, some fleur de sel and a drop of water; set aside. Take apples from the molds and place on puff pastry. Heat everything in the oven at 100°C/210°F for a few minutes. Glaze tarts with caramel and garnish plate with caramel as well. Place half of the small tart on the plate with a quenelle of ice cream. Decorate with physalis and dried vanilla.

White peach candied with star anise and fresh basil sorbet

***For 10 people:* 5 white peaches, candied basil leaves, star anise.**
***For the syrup:* 3 litres water, 400 g sugar, 100 g brown sugar, 40 g fresh basil, 5 pieces star anise, 45 g lemon juice.**
***For the sorbet:* 500 g water, 500 g white wine, 230 g sugar, 60 g lemon juice, 15 g basil leaves, 4 g gelatin (2 leaves).**

Prepare syrup with above mentioned ingredients. Place peach halves in a Gastrovac and pour syrup over it. Vacuum to 1 bar and wait 2 hours. Raise temperature to 47°C/116°F and let simmer for 3.5 hours Reduce pressure, remove peel from the peaches and let peaches cool in the syrup. For the sorbet, prepare the syrup with water, white wine, sugar, lemon juice and basil. Bring everything to a boil and let sit in the fridge for 24 hours. Heat syrup to 45°C/113°F, add gelatin and pour in a Frix or Paco beaker. Put in the freezer. Quarter the peaches. Put 3 pieces in a glass with a quenelle of sorbet. Garnish with the candied basil and star anise.

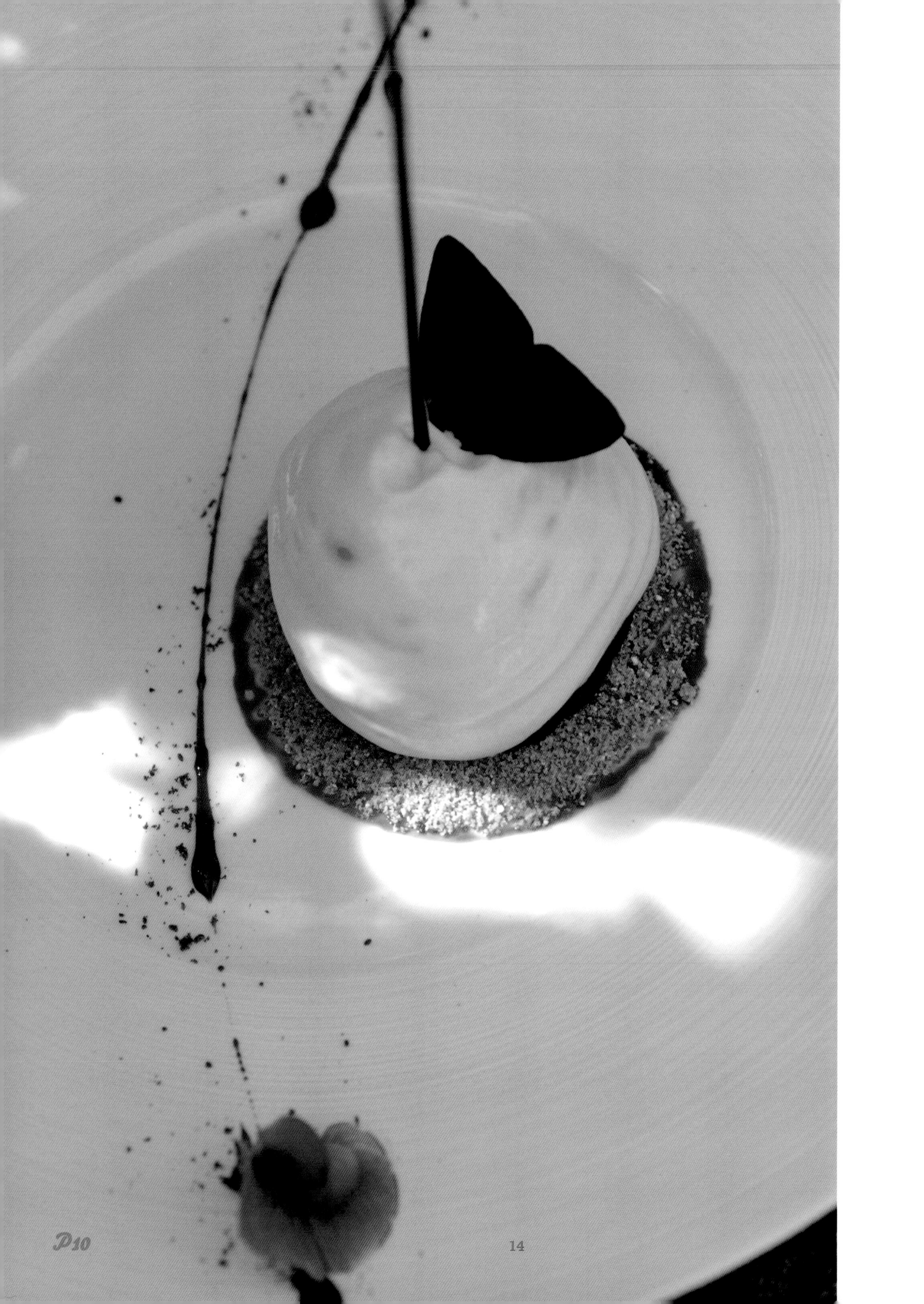

Magnus Ek
Oaxen Krog

A trip to Oaxen Krog is more than going out for dinner, it is a total experience. Oaxen is located on a very small island with fascinating vistas. Here you will enjoy genuine Swedish hospitality and a kitchen that is incomparable.
World top-100 chef Magnus doesn't like to be rated in a box but we feel that he belongs to the top three in Scandinavia. This chef is constantly looking for the roots of the Swedish kitchen. The classics are translated in modern versions, but the traditions are still respected.
The restaurant is only open from early spring to fall, the rest of the year there is too much ice and snow so the doors are closed.

Pudding of cottage cheese with a crust of white nougat and burnt sugar

For the pudding: 100 ml milk, 400 g cottage cheese, 17 g egg, 2 egg yolks, 20 g sugar, half a leaf of gelatin, 100 ml cream, 11 g stabilizer.
For the jam: 70 g raspberries, 5 g sugar.
For the white nougat crust: 25 g butter, 1 egg, 100 ml sugar, 90 g flour, 1 tsp baking powder, 50 ml milk, 100 g white praline paste.
For the ice cream: 5 g potato starch, 200 g milk, 4 egg yolks, 1¼ leaf of gelatin, 350 g cream.
For the burnt sugar: 114 g glucose syrup, 2 tbsp water, 16 g sugar.

For the pudding combine cheese, egg, egg yolks and sugar and pour in the Thermomix set at 65°C/150°F. Dissolve soaked gelatin in it and cool. Add cream and stabilizer. Pour mixture in a siphon and attach a charger. Let rest for one night and shake well before use. For the jam boil all ingredients and reduce to a syrupy consistency. For the crust, beat egg and sugar fluffy, add the milk, the flour and the baking powder and mix well. Pour batter in a cake form and bake in the oven at 175°C/350°F for 12 minutes. Invert the cake, crumble it and mix with the praline paste. Spread on a baking sheet and bake at 160°C/320°F for 10 minutes. Cool and crumble again. For the ice cream, bring milk and starch to a boil, pour in a Thermomix, add egg yolks and sugar and process on medium speed at 65°C/150°F to get a strong composition. Dissolve the soaked gelatin in the mixture and pour in Paco or Frix beakers and spin. For the burnt sugar, caramelize sugar and water, add the glucose and cool. Using a metal ring, put some nougat powder on the plate, lay a little jam on it and generously pipe pudding over it. Spoon a few strips of burnt sugar on the side and garnish with small edible flowers from your garden.

Structure of blueberries and licorice root

For blueberry ice cream: 5 g potato starch, 75 g cream, 5 egg yolks, 40 g sugar, 350 g blueberry puree, 50 g cream.
For the granité: 75 g sugar, 250 ml blueberry puree, 1 star anise, 15 g Spanish chervil, 250 ml water.
For the macaroons: 49 g egg white, 19 g sugar, marrow of 1 vanilla bean, 100 g icing sugar, 56 g almond powder.
For the blueberry cream: 100 ml sugar, 4 egg yolks, 12 g potato starch, 100 ml blueberry puree, 100 ml lightly whipped cream.
For the licorice root powder: 2 Tbs sugar, 15 g butter, 20 g flour, 10 g ground licorice root.

For the ice cream bring cream and potato starch to a boil, pour in the Thermomix and add egg yolks and sugar; mix at 65°C/150°F. Pour in

beakers and spin. For the granité bring all ingredients to a boil, except for the chervil, pour in a shallow bowl, add the chopped chervil, freeze and stir regularly with a fork. For the macaroons, beat egg white with sugar, mix the rest of the ingredients and combine with the foam.
Pipe foam in drops on a baking sheet and bake macaroons in the oven at 130°C/265°F for 20 minutes.
For the berry cream, bring puree close to a boil. In the meantime beat sugar, egg yolks and potato starch and add the hot puree. Put back on the heat and prepare as an anglaise. Let cool and using a spatula, stir whipped cream in it. Make a dough with all ingredients for the licorice root powder. Bake 2/3 of it in the oven at 160°C/320°F, cool, crumble, mix with the unbaked dough and sprinkle on parchment paper. Let dry overnight and crumble to a fine powder. Spoon granité on a plate and lay a scoop of ice cream and macaroon on top. Draw strips of cream on the plate and sprinkle with licorice powder.

Jam of green tomatoes with cream puffs, cream cheese ice cream and cocoa meringue

For the tomato jam: 6 green tomatoes, 100 g sugar, 100 ml glucose syrup.
For the cream puff batter: 100 ml water, 33 g butter, 12 g sugar, 70 g flour, 2 eggs.
For the cream cheese ice cream: 2.5 grams potato starch, 100 ml milk, 50 g egg yolk, 33 g sugar, ½ leaf of gelatin, 175 g cream cheese, 25 g milk.
For the vanilla cream: 120 g sugar, 2 egg yolks, 10 g flour, 100 ml cream, marrow of 1 vanilla bean.
For the meringue: 50 g egg white, 150 g sugar, 50 g water, 1 tsp cocoa powder.

Cut and peel tomatoes. Boil sugar with the glucose until it gets colour, add the tomatoes and cook again. Take tomatoes out of the syrup and bring liquid to a boil at 119°C/245°F. Cool. Pour in the blender with the tomatoes and let rest in the fridge overnight. For the cream puffs make a classic batter and pipe small amounts on a baking sheet.
Bake cream puffs in the oven at 180°C/355°F for 10 minutes. Cool and slice before serving.
For the ice cream bring milk and starch to a boil, add egg yolks and sugar, pour in the Thermomix and process at 65°C/150°F. Dissolve the soaked gelatin in it and carefully add the cream cheese. Pour mixture in beakers and spin before serving.
For the vanilla cream, keep 50 ml cream aside and make an anglaise with the rest of the ingredients. Cool and mix with the 50 ml cream; whip before serving. For the meringue boil sugar and water to 121°C/250°F and beat egg whites to stiff peaks. Add syrup one drop at a time and beat until cold to get a tough foam. Blend in cocoa powder last. Spread a thin layer of meringue on a baking sheet and bake for 6 minutes in the oven at 160°C/320°F. Turn heat down to 60°C/140°F and dry a while longer. Crumble the meringue. Spoon some vanilla cream on the plate and sprinkle generously with the meringue crumbs. Add a good size quenelle ice cream and put a cream puff on the side. Finish with a quenelle of jam, small herbs and flower leaves.

Jean-Georges Klein

L'Arnsbourg

The 3-star restaurant L'Arnsbourg in Baerenthal, member of our own club Les Amis Saisonnier and owned by Jean-Georges Klein, is very special. And we are not talking about the beautiful location or the modern interior. We are talking about the kitchen that is classic as well as ultra modern. Guests can dine here on classic dishes with a German or French influence or treat themselves to lots of trendy techniques and all kinds of flavours. The creations of this pâtissier are recognized by his signature dish: the butterfly tuille.

Mascarpone tart with anise flavour and a sorbet of vodka

For 10 people: fennel powder, dried brioche crumbs, double cream, dill tips, olive oil with lemon, 10 butterfly tuilles.
For the mascarpone tart: 125 g mascarpone, 125 g milk, 62 g cream, 3 g kappa (tapioca), 45 g sugar, 2 g agar-agar.
Dill syrup: 500 g water, 75 g sugar, 1 bunch dill, 1 g agar-agar.
For the vodka sorbet: 300 g water, 50 g glucose, 50 g sugar, 200 g vodka, 1 gelatin leaf.

For the tart, heat all ingredients and pour in a shallow dish. Cool and cut in rectangles of 4 x 3 cm and cover immediately with brioche crumbs. For the syrup, bring water and sugar to a boil and simmer dill for 4 hours; put through a fine-mesh sieve. Add agar-agar, bring to a boil and pour in a bowl. Stir now and then to get a semi-jelled syrup. For the sorbet make a syrup of water, glucose and sugar and add the soaked gelatin. Add the vodka and spin in the turbo machine. Spoon syrup in a soup plate and sprinkle some olive oil over it. Place tart in the syrup with a quenelle of sorbet. Finish with a few drops of cream, small dill tips and fennel powder.

Textures of brownie

For 10 people: candied lemon zests, roasted pistachio nuts, shaved white chocolate, 10 chocolate Florentines.
For the passionfruit gel: 250 g passionfruit pulp, 25 g sugar, 2 g agar-agar, 1 g gellan.
For the crème anglaise: 500 g whipping cream, 100 g egg yolk, 100 g sugar, 1 vanilla bean sliced open, 2 gelatin leaves.
For the brownie powder: 120 g butter, 60 g couverture 66%, 100 g egg, 175 g sugar.
For the chocolate ice-cream: 250 g milk, 250 g cream, 100 g egg yolk, 90 g sugar, 140 g couverture 72%.

Bring all ingredients for the gel to a boil. Whisk with a hand blender and cool. Then whisk again with the hand blender and let cool completely.

Make a classic crème anglaise with the ingredients and combine with soaked gelatin. Make a dough with the brownie ingredients and bake in the oven at 170°C / 340°F for 45 minutes. Open oven door, let dry for 3 hours at 100°C / 210°F. Freeze brownies and when frozen grind them to a powder. Turn ice cream into an anglaise and dissolve the chopped chocolate in it. Pour mixture in frix beakers and spin immediately. Put a bit of the gel in the centre of a soup plate and fill plate with the crème anglaise. Sprinkle brownie powder over top and garnish with shaved white chocolate, pistachio nuts, lemon zests, a florentine and a quenelle of ice cream.

Rhubarb and strawberry terrine

For 10 people: **1 kg peeled rhubarb, 800 g washed strawberries, chopped almonds, strawberry coulis, 10 butterfly tuilles, 8 gelatin leaves, 500 g freshly grated coconut.**
For poaching liquid: **1 litre water, 200 g sugar, 300 g almond syrup.**
For yuzu ice-cream: **500 g milk, 125 g sugar, 50 g egg yolk, 125 g cream, 150 g yuzu fruit. (Yuzu is an Asian citrus fruit).**

Boil ingredients for the poaching liquid and reduce to a syrup. In it, poach whole rhubarb stalks until cooked and cool. Heat 1 litre of the liquid and dissolve the soaked gelatin. Divide rhubarb and strawberries neatly on a rectangle plate, cover with the gel and let set in the fridge. Put coconut in a Thermomix, run it at the highest speed until it becomes liquid. Spread liquid on a silpat, using a template to create rectangles and set aside when cold. For the ice cream, make an anglaise, let cool and mix with the yuzu juice. Pour mixture in Frix beakers and spin immediately. Cut small squares of the rhubarb-strawberry terrine and place a coconut cookie against it. Place a quenelle of ice cream on one side of the plate and garnish with chopped almonds and a butterfly tuille. Finish with a line of strawberry coulis.

A walk through the forest

For 10 people: **600 g blackberries, small young fir buds, 10 butterfly tuilles.**
For the anglaise of fir needles: **500 ml milk, 6 egg yolks, 120 g sugar, bourgeons de sapin (liqueur made of young fir buds).**
For the sorbet of bourgeons de sapin: **1450 g sugar, 400 ml water, 250 g fresh fir buds, 200 g boiled lemon juice.**
For the marjoram waffles: **150 g cream, 25 g milk, 2 egg yolks, 10 g sugar, 90 g flour, 50 g melted butter,2 egg whites, 20 g sugar, 15 g marjoram powder, dash of salt.**

Make a classic anglaise and add liqueur to taste. Set aside until it is very cold. For the sorbet, boil water and sugar to a syrup, infuse with fir buds and add lemon juice. Pour through a fine-mesh sieve and pour inFrix beakers and spin immediately. For the waffles mix cream, milk, egg yolk, sugar, salt and flour to create a smooth batter. Pour through a sieve and add the melted butter. Beat egg whites and sugar till fluffy and spoon carefully through the batter. Slowly add the marjoram and bake waffles with a waffle iron. Pour crème anglaise in a soup plate with the blackberries, fir needles and a good size quenelle of ice cream. Place butterfly tuille on top and set a waffle, cut in two, on the edge of the plate.

Red

A colour full of flavour and love

Culiversum is a company run by Jeroen van Oijen where they develop products and concepts to inspire gastronomy. Culiversum likes to inspire passionate chefs as well. Ideas that come from innovative projects are used again to look at "average" products to being developed and work with these in different ways. It is very obvious that both sides can learn a lot from each other. In this article Jeroen shares his passion for colour and taste of red fruits and vegetables.

Culiversum, Food, design and innovation
www.culiversum.nl

Tasteful colours

Red is an intense colour. Love, the devil, blood, danger, speed and erotica, all of these are expressed visually by this attractive colour. While red is usually applied to express beauty and love, it's totally in but also totally out. Red supports the power of fast cars, but ironically is also the colour to stop overzealous drivers. But in the kitchen the colour red is an all time favourite and loved for its decorative character. Just think of vegetables like red peppers, beets, tomato, red cabbage and rhubarb, or fruits such as strawberry, raspberry, red currants, blood orange, watermelon or other exotic fruits. In this article we will show how red fruit, but definitely also red vegetables, can make a dessert much more appealing and reach a higher level.
There are infinite possibilities, but we will feature the most interesting and trendy ones. To give you an idea how to apply the structures, we developed a dessert where the colour red will be the heart of the matter. Of course taste and experience remain the most important goal, but the visual aspect will always be part of the experience of the food.

Segments of raspberry

Ingredients: **fresh raspberries, liquid nitrogen, silicon paper.**
Note: *before you start working with liquid nitrogen, read all the safety instructions you will find in Pastry in Europe 2009 and follow the instructions of the supplier.*

Carefully drop the desired quantity of raspberries in the liquid nitrogen; once they have reached the bottom, they will be totally frozen. Take them out of the liquid nitrogen and put them between two sheets of parchment paper. Move a rolling pin over it so all the juice releases from the small pockets and separates. Transport to a small container and put in freezer to reach the desired temperature. NEVER serve it straight from the nitrogen, as the coldness will be extreme!

Gel of red fruit

Ingredients: **200 g red fruit puree, 50 g sugar water 1:1, 2.5 g agar-agar.**

Bring all ingredients to a boil, pass through a fine mesh sieve and cool to gel. Whisk in blender to get a glossy gel.

Strawberry spaghetti

This spaghetti can be made with any liquid, but make sure it has good flavour and a very low dose of agar-agar. To make this spaghetti, a special set is available at specialized wholesalers.

Ingredients: **250 g strawberry coulis, 50 g water, 100 g sugar water 1:1, 7 g agar-agar.**

Bring all liquids and agar-agar to a boil. Pass through a sieve and remove foam with a spoon. Fill a syringe full of liquid and squeeze the content in small silicon tubes. Immediately immerse in ice water to gel. Squeeze the spaghetti out of the tubes using a siphon with a special adapter.

Dry strawberry toffee

Ingredients: **180 g crystal sugar, 125 g glucose, 150 g whipping cream, 100 g reduced strawberry coulis, 50 g unsalted butter, 40 g maltodextrine.**

Boil sugar, glucose, reduced coulis and butter to 110°C/230°F. Pour on a silpat and cool to room temperature. In a KitchenAid, mix 100 g of the obtained caramel with maltodextrine to get a dry powder. Serve powder as part of a dessert or serve separately as a pre-dessert. The flavour can be enhanced with a dash of sea salt.

Cherry paper

***Ingredients:* 500 g cherry puree (maximum 10% sugar)**

Reduce puree by half. Cool to 40°C/104°F and spread a very thin layer on small silpats using a pallet knife. Dry in the oven for three hours at 50°C/120°F. Take out of the oven and immediately pull the sheets from the silpats. Let harden and keep in a tight container with silica grains.

Instantly prepared cherry sponge cake

***Ingredients:* 50 g almond powder, 100 g cherry coulis, 125 g pasteurized egg white, 80 g pasteurized egg yolk, 50 g sugar, 65 g flour, 12 g reduced cherry juice.**

Mix all ingredients in a blender to a smooth consistency. Pour through a fine mesh sieve in a half-liter siphon. Attach two chargers (N20) and put aside. Take small carton cups and pierce a little hole in the bottom.
Fill cups 1/3 full with the mixture and put 50 seconds in the microwave. Cool for one minute and cut the cups open.

Ice cold pearls of watermelon and red vodka

Using a melon baller, make balls from the watermelon and mix with sugar water and red vodka. Put in the freezer so they will get ice cold. Serve as part of a dessert or as a pre-dessert. The best temperature to serve at is -7°C/20°F.

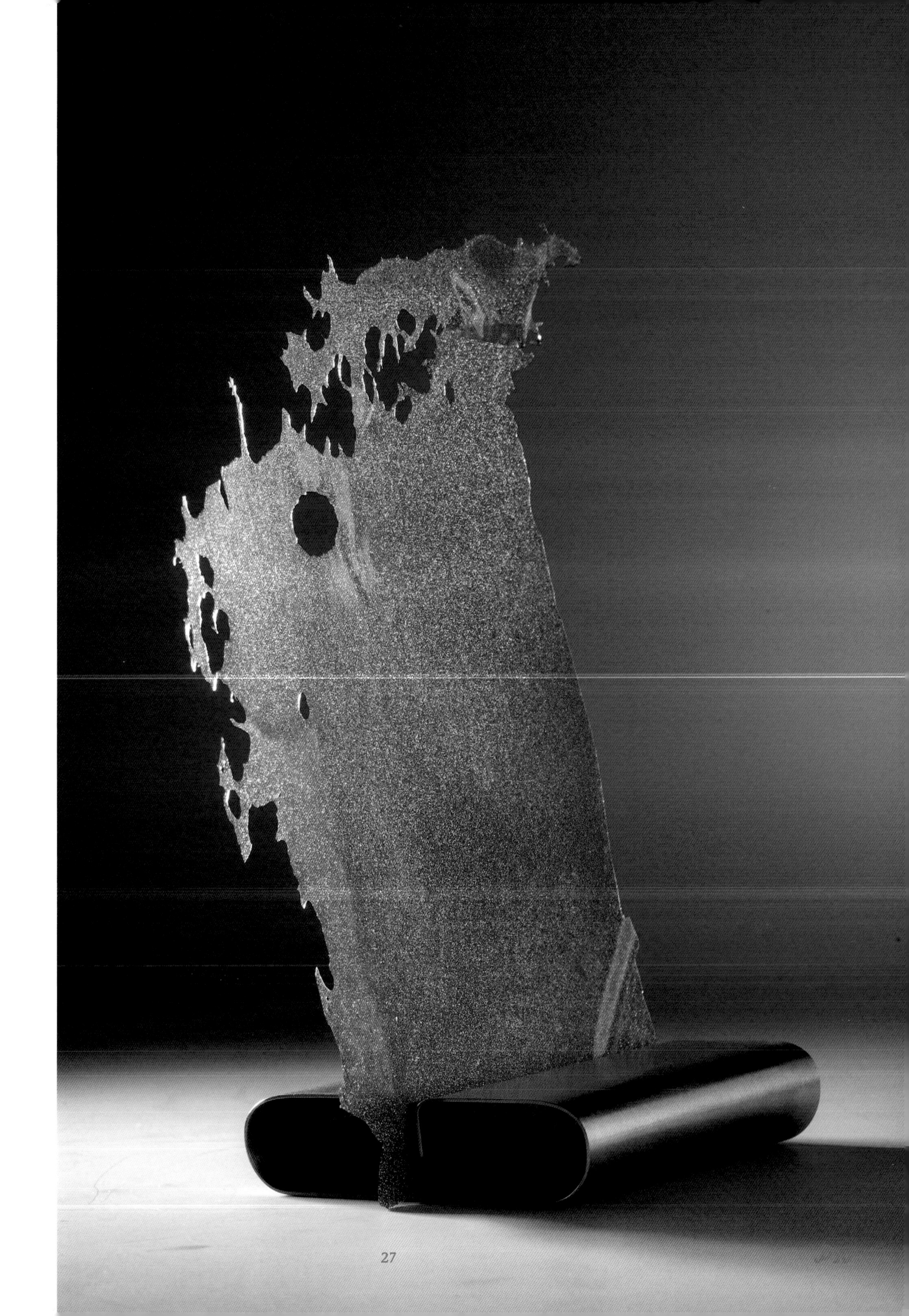

Beet syrup

This syrup goes well with red fruit, yogurt or cheesecake, and is great with cheese. Reduce beet syrup with 1/10 glucose syrup to get a light syrupy mixture. Cool and pour in a squeeze bottle. Instead of piping the beet syrup, you can also use a brush for extra effects on a plate.

Sugar-free sorbet

Sorbets usually contain a lot of sugar. Besides flavour they create structure by forming ice crystals. Sorbet without sugar is often watery and melts easily. Culiversum, together with one of its gastronauts, has developed a technique to create sugar-free ice cream with polydextrose. This ice cream is perfect with savoury dishes and with desserts that require less sugar.

Ingredients: **1 litre fruit coulis, 600 g polydextrose, 7 g gelatin leaves.**

Heat some of the coulis and dissolve the pre-soaked gelatin in it. Mix with the rest of the coulis and using a hand blender, add the polydextrose. This mixture can be made in a sorbet using a sorbetière, PacoJet or Frix-Air.

Chewing gum ice cream

A piece of nostalgia: ice cream with the flavour of chewing gum! By infusing the chewing gum in milk you get the flavour of gum and using a sieve you get rid of the gum. Delicious with yogurt and fresh fruit.

Ingredients: **120 g bubblegum, 1 litre milk, 100 ml unsweetened whipping cream, 190 g crystal sugar, 60 g glucose, 200 g pasteurized egg yolk, 9 g ice cream stabilizer, 60 g unsalted butter.**

Infuse bubble gum and milk on low heat for 15 minutes. Pour through a fine mesh sieve and add the rest of the ingredients. Heat au bain-marie to 84°C/183°F, and keep stirring until it thickens. Cool down to 4°C/39°F and keep in the cooler for 24 hours to set. Spin in the ice cream maker and serve at -12°C/10°F in order to create beautiful quenelles.

Strawberry tuilles

***Ingredients:* 100 g strawberry puree, 20 g glucose, 60 g unsalted butter, 60 g flour, 40 g icing sugar, 60 g pasteurized egg whites.**

Reduce strawberry puree with glucose to a paste; you can add some red food colouring if you want to enhance the colour. Soften the butter and mix with strawberry paste. Add the flour, egg whites and icing sugar and blend to till smooth. Spread mixture using a template over silpat. Bake in the oven at 160°C/320°F. Store in a tight container with silicon grains.

Raspberry bonbon

A beautiful contrast between tart flavours and fresh raspberries is the taste of white chocolate in combination with Greek yogurt. The Atsina cress (from Koppert Cress) is not only decorative, but gives a fresh anise flavour to this fabulous friandise as part of a dessert.

***Ingredients:* 20 g raspberries, 150 g chocolate couverture, 90 g yogurt, Atsina cress.**

Heat Greek yogurt and the white chocolate to 35°C/95°F and pour in a small container. Let set in the cooler and transfer later to a piping bag that has a thin smooth tip. Take some beautiful firm raspberries and fill these carefully with the yogurt-chocolate ganache. Garnish with a small sprig of Atsina cress. Serve as a friandise or as part of a dessert.

Meringue of Red Beet

This is a super delicious variety of the classic meringue. Here, dried egg whites are used and mixed with the juice of red beets. This replaces the classic egg whites with a base that has a specific flavour. It gives also a very nice structure, is crunchy and melts on your tongue, which releases the flavour instantly.

Ingredients: **200 g beet juice, 11 g egg white powder, 75 g sugar water 1:1, 0.1 g xanthan gum, 50 g crystal sugar.**

Mix all ingredients, except the sugar, with hand held blender but don't beat air in it. Put covered in the fridge for 12 hours. Beat mixture in KitchenAid until strong peaks form. Mix with the sugar and pour in a piping bag with a smooth tip. Cover baking sheets with silpats, pipe small drops of the meringue on it and dry for 2 hours in the oven at 70°C/160°F. Store in a tight container with silica grains.

P10

Raspberry toffee

Ingredients: **300 g raspberry puree, 300 g unsweetened whipping cream, 250 g sugar, 75 g honey, 25 g lemon juice, 3 g salt**

Bring all ingredients to a boil, stir regularly, cool and pour in a squeeze bottle.

Bouillon of red fruit

Ingredients: **1000 g fresh red fruit, 125 g red wine (Cabernet-Sauvignon), 100 g sugar, 1 sprig fresh mint.**

Cut red fruit in pieces and put in a vacuum bag with the rest of the ingredients. Process sous vide and stop when the liquid starts to bubble. Heat in a warm water bath 65°C/150°F for 45 minutes and immediately put bag in ice water. Let rest overnight in the fridge. Drain fruit through a sieve but don't press the fruit. Use as consommé for a dessert or as a basis for a nice clear gel.

Sugar strips of small red beets

Ingredients: **150 g small red beets (cooked), 20 g icing sugar, 25 g isomaltose, 5 g glucose.**

Cut the beets and put in the Thermomix together with other ingredients. Heat to 80°C/175°F on medium speed. In case you don't have a Thermomix, use a hand held blender and a measuring cup heating au bain-marie to 80°C/175°F. Put mixture through a fine mesh sieve and cool. Cut straight sheets of silicon paper the same size at the silpats. Put paper on silpat and spread beet mixture on it, remove paper and repeat. Let dry for 35 minutes in the oven at 125°C/260°F; keep in tight container with silica grains.

RED, the dessert

Structures of red fruit and red beet with sugar free sorbet of Greek yogurt

Ice cold pearls of watermelon and raspberry with dragon gel.

On the plate you will see a spiral of two flavours of spaghetti, one with strawberry coulis and one made with blackberry liqueur. In the spiral is some raspberry toffee with a quenelle of sugar free yogurt sorbet. It is garnished with pieces of raspberry, drops of dragon gel and ice pearls of watermelon and vodka. To balance the structure we have added sugar strips and red beet meringue with a cherry sponge cake. This is just a suggestion for dessert. Needless to say, there are endless varieties.

Mol d'Art

Where passion and quality come together

**Any chocolatier who has never heard of Mol d'Art ought go back to school! This company has been tops for many years when it comes to machine building, chocolate moulds and packaging.
The products are shipped worldwide.**

Jozef Vanelven was established as a chocolatier in Bekkevoort, Belgium, where he worked with machines he didn't like. One of the things that bothered him was the noise they made. He wanted to make a change: "You can get quite far with a bit of basic knowledge. I decided to develop a chocolate molding machine which I did together with some technical people but I was the chocolatier." This was the early 1980's, and that's when Jozef developed other products as well. "I liked beautiful packaging for my pralines but in those days there was only one production company that could do that. I had to order so much at once that I had enough packaging for years at a time! With the help of the local technical school we developed a machine that could make thermoforms. Before that I could make about 150 sheets a day and that meant a hard day's work. Many colleagues came to me asking where I was getting the praline packaging, but I didn't tell them anything." After three years Jozef realized that his packaging material and mould machines had a good chance to bring in some income. The result was five thousand square meters of in-house working space.
In the showroom are thousands of moulds and other forms next to several types of chocolate machines. It is a Mecca for a chocolatier. "In the eighties I developed chocolate melting containers. It used to be done au-bain-marie but that was a lot of work, so I started developing new machines in my own work shed. I went to a pet shop and bought a water container for dogs, made a mould of it with a heating element and a very precise thermostat. The materials we sell have to be practical and

have to be of great quality. Take the magnetic mould. As a chocolatier it drove me crazy to have to work with clamps. You always lost them or they disappeared in the chocolate bin. Working with these was very unpractical." After producing his first magnetic mould it took another five years to perfect it for the market. Now he makes about eight hundred different magnetic chocolate moulds. Our master is full of passion; he is still looking to developing new things as he has done for years. "When my children were young and got presents they knew that I would take these away one day later to make moulds of it."

CNC machines

Our tour continued in the heart of the company, the production room. Almost everything is made in-house. At the packaging machines, a large roll of polyethylene terephthalaat, or PET foil, is rolled out. This roll can have a diameter of up to one metre. A hot mould of 360°C/680°F forms the foil into a template and another machine cuts through the foil with knives that are heated to 160°C/320°F. The foils exist in different colours and thickness; the machines can process from one hundred microns (one micron = one millionth of a metre) to eight millimetres.
"We have four machines. I used to do 150 packages in one day, but now it takes one minute!
We are taken to another building. It is the metal section where swinging machines, moulding and tempering machines are made by hand.
"We always carry a small supply of something. If people want to buy anything they shouldn't have to wait six months. You wouldn't want that yourself." In the technical department, Jozef shows us the interior of a moulding machine. Our friendly master thinks back to the way it used to be. "Now we work with heated threads that go around the whole container comparable to a heated floor in a house. We used to have only two or three separate elements but those could burn the chocolate easily." We notice that the machines are almost soundless and according to Jozef, that is a must. "Just imagine that chocolatiers are working with these machines day in, day out, you wouldn't want these to be noisy. Comfort in the workplace is very important." In the metal department the inox machines are assembled with utmost precision. Jozef is a very proud man and likes to show us everything; it is clear that he knows his production process in every detail. To create forms one needs aluminum moulds, and even these ones are made in-house. To get a better look we are taken to the CNC machines. Mol d'Art has two of those, each with their own engineer. Computer controlled and fast, this device creates forms from a block of aluminum. "The computer has a jewelry program that works with very fine details. We customize everything for our clients and that is not simple. A form cannot have too many levels of depths and should be tapered. If we are finished with a mould, I am the one who pours the first session. This way I will know if the mould loosens easily."

Flexible

A company, like Mol d'Art, is, in spite of its worldwide recognition, still a small business with only fifteen employees. Because everything is done in-house, one can be quick and flexible. "We had one client who was in a hurry to get some customized packaging. While he was having coffee, we worked like crazy to deliver. He had his packaging that evening. Although this was an emergency, it proves our thinking and our ability. Besides that, chocolatiers are my colleagues. We speak the same chocolate jargon. I love to meet people with a passion. I love my work, I travel the world, if not by plane then by e-mail. We try to be the best player on the world market." It doesn't seem to matter if it is the King of Pralines, the famous Marcolini or a local chocolatier; the door of Mol d'Art is open to everyone.

Mol d'Art
Industriepark 16 – Webbekom-Diest
T +32-13 33 41 77
www.moldart.be

Mol D'art

27
31
32
34
51
63
65

Vienna

A Symphony of Pâtisserie

Most people who think of Vienna think of Mozart or other famous composers and coffee with sacher torte. But this city can truly call itself the city of pâtisserie. We are on our way to discover some of the secrets.

You will find a konditorei on almost every street corner, often of high quality and well worth a visit. At most of these you can enjoy a nice cup of coffee and of course a Wiener mélange. About two or three times a week people go to their favorite bakery to pick up some delicacies, but often they stay for hours to enjoy a delicious piece of pastry. Austrians love their cakes. Traditionally these slices of cake are made with heavy butter cream, whipped cream and of course chocolate. Further on we will explain why these cakes are so heavy and rich.
Walking through this city gives you a feeling of being in the east bloc of Europe. However this feeling disappears quickly when we see all the impressive buildings downtown that were built in the time of Emperor Franz Joseph. Everywhere you see reminders of famous musicians from the past: Strauss, Bach and Beethoven being the leaders. Most hotels have some kind of plaque showing that an artist once lived there. But let's forget operas and operettas since we are here for pâtisserie. We visit the main establishments and also find interesting places along the way.

Indianer Schlagober

On the Wollzeile we find Konditorei L.Heiner with a sign displayed on the front of the building that says that they deliver to the Royal Family. It's not for show; they really do. Then we find a konditorei that dates back to 1840. The saleslady tells us that this is the fourth generation of the family business. In the showcase we find several classic Viennese products we will introduce to you, Topfen Golatsche, a quark filling that is put on a sheet of puff pastry folded in a square and then baked lightly. Another classic is the Indianer Schlagober, a sphere of biscuit covered with chocolate. When you order these, they are sliced in the middle and filled with whipped cream. On the counter we see a delicacy that we have never seen. It is called nuss beugl or little nutcracker. Although our saleslady tries her best to explain which dough is used, we don't understand it at all. The only option is to taste it. It tastes like a sweet sausage roll with a filling of ground walnuts.
The Viennese people love to bake cakes and that shows when we visit another little bakery called Reimer, in the same street as Heimer.
Our curiosity gets the best of us when we see a serving tray with chocolate tulips from Amsterdam. Once inside you can find all kind of garnishes to uniquely decorate a cake. We see at least hundred different flowers made of marzipan, fondant and sugar. Next to it is a showcase full of marzipan figurines in every shape and form. Everything is made by hand; the sky is the limit. Owner Eva Reimer only wants to make products that are fully edible, which is why all the figurines are small. No inedible little sticks or anything like that are used. For people who want to make things themselves, Eva has already written two books and sells all ingredients and materials. In every bakery we find sacher torten, all packaged in small wooden boxes just like the original ones. It seems that the whole city wants to share in the success of this famous tart.
We were fortunate to meet the maker of the real sacher torte.

Pupperl
oder

Eva Reimer
Kinder-Torten
A&M
Kunstwerkstatt

SCHOKOLADE
TULPEN
aus Amsterdam

Sacher Torte

This chocolate cake with apricot jam has a rich history and celebrated its 175th anniversary last year. The recipe is a well kept secret that has been hidden in the safe of the prestigious Sacher Hotel, located in the Philharmonic Strasse. The history doesn't start in the hotel but in 1832 when the hotel didn't even exist. At the palace of Prince Metternich, a sixteen-year-old apprentice-cook, Franz Sacher, had to replace a chef who became ill. Just that day the Prince had some important visitors and wanted to serve something special. Franz wanted to show his very best side and created a new tart. This soft chocolate cake with apricot jam and smooth glazing would melt in your mouth. The student became famous for his cakes and moved to Bratislava and then Budapest to work for the Earl of Esterhazy. After he finished his training he returned to Vienna with the secret recipe. The pâtissier started to work for Dehne and made the famous tart. When Franz's son opened the famous Sacher Hotel in 1876 the tart was made again. After the Second World War the competition started: who made the original Sacher? In the end, the Sacher Hotel won the battle and that is where the original tart is still made, covered with a chocolate seal and patented so the recipe can never be changed. The tart will always be sold in the famous small wooden boxes.

Thanks to our well-known pink pastry books, we are a few of the lucky ones who were allowed to witness the making of the original Sacher Torte. The bakery is located about 10 kilometres from the Sacher Hotel, where we receive a warm welcome by chef pâtissier Alfred Buxbaum, or as they call them in Austria, Chefkonditor. This chef has already been working with the Sacher flag for 18 years and has experience in famous establishments. "As a young student I would never have dreamed that I would ever make the Sacher Torte, let alone becoming the chef. Sacher has always been a true philosophy, not only in Austria but far beyond."

When we go through the revolving doors, the smell of chocolate wafts over us. It is a delicious smell, but means nothing to the staff, as it is so common to them. We notice a lady who is separating eggs. "We make everything with top quality and fresh products," says the chef. When we ask the lady how many eggs she breaks per day, we are shocked because chickens would have to do a lot of work to lay seven thousand eggs!

Our primary question is the tart, what is in it? Without giving away the secret recipe, Franz tells us how the tart is made. It is very simple.

"The biscuit consists of butter, sugar, egg yolks, chocolate and of course

beaten egg whites. The biscuit is baked at 189°C / 372°F after which it is cut in half and then spread with apricot jam. The layers are put back together and covered again with apricot jam. It then goes to the glazing department to be totally covered with a layer of chocolate, which can keep the tart for 3 weeks at room temperature. Next we let the tart harden in storerooms at 18°C / 64°F and then they are packaged in the traditional wooden boxes. Every tart will get its original seal." Walking through the bakery we see step by step what has been explained to us. 1000 to 1300 tarts are produced per day, depending on their size. During the Christmas season the production is 3000 tarts per day. Okay, don't feel sorry for the lady who separates the eggs because they do take turns within the bakery. The tart has many secrets; one of them is the chocolate that is made with three varieties. After making the right guess we can disclose that two of them come from Belgium. The bakery has been built with help from Alfred. "We used to work in the cellar of the hotel with eleven people. Something had to change. We established a production line, starting with the eggs and finishing with the packaging. The new bakery has now 35 employees." Anyone who thinks that they just produce sacher torten has it wrong.

The secret recipe

The recipe is still a mystery to us. There is no option to change it, as the chef is obliged to keep the original recipe. This is so strict that even the cocoa percentage of the chocolate is carefully watched. Even with all these strict rules they still have room for creativity as we found in the lobby where we see a base set up for a tart that has a diameter of one and a half metres to later be made into a Sacher Torte. The biggest one ever made was two and half metres in diameter. We take a side tour to the Sacher Hotel, which has lots of charm and class. One of the wings in the hotel has a large shop that doesn't just sell sacher torten but a variety of other merchandise. From here the Viennese can ship their specialty all over the world. There are also four other places and plans are under way to open a Sacher café in China.

Demel

Our trip of Vienna continues; a visit to Hofzuckerbackerei Demel is a must. The minute we enter the store we are back in the time of Mozart. The beauty and splendor make a great impression on our editors.
We needed to know a bit of history to understand this konditorei.
It started with a different name and a different location. In 1786 the Gefrorenes Salon on Michaelerplatze was opened by Ludwig Dehne.
As the name implies, this salon sold only frozen desserts, unique for that time. The salon had many customers from the theatre across the street. When Ludwig passed away, his wife took over the business and later his son August. In 1857 the son handed over the business to Christoph Demel and a new name was created. The empire of Franz Joseph was growing fast and that made it necessary to move. In 1888 they opened a shop on the Kohlmart where they are still today. The family lived above the bakery.
The memories of those days are still evident in the building, as in the gorgeous old kitchen and hand painted wallpaper. It is probably not easy for the staff to work there. Every floor has its own work area and the old rooms have been made into salons where one can enjoy Wiener mélange and a piece of pastry. It is hard to imagine that we are walking in an active working bakery; it feels more like visiting an old king in a castle.
A major change took place when Anna Demel took over the business. This lady made the store even more famous, mainly by her involvement in the production. Her personally created tart, the Annatorte, is still available at Demel today. The famous history continued. Anna adopted her niece Klara who married an architect and artist by the name of Frederico von Berzevicry-Pallavicini. He had a great influence on the success of the konditorei through his presentations and packaging.
After his death the Demel business was taken over by many different people. Currently it belongs to a large culinary entertainment business Do & Co. Although this company is very commercial, it has not changed the soul of the Demels. The store is a treasure and still carries the atmosphere of 1888. All sweets are displayed in wooden showcases and all walls have mirrors that make the store look much larger. Some specialties we discover are Fächertorte, of course the Annatorte, the Fragilité, the Sachertorte, the Crèmeschnitte, the Russian Punschorte and the Katzenzungen. We move to the coffee area where it is very busy. Behind a glass window many pâtissiers are in action. Modern equipment sits next to marble counters and marble washing basins. Our eye catches two tarts with two sculpted busts on top of Bill Clinton and Kofi Annan. The busts seem to be a world famous specialty. The same were made of Mohammed Ali and tennis star Rafael Nadal. We move on, going through little corridors and over little steps, as Chef Dietmar Muthentaler waits to show us all the workstations.

Artistic

Dietmar gets right to it while we are still mulling over the impression we have of the busts. "These decorations are made by Kurt Nitsche, a man who is more like an artist than a pâtissier and who has done this for more than 37 years. We try to work together with our customers to fulfill any special requests. Kurt is extremely creative. He is the maker of the busts that are the ornaments on top of the tarts. The head is made of styrofoam covered with marzipan and a bit of alcohol to thin it. Once the face has been molded, it is set to dry. The alcohol evaporates and the marzipan hardens." We see eight people working on it. "We have twenty-five people working in the pâtisserie. Fifteen steady employees and ten students." Demel has seven different departments. In the demonstration area we find the Sacher section, the Strudel section, the Cookies section and the Decoration section. We walk through the large building and arrive in the kitchen where tarts and cakes are made with several kinds of dough. There is no dull moment here as they make fifty different kinds of tarts depending on the season. We take the elevator one floor up to the chocolate department where bonbons, pralines and chocolate cookies are made. One corner is set aside for the Annatorte that consists of chocolate biscuit, nougat and orange liqueur. Finalizing the tart is a specialty. Tempered chocolate with praline keeps moving on a cool marble slab until it starts to harden. This mixture is spread out in a thin layer and cut in slices used for decorative garnish around the tart. History is evident here because next to the synthetic chocolate moulds we find hundred year old metal forms that are still used today.

Demel's Sacher Story

From the chocolate section we descend to the Demel museum where you can learn everything about its history, where famous showpieces are displayed and where you can taste the history. We like to hear Dietmar's version of the Demel Sacher torte. "This is the seventh time I am telling the story this week, but that's the way it is. There are several stories being circulated. Eduard, son of Franz Sacher, was a student here before he opened the famous hotel. Here the tart was first introduced. Franz Sacher and Anna Demel have always been good friends so it wasn't a problem. They do have the original certificate, but does it matter? Besides 50,000 sacher torten we sell a lot of other specialties." We wonder if there is a difference between the tarts of Demel and Sacher. "Just a little bit. We only use one kind of chocolate; Sacher uses three. We don't slice the tart in the middle to fill with apricot jam, which our colleagues do. It is all about taste that cannot be disputed." Demel has the certificate K.u.K. that means the bakery delivers to the Royal Family, but what makes Demel stand out? The chef: "As you just heard, Demel is a business with lots of history and is highly regarded. We stand firm by our values, so we keep our customers. We use the best ingredients and make almost everything ourselves. We expect that everyone working here has a passion for the job."

Russian Punschtorte

Tart for 8 people: butter, flour, rum.
For the biscuit: 4 eggs, 145 g sugar, 145 g sifted flour, 45 g melted butter.
For the vanilla cream: 400 g milk, 200 g whipping cream, 120 g sugar, ½ vanilla bean, 45 g cornstarch, 150 g egg yolks.
For the foam: 125 g fresh egg whites, 200 g sugar, 100 g icing sugar.

Grease a form of 20 cm in diameter with butter and dust the inside with flour. Beat eggs, butter and sugar au-bain-marie to 50°C / 120°F. Then beat again until it is cold and combine with the flour. Pour batter in the form and bake in the oven for about 45 minutes at 165°C / 330°F. Invert the biscuit and let cool. For the vanilla cream, stir sugar, cornstarch and egg yolks to make a smooth batter.
Bring milk, whipping cream and vanilla bean to a boil, prepare as an anglaise and let cool. Slice the biscuit twice horizontally, brush with some rum, spread some cream on top and put layers back together.
Beat egg whites with icing sugar. Use rest of the sugar and a bit of water to make a syrup at 121°C / 250°F and prepare as Italian foam. Pipe a layer of 2 cm foam around the tart, caramelize the foam with a torch and garnish as you wish.

Demel

Konditorei Oberlaa

On the outskirts of the city we find a very special konditorei, where, besides two skilled employees, we discover the secret of Austrian pâtisserie. Most of the konditoreis are downtown, and while Oberlaa has some shops there as well, the source of this famous konditorei is quite far away from the town centre. Oberlaa used to be a suburb of Vienna, but has now become part of Vienna. The story starts in 1974 with an international exhibition in the park that included a health resort, a wellness centre and a sauna. As strange as this sounds, the owner felt that a konditorei should be part of this. Karl Schumacher, a well-known figure in Vienna, was assigned to set this up. He had his own style, something the inhabitants were not used to. For example, he didn't like heavy pieces of cake that were quite common everywhere. The park exhibition was a huge success and the konditorei did very well until the exhibition was over. Customers stayed away and Karl refused to change his methods. When he was close to bankruptcy, the culinary supermarket Meindl decided to sell Oberlaa's products and the business got back on its feet again. The city people appreciated Karl's style and Karl even opened another shop. Now, seven years later, there are seven shops and Oberlaa has become an institution in Vienna and far beyond its borders. Karl is now retired so we met the chefs in charge, Leopold Forsthofer and Vinzenz Bäuerle.

We enter the bakery via a labyrinth of musty and stuffy corridors and doors. Leopold: "It all started here in a few square metres. Our production and staff has increased so much that we now need every space in the building. Fortunately, we are getting a totally new work place in three years." There are about forty people working in the production where everything for the pâtisserie is handmade and packaged for their stores. Thirty different kind of bonbons, more than twenty different tarts, you can imagine how busy they are. The bakery looks older and it is warm and humid, but the working atmosphere seems to be the same. Both chefs have been colleagues for years and are good friends. Leopold has been at Oberlaa for twenty years and Vinzenz seventeen. Leopold is into competitions and is very proud to show us his showpiece that will represent Austria at the Callebaut Chocolate Masters. "I can do fun stuff here, like making decorations, beautiful wedding cakes and travel abroad to judge competitions. Vinzenz is the real chef in charge of administration and production. Together we form a great team." Vinzenz confirms that. "I am happy that Leopold does the competitions, which are good for business. I don't need the publicity."

The kitchen is divided in different sections. A few years ago the chocolate section upgraded to a tempering and glazing machine, saving a lot of time and effort. "In the past, six people did the work of this one machine. Now we can temper and glaze six-hundred molds in one hour." We are surprised to see a Panettone coming out of the oven, to us better known as Italian Christmas bread. Panettone in Vienna? Leopold: "Austria borders on eight countries, and each country has put its stamp on our pâtisserie. Our predecessor Mr. Schumacher was fascinated with Panettone and he spent the last two years of his career here to make the right levain for it. He gave us the recipe as a farewell present. I believe it is the best Panettone in the world."

Conservative

We are curious as to why these two chefs believe that Vienna is one of the pâtisserie capitals of the world. This question gives us an insight in the secrecy of the pâtisserie in Vienna. "As I just mentioned, Austria is situated between eight countries. In the beginning of the nineteenth century, Vienna was the centre of trade and politics in Europe. Where do you meet? Exactly…in a coffee shop. Everyone knows that coffee and pastry go hand in hand. That's why I think pâtisserie and Vienna belong together." Vinzenz explains why traditional pâtisserie is a serious business. "Austria is a conservative country. People here don't like change, and that is why you see totally different pastry here than in Spain. In the old days, when people really had to work hard, a substantial meal was a must. It's not so necessary now, but they still eat substantial meals. We also find it difficult to change; people are not ready for that yet. We can try something trendy that is hype for a while and then it is over. If we really want to advance, all konditoreis have to do it together. But people are slowly changing. Just think that ten years ago, people would only eat milk chocolate and very little pure chocolate. Now it is almost the opposite."

One product that we cannot find anywhere is macarons. Oberlaa started to make them and called it Laa Kronen; they are a huge success. The name Kurkonditorei says it all. The shop is close to a wellness spa. You find this also in their salon. Every table displays a card showing "healthy" pâtisserie without gluten, lactose, sugar or eggs. Vinzenz: "It might sound strange but pâtisserie can be healthy. We use fresh fruit and natural chocolate. There are also brands that use animal fats that are not healthy. It is not easy to talk about quality, because everyone does that. We work with the best and most authentic products and leave it up to the customer to see if it is quality. For us, taste is the most important; therefore the tart might not always look the best. We don't want to compensate the taste."

It is time to leave a city that has conquered our hearts. Both chefs briefly talk about their dreams. "Our own school where we can get our colleagues excited and teach the customers to appreciate what quality is all about…." It is clear to us that an extended visit to Vienna should be a must for the education of every pâtissier; to discover the roots of his or her own profession.

Because of its strategic location, the little French harbour village of Sète on the Mediterranean Sea has a rich history. Here we found a very classic cake.

In Sète, we are getting a lesson from Serge Aprile, who together with his wife Michelle owns the patisserie shop Bladier Aprile. A cake called Frescati has been the life for Serge. The cake's history goes back to Paris in 1914, the era of La Belle Epoque. At that time it seemed a cake named Frascati had always existed and was made by just about everyone. Pâtissier Fourniol made them for banquets and they were served after an opera performance. Fourniol was a famous pâtissier who had many students, including Gaston Bladier. He took the recipe to Sète and taught it to his sons Louis and Fernand, the father of Michelle Aprile. The cake was forgotten in Paris but not in Sète and this is the only place in the world where you will find it. According to Serge, the cake is very sweet and therefore doesn't have to be refrigerated. Sète cuisine had a lot of Italian influence and thus the cake was made with Italian foam; so Frascati was re-named Frescati.

Three elements

The fire in Serge's eyes tells everything about his passion. He won't share the recipe here, but he is willing to tell us everything about the cake. It starts with the bottom. This is made of dough that first looks like normal sablé dough (sand dough). Serge: "The bottom consists of a very hard and heavy dough. It is different than the sablé that is too delicate and would break under the weight of the cake. For the dough I mix the flour and the sugar and blend in some liquids." Italian meringue is piped onto the baked bottom. If you think that meringue is meringue, think again. Serge comes up with a story that makes us really think. "Recipes don't always work; this is because you have to have the right proportions. Sometimes a recipe asks for 3/4 of an egg, but that doesn't exist. A lot of factors are involved that will make or break a recipe. First you have to look at the ratio in a recipe, like how many parts of sugar does it need to make a great meringue. For example, the weather! It might seem unimportant but humidity in the air plays a big role. In that case you

have to change your proportions. You can't just add a handful of sugar as it depends on protein content. How much do you want to make? The ratio for a small portion is different than a large portion. I found that out when the dough mixer from Michelle's grandfather broke after years of service. I bought a new one and the result was totally different. It is easy to beat a small amount until it is cold, but we make 40 litres of beaten egg whites for a meringue. How do I get that cold? We have a working bench with a cooled marble slab. I temper the foam this way." Great concentration is needed to make this cake. If just one thing goes wrong you have to start all over again. On the layer of meringue comes a slice of biscuit; this is as special as the foam. The chef beats egg yolks and sugar and makes foam with egg whites. The beaten egg whites are mixed with the yolks. Then flour and raisins soaked in rum are added to the mixture using a spatula. "The same proportion as for a normal biscuit, except the order of mixing is different. It stays more airy that way." The biscuit goes into the oven at 190°C / 375°F. When that is baked, rings of 3 centimetres in height are cut out. The cake is drenched in syrup with lots of rum. This slice is placed on top of the meringue bottom. It is then topped with Italian foam that according to Serge has an insulation effect. The foam is spread generously as half of the cake made of meringue. The cake is now 20 centimetres high and ready for the finishing touch. One sweeter layer is added, made of caramel deglazed with coffee extract. Soft fondant is added and the soft hanging mixture is poured over the cake which gives it a very shiny appearance. The cake is garnished with red bigareaux confiture.

Exploding rockets

For Serge, this cake is his work and purpose of life. "You don't choose to make a Frescati, the Frescati chooses you." He learns something every day, if not the day is wasted. "I see it as working in space. If one launches a rocket and nothing goes wrong, than nothing has been learned.

One can only learn from exploding rockets. It is the same for pâtisserie, so really pâtissiers are astronauts." The cake is cut with a hot knife, because at Pâtisserie Aprile strict rules are in order. Serge takes a knife and puts it on an open fire. Once the knife is red hot, the cake is cut. The action releases much smoke like an exploding rocket; the meringue is burnt with it as well, a great idea and a flavour enhancer. Then the cake is done. "In the old days we had no electricity or cooling. Since no cream is used the cake stays good for a while. August 25 is the celebration of Saint Louis. That day everyone buys a cake in the morning and eats it in the evening on top of Mount Saint Claire."

You have probably figured out by now that our pâtissier is very proud of his product. He doesn't want to share his recipe and we respect that. Since there is no successor trying to make this complicated cake he is already busy to keep the tradition going in a special way. Serge: "When I die I want a gravestone with a large Frescati on every corner with the recipe in every language. The cake has kept me alive but has also caused me death." We ask him why he doesn't have a student. "I have had a few students, but learning to make this cake takes years. If you put three lines on a wall are you then a painter? You can only paint if you know how to work with pigments and how to create the perfect colour."

Secretly our pâtissier is dreaming of a stamp with his Frescati on it so that the whole world will be introduced to the Frescati de Sète.

Belgian jelly gums

In the European capital of Brussels (Belgium) we find Suikerbakkerij Joris (Sugar Bakery Joris), established in 1938. The business has earned a reputation for its candies of classic jelly gums.

Hans Van Den Driessche is the third generation; his grandfather and father came before him. The business used to make mostly chocolate products but when World War Two broke out, the ingredients became very scarce. It was easier to get sugar or invert sugar and gelatin. The only way to continue the business was to change and start making gums. Hans began helping in the business at sixteen and went to the confiserie school in Solingen (Germany). "I never have left the profession since." Today this sugar bakery only makes jelly gums. But what are these gums? It is a broad concept that involves lots of different candies. There are two kinds: hard and soft ones. The hard ones are made with Arabic gum and the soft ones with gelatin. We will explain both.

Arabic Gum

Hard gums are made with a binding agent like Arabic gum, which is the resin of acacia trees from the African countries Sudan, Nigeria, Chad or Senegal. At Joris' they use the one from Sudan, as this seems to work best. The wrong gum that doesn't have the right thickening agent can lose its strength after a few days. There are dozens of different kinds of Arabic gum, but only fourteen can be used in confiserie. To extract the resin, incisions are made in the acacia tree with a machete. After a few weeks the sap hardens and forms little balls that the farmers gather and pack in canvas bags. These are then available for sale at the gum market in Sudan where prices can differ on a daily basis. If the price is right Hans buys a lot to stock up for the future. Arabic gum is not cheap; right now it is $2.50 per kilo, sometimes as low as $1.50 but also as high as $10.00 per kilo. The Arabic gum arrives in bulk in large canvas bags at Joris.
First the gum is ground into small pieces and melted in water of 80°C / 175°F. The temperature has to stay the same for 45 minutes. All impurities are removed by means of a centrifuge which gets rid of residues like little branches, sand or small leaves. The machine also takes out some

colour and leaves a transparent brownish solution with a very light sweet taste. This is one of the reasons why the Sugar Bakery still uses the real Arabic gum. Hans: "Because of the high price of the Arabic gum, some colleagues are using cornstarch. The advantage of gum is that it dissolves in your mouth and doesn't stick to your teeth. It is low in calories and has its own flavour." Low calories? So eating candies is healthy? "Yes, Arabic gum is a good fibre, in our jelly gums you will find about 40% fibre. It is good for the intestines, but is not really a laxative. Besides that it contains fifty elements that can't be replaced by cornstarch, which has only three. Another disadvantage of cornstarch is that it doesn't dissolve in the mouth and has no flavour."

The solution is mixed with sugar and glucose. The hard gums are cooked in a covered pot with an inside stirring mechanism and heated to break it down to 70% dry material. The pot looks like a small submarine. It is hard to exactly guess the temperature inside because the sugar quickly forms a film around the thermometer. A pump sucks the mixture in this pot and this makes it possible to cook under pressure that lowers the temperature in one minute instead of five minutes. When the mixture has reached the right consistency, colouring and flavours are added. Hans does his best to only use natural products but that is not always possible. These can be fruit flavours but also licorice root to make licorice. On the bottom of the pot is a tap to drain the mixture for further use in a mogul, a molding machine, which we will explain later.

Soft gums

The base of the syrup is the same: sugar and glucose, but instead of gum, gelatin is added. There is a huge difference in using gelatin that gels or gum that thickens. Gelatin takes nineteen times its own weight in water but only a 5% solution is necessary in a soft gum recipe, unlike the hard gums using Arabic at 40 to 50%. The syrup is cooked in an open copper kettle that weighs 250 kilograms and is stirred carefully with a wooden spatula. The gelatin, flavour and colouring are added. If colour and taste are satisfactory, it goes in the mogul as well.

The Pouring

The gums come in hundreds of shapes and sizes. Hans shows us a cabinet full of forms that are small plaster contramals (molds) glued to a fabric. We count about 40 different molds. The mixture is poured in a molding machine, the mogul, to create the shapes. This presses the molds in a container of starch and that creates the forms to pour the syrup in. Plaster forms are used to prevent electric static. The forms are glued to a coarse fabric to make sure that air can get to it and to prevent a vacuum problem, which could cause the cornstarch to stick to the plate. Cone shapes are also used for the same reason to get air, preventing a vacuum. The quality of the cornstarch is very important. It should be somewhat old, because fresh cornstarch makes it too soft. Compare it to sand on the beach and sand to build sand castles. Old cornstarch is added to fresh cornstarch to get the desired effect. Cornstarch is used because it can absorb and reject water. The mogul has lots of knobs and levers for adjustments because it is important that the syrup is poured with the right quantity and frequency.

Thus it starts with the pressing of molds in the cornstarch and then syrup is poured in the molds. A dispenser is used to get the right quantity in the molds. The spout is made in such a way that it moves along with the belt so it extends the pouring time, even if it is just a few seconds. The temperature is again very important. If the material is too hot it mixes with the cornstarch. We follow the little gums called "noses". They are soft on the inside and hard on the outside. The machine accurately pours 4-5 grams in the form with a small layer of cornstarch on top. This is to create a skin on top of the soft gum. The cornstarch that is left goes through a sieve and is used again, which is understandable since the machine uses three thousand kilograms of cornstarch per hour.

The Hardening Process

This process shows a big difference between the hard and the soft gums. The soft gums only have to cool to let the gelatin set. Hard gums contain more water and need to dry longer. This happens in a drying chamber where the temperature is 60-80°C / 140-175°F. It takes three to five days

for the hard gums to dry in cornstarch forms. The chambers draw in heated air and ventilators are used to blow the hot air over the containers of cornstarch and gums. The same machine releases the forms again. The starch is collected, purified and re-used. The gums are well cleaned. A bit of oil is added to make the gums shine, just one gram per kilo. At Joris' the hard gums are steam cleaned, so they shine more and are called "washed gums". This method is not possible with the soft gums, as that would melt the gelatin. The candies can also be covered with a sweet or sour layer, which is done with a special tool. The soft gums only need a few hours to harden on large tables after they have been processed even after they have been dipped in a sugar bath. They contain more liquid than the hard gums. Gelatin allows more fluid in the candy without making it sticky, and is much softer and done quickly. When everything is ready packaging can start. At Joris' they use boxes in the style of the house, real retro, although the packaging hasn't changed in 40 years! The warehouse is filled with 80,000 kilograms of gum fun. We feel like kids in a candy shop.

Copenhagen

From Flöderböller to Sømods Bolcher

It is one of the trendiest cities in Europe. Everything around us seems to be a design. Copenhagen is also becoming the rising star in gastronomy, but is it the same for pâtisserie? The city might not be as rich as Vienna or Paris, but has some very interesting spots that we would like to share with you.

Our agenda is filled with places to visit so we assumed that we needed to rent a car, but it wasn't necessary. The downtown area with all the "sweet" attractions is very small. We could walk everywhere. This way we discovered places we would have never seen if we had been driving fast and furious along the roads. Although most of the gastronomes and pâtissiers are still looking at Barcelona in Spain, it is amazing to see what has happened in the north. The city has at least a dozen renowned star restaurants and many are up and coming. The Danish people must love going out for dinner as most of the better restaurants are fully booked weeks ahead. Let's start with our "sweet" inspection tour.

Braendle Mandler

We are on our way to the first address and the oldest pâtisserie in the city and arrive at the very busy Strøget Kamilla. It is obvious that Kamilla enjoys serving dozens of people with her caramelized almonds. These are boiled in heavy sugar syrup and vanilla and then rolled through sugar. Next to the nuts being prepared in front of the customers we see many other kinds of nuts as well as dried and caramelized fruit. Although there are many of these stands in any city, Kamilla ensures us that these caramelized almonds are typically Danish.

Keeping traditions alive

If you can imagine what a pâtisserie looked like in the 19th century, we don't have to describe Konditorei La Glace. Everything looks perfect and nothing seems to have changed since 1870 when the store first opened. The very friendly Marianne Kolos is joining us and we are overwhelmed with sweets and hot chocolate with whipping cream. In the meantime she is happy telling us about the history but wants to have something cleared up before we start: "In spite of the age of La Glace, we are a young and hip business where traditions are honoured. I don't want to be a museum for tourists. We do have all the information and names in English but only show that when people ask for it." When Nicolaus Henningsen opened his doors two centuries ago, he had no idea how famous his store would become. Three generations of a German family built the business until 1977 when history was almost finished. There was nobody in the family to continue and the business had to be sold. Marianne's mother, a lawyer, was looking for an office and fell in love with the charming building. She realized how valuable this bakery was for the city and decided to exchange her lawyer's robe for the traditional clothing of sales ladies. Marianne intended, just like the rest of her family, to be part of the law business but felt that a business like this would suit her better. She followed in the footsteps of her mother and in the meantime, even the third generation is keen to get involved. "In the history of La Glace there have been three incredibly important instances. First the phone connection in 1896 that suddenly made it possible to receive orders. Then in 1923 electricity came to us and we could expand production. The last big step was the arrival of internet in 2002 which provided access to the whole world." Marianne is a good and wonderful woman who tells you like it is: "We are one of the few shops in Northern Europe where you cannot get anything besides pastry and a hot drink. Anyone else serves sandwiches or a glass of wine; we don't want to do that. I only think of quality and work with the best ingredients. Because we use a lot of whipping cream, our cakes don't keep long and are hard to cut. They are not suitable for people on a diet, so just enjoy them and don't watch calories."

Their most popular specialty is the Sportskage. This recipe has not changed since 1891 and is made of chopped nougatine and whipped cream on a bottom of macaron and garnished with caramelized cream puffs. A large sandwich early in the morning! There are always 18 layered cakes in the window, but one comes to La Glace for ice cream tarts as well. "We were one of the first in Copenhagen making ice cream the old fashioned way with dried ice and a salt solution. We still use the old molds that we started with in the beginning."

We were told that the working area is very special but also heard that no one is allowed to visit. "I will make an exception for you; my chef pâtissier would love to show it to you." A small building with five floors is adjacent to the shop and our first impression is that nothing has changed since the time they started, except for a few necessary adjustments. Every floor has a separate department where nearly ten people work in a very small area. You don't find fancy KitchenAids or ice cream machines here, no new baking forms or molds. The practice of decades ago still counts. "We make ice cream in a machine from 1923 and whip cream in the same fashion." Pâtissier Arne has been working here for 45 years and it is a joy to watch him. It is difficult to describe the working area; you have to have been there. Once a year, the day before the school holidays start, Marianne opens her doors to the public, so that is your only chance!

Before we planned our trip to Copenhagen we searched for specialists in viennoiserie, as we believed it would have a Danish history. In the English language viennoiserie is called Danish pastry. The Danish call it wienerbrød. It is available in every bakery and Marianne has a great assortment but we never found out why it is called Danish pastry. Happily our lady has an explanation. "The recipe comes from Vienna. There was a time when many labourers from Austria came to work in Denmark and some happened to be bakers. They brought in the dough made of thousands of layers and perfected it here."

ROM
NMA
KARAMEL
TRØFFEL

Everything in your own hands

When we tried to confirm our appointment with Peter Beier, we received an e-mail that he was at a cocoa plantation. We found out later that indeed he owns his own plantation but that's not all. With twenty years of experience Peter knows what he is talking about. He doesn't want to think about anything else but chocolate. This philosophy must have helped him because he now owns four shops, another three franchises and a large production facility outside the city, because in his shops they only make hot chocolate. "I sell the most chocolate in Copenhagen. We have just one product and that is chocolate and I want to be the best in that. By making everything in a central location, I know that the flavour will always be consistent and good. The big difference between others and us is that we have the complete process in our own hands from bean to bonbon. I have my own cocoa plantation in the Dominican Republic and also my own orchards of apples, pears and soft fruits. We even have our own almond trees and they are so difficult to maintain that no one else wants to do it, so we are ahead of others in that respect." Even in Copenhagen Peter has his own learning institute where a small plantation is built. "A good employer should know everything. We deliberately choose to have our own plantation so we don't need to compromise when we import. It is not a matter of money, but a way to make the very best and you can adapt the flavour to your own liking." His ambition for perfection goes even further; he only employs people who are fully trained in the business. "It is more expensive, but I know what I have. We treat everyone to a nice breakfast and a free lunch. It is motivational and you are not eating sweets all day. Every store has fruit plates for our staff. It has to be a pleasure to work for us and that results in quality."

Peter tells us that the entire process is in his hands but we haven't heard any mention of a small dairy factory. Does he own that too? "That's not necessary since we work with hardly any dairy. I don't use butter or cream in my ganache. The Danish like concentrated flavours and a ganache contains mostly chocolate with a bit of milk and maybe cognac. It gives a much purer taste." Peter is pretty clear when it comes to prices. It doesn't matter if you buy one gram or one kilo bonbons, the price is the same. "I don't force people to buy more; they should take what they like." We don't see anything strange in the store, some nicely displayed pralines and some pre-wrapped little boxes. The boxes are special as they are made of the waste of the cocoa beans. The chocolatier has his own opinion on flavours: "It is pure chocolate or marzipan with a suitable flavour, no whipped butter cream or heavy ganaches. We pack our boxes to the rim; people are not here to buy air."

Luxurious to extreme

Our hotel is a stone's throw away from the famous Tivoli Park, a large amusement paradise for young and old, even for gastronomes because the park has a very trendy restaurant called The Paul. When we walk around the edge of the park, our eyes catch a very luxurious delicatessen and we stepped inside. What we see is beyond our imagination. The shop is apparently part of the brand new Hotel Nimb that opened just a few days before we arrived. In the centre of the shop is an enormous chocolate line where chocolaterie Summerbird exclusively makes flöderböller. Before we visited we wanted to look around as we saw a large glass wall with a dairy factory behind it. The only purpose of this factory is to provide fresh milk for the hotel and the shop. No cost was spared to construct this most luxurious hotel of the city.
It all started at the end of the 19th century when the Nimb family opened a restaurant at the edge of Tivoli in the famous Carstensen's Bazaar. Although the name of the restaurant was Divan 2, the people knew it better as Nimb's. The family had a great sense of business and for decades it was the meeting spot for gastronomes. At a certain moment no successors were available and the business went downhill. The famous gourmet shop Løgimose didn't want this history lost and decided to invest. They have all the experience in gastronomy and own several businesses that are on top of the list. In Tivoli all facets of business have to come under one roof in a luxurious way and must be very transparent. Dairy manager Kim Erntsen gives us a tour. "We have put our factory in the store so the clients can see what happens. On all sides the factory is surrounded by glass so people can also see in from the street. We work with the most modern, closed dairy system." The milk is delivered fresh daily by two organically certified farms located on the other side of the large bridge in Sweden. The morning milk is guaranteed to be processed by evening and is then displayed on a shelf in the store. "There are no other factories where consumers can be this close." The little factory has only been open for a short while and the assortment is minimal to guarantee quality. "We only produce cottage cheese and fresh cheese, no hard cheeses. We also have butter and fermented milk products like yogurt, natural buttermilk and sour cream. We have different kinds of yogurt flavoured with our homemade jams." The assortment is completed with fløde, (38% whipping cream), regular milk and chocolate milk, made with Valrhona chocolate from the store. "Our most important

goal is to make sure that the guests have everything they need for breakfast and of course the chefs in the restaurant have the best dairy products to work with. Smell and flavour are of utmost importance to us. More and more people want light products, but you need butter for good flavour so we leave it in. To avoid butter you have to start working with additives and we don't do that. Therefore we don't make cream or milk ice cream."

Flöderboller

We stand in front of the chocolate line and try to guess how many pralines are made each day. We were told that these are only used for flöderboller; the rest of the chocolate comes from the central area. These cones are typical Danish and one believes that the recipe for these was developed 300 years ago. It is a crunchy bottom with a cone made of Italian foam on top that is finished with a thin layer of chocolate. Kim Ilardo is the expert here who takes his work seriously. When we ask him how he makes the flöderboller he replies that it is a secret. Eventually we hear that the filling is made with egg whites, sugar and vanilla. For the rest he refuses to say anything. Fortunately one of his

female colleagues is a bit more open and tells us that Italian foam is the key. Where others choose a crunchy cookie as bottom, here homemade marzipan is used. The foam is piped on this bottom and immediately disappears in a chocolate bath and cooled quickly to harden, a process that takes 15 minutes. Kim: "We only use basic meringue. Garnish or enhancers make the meringue collapse quickly. Good flöderboller stays firm for 3 hours, commercial ones much longer. Therefore we make fresh flöderboller all day long." In Tivoli there is another variety. Every month it is made with a different vegetable or fruit flavour, right now it is rhubarb. But we thought that you couldn't add garnish? Once again Kim keeps his mouth shut as to how he does it. But when we get a chance to taste the flöderboller, we discover the secret! The rhubarb goes in the chocolate cone before the meringue is piped in.

Sømods bolcher

If there is anything that is constantly offered to us it is the so-called bolcher or sour candy. In every shop in Tivoli and almost at every tourism attraction you will find jars and bags of this candy. It all goes back to the original sømods bolcher that has been made the same way since 1891. Although we had seen it produced in many places we decide to have a look. If we look in the shop and the working area, we feel that the only thing that has changed is the people. The process is an attraction that is anxiously protected. The public has been allowed to follow its process since day one. This is a work of passion, and tourists are crowded around the tables. We get the same short explanation as they make no exception for journalists. Per batch twenty kilograms of sugar is boiled to 180°C / 355°F when the mass is poured on a greased metal table; flavours and colouring as well as tartaric acid are added. There are about 80 flavours with different colour combinations and forms. The only mechanism used is an old fashioned form to shape the candies. You hear oohs and aahs when the men throw caramel over a hook and start pulling. Three confectioners work 140 kilograms of sugar a day. If you realize that each kilo of sugar produces 2000 candies you can figure out the production.

Lagkagehuset

A bakery where everyone sends us is Lagkagehuset, located in the heart of Christianshavn where it seems that hippies would like to create their own government. We don't notice this in the bakery, but it is busy there. It was seventeen years ago that Ole Kristoffersen started a bakery next to the present one. The building dates back to 1930. "When I started it was a traditional bakery. I got rid of 95% of it to become more specialized. In 1992 we put a large brick oven in the walls so our clients could see what we were doing. Authenticity gives them confidence and it creates the old baker's tradition." Popularity grew and Ole could soon expand. It is now 1000 square metres. "I started with 16 people, now we have 110 on the payroll. We are well known for our bread that really takes 24 hours to make. We bake all day long. When our bread is older than 10 hours we don't sell it anymore. 85% of the bread is baked during opening hours. This is not the same for rye bread, which should be older. Danish bread is a lot heavier than the French bread. One slice of our rye bread with pumpkin seeds will fill you up." We noticed that the traditional products are most popular but even for stuffed sandwiches people drive the extra mile. Three people are fully occupied with this. We heard that more than 2300 people come to the bakery every day and we are still talking about getting the highest quality products. They also deliver to top restaurants and airlines. We look around and see fourteen ladies running off their feet to help everyone in the shop. Two ladies do nothing else but fill the racks. Not only is Lagkagehuset known for their best quality but also for their interior, that reminds one more of a jewelry store than a bakery. "It doesn't matter where a client is located in the store, he can see all the assortments." The pâtisserie is built with arcs just one floor high and the sides and top are completely made of glass, whereas the base is made of wood. The display counters have no fluorescent lights, but hanging lamps. "This way you see the product in a more natural way. People don't wait in line here but can order from every corner and see what they order. I was the first baker with this kind of interior and in 2005 we were even acclaimed as the best store in Copenhagen. Many colleagues come in to get inspired which is a real compliment to us."
After a few days here our Danish language has not improved. Yet we do recognize that the name of the store has something to do with layered cakes. We seem to be right and Ole immediately starts to explain: "The architect came up with the name. He designed the building is such a way that you should be able to see layers of cake." At La Glace we saw layered cakes with a hundred year old history that never changed. Ole is more relaxed about it. "To me a Lagkage is a cake that gives you the freedom to combine and vary the layers any way you want... The bottom and layers are made of light and airy biscuit, but it makes no difference if they are filled with whipping cream, a mousse, fruit or chocolate."

70 % rugbr
32,-
Filonebrød
32,-

René Mathieu

Château de Bourglinster

This ambitious chef from the Château de Bourglinster in Luxembourg has enormous talent. His desserts are advanced and innovative.

Exotic shooter of blood orange, coconut, pineapple and an emulsion of old rum

For 4 people: **250 ml pineapple coulis, 250 ml blood orange juice, 100 ml cane sugar syrup, 250 ml coconut coulis, 200 ml coconut liqueur.**
For the rum foam: **250 ml milk, 30 ml old rum.**

Mix the pineapple coulis with half of the sugar syrup. Fill each glass one quarter full and freeze. Mix the coconut coulis with the coconut liqueur, pour on the frozen pineapple coulis and freeze again. Mix the orange juice with the rest of the sugar syrup and pour on top of the frozen coulis. Heat milk and rum to 80°C / 175°F, whisk with a hand blender, let rest for a few minutes and scoop foam on the thawed shooter. Serve with a small black straw.

Sweet Symphony of fruit, confiserie and chocolate

For the crème with kirsch: **250 ml slightly whipped cream, 100 ml milk, 1 vanilla bean, 30 ml kirsch, 50 g sugar, 2 gelatin leaves.**
For the pure chocolate crème: **250 ml milk, 250 ml cream, 75 g sugar, 100 g egg yolk, 200 g pure chocolate 70%.**
For the biscuit: **100 g egg, 50 g sugar, 35 g corn starch, 15 g cocoa powder.**
For the garnish: **20 amarena cherries with syrup, 4 chocolate cigarettes, 4 pieces of Atsina cress, cherry marshmallows.**

For the biscuit beat eggs and sugar, add cornstarch and cocoa powder, bake 10 minutes at 180°C / 355°F with a bit of steam and freeze to make the slicing easier. For the chocolate crème bring milk and cream to a boil, pour on the egg yolks and stir well. Put back on the heat and cook to 86°C / 185°F, then add melted chocolate. Mix everything thoroughly and cool. For crème with kirsch, infuse vanilla bean in milk, cool and add slightly whipped cream and sugar. Dissolve gelatin in a bit of warm kirsch and add to the mixture. Add the rest of the kirsch till you get the consistency of yogurt. Get nice stem glasses and put four amarena cherries on the bottom of each glass. Pour a bit of kirsch crème on it. Put a round slice of biscuit on top and finish the glasses with the chocolate crème. Finish with garnish.

Ice cream of micro-greens

For 1 litre ice cream: **500 g milk, 150 g whipping cream, 100 g crystal sugar, 30 g glucose powder, 20 g invert sugar, 35 g milk powder, 40 g Lime cress, 40 g Atsina cress, 1 tbs candied lemon peel, brunoise of finely sliced licorice laces, 4 small candy flosses, crushed pistachios.**

Heat milk and infuse with the different cresses. Mix, drain and add milk powder, the invert sugar and the glucose. Add the crystal sugar and heat to 86°C / 185°F. Cool and spin in ice cream maker with the lemon peel and licorice brunoise. Freeze. Fill glass with a scoop of ice cream and garnish with candyfloss and crushed pistachios.

Strawberries, Almond Foam and Pistachio Ice cream

For 4 people: **500 ml whipping cream, 300 ml strawberry coulis, 2 g xantana (thickener), juice of 1 lemon, 50 g sugar, 200 g strawberries, 100 ml strawberry syrup, 4 scoops pistachio ice cream, 1 small bunch of chopped mint, 6 g agar-agar, 100 g sugar, 200 ml water, 4 mint leaves dipped in chocolate, fresh strawberries (sliced).**
For the almond foam: **500 ml whipping cream, 20 ml almond milk, 2 g xantana.**

Pour 1/4 of the strawberry coulis with 50 g sugar, lemon juice and xantana in a siphon and insert two charges. Heat the rest of the strawberry coulis with the agar-agar and the chopped mint. Fill a shallow dish up to 3 cm deep and let cool for 10 minutes. Cut in cubes of 3 x 3 cm. For the almond foam, pour cream, almond milk and xantana in a siphon and insert 2 charges. Cut strawberries and mix with strawberry syrup. Make a caramel with water and sugar. Dip the rim of glasses in this caramel and let cool to get a nice looking brim. Place slices of strawberry on the bottom of each glass and top with a scoop of pistachio ice cream. Cover this with pieces of strawberry and mint and finish piping almond foam and strawberry foam on top. Insert mint leaf and strawberries and serve immediately.

Smoked crème brûlée au chocolate, candied pear and spice cake

For 4 people: **cane sugar, a few black licorice laces.**
For the pear compôte: **two pears poached in syrup and sliced as brunoise, 50 g brunoise of spice cake.**
For the crème brûlée: **250 ml milk, 250 ml cream, 4 egg yolks, 100 g pure chocolate, 75 g sugar, 50 g cedar plank.**

Bring milk, cream and sugar to a boil; remove from the heat, add chocolate and mix well. Pour mixture on the egg yolks and put in a small bowl. Place bowl in a tall pot, put cedar wood next to the small bowl and light the cedar to smoke. Cover with an airtight lid and refrigerate for 24 hours. Next day mix pear brunoise and the spice cake and fill four ovenproof glasses. Pour crème brûlée in the glasses and put in the oven for 6 minutes at 100°C / 210°F. Sprinkle with cane sugar and torch. Wrap licorice laces around a sharpening steel and deep-fry for a few minutes for garnish.

Ice cream lollipop of white chocolate and an emulsion of rose petals

For the white chocolate sorbet: **800 ml water, 75 g sugar, 200 g white chocolate, 60 ml eau de vie of cocoa.**
For the emulsion of rose petals: **10 ml rose water, 250 ml milk, 250 ml cream, 6 non-sprayed Sonia roses, 50 g sugar, 2 g methyl cellulose.**

Bring water and sugar to a boil. Once boiling add 100 g white chocolate and eau de vie, mix until homogenous, cool and spin. Fill forms (4 cm wide and 2 cm high), insert a little stick, and put in the freezer. Melt the rest of the chocolate, dip the frozen lollipop in it and put back in the freezer. Make emulsion of rose petals, rose water and sugar and add the methyl cellulose. Drain, pour in a siphon and insert two chargers. Pipe rose emulsion in a glass and put ice cream lollipop in it.

Violet foam with explosive cocoa-ravioli

For the violet foam: **500 ml water, 2 g methylcellulose, 2 g soya lecithin, 75 g violet candies (sour candies made with violet flavour).**
For the ravioli: **4 sheets of ouwel (edible paper), 5 g citric acid, 5 g crackling sugar, 5 g ground violet candies.**

Heat water with candies, the soya lecithin and the methyl cellulose, pour in a siphon and insert two chargers. From edible paper, create 8 rounds of 5 cm in diameter. Make a mixture of citric acid, candy powder and crackling sugar and put in the middle of four of the rounds. Wet the edges with egg white and cover each round of ouwel with another one. This creates the ravioli. Put in the oven for 3 minutes at 175°C / 345°F to make a soufflé. Sprinkle with cocoa powder. Fill a glass with violet foam and stick a ravioli in it.

Maison Pic

Philippe Rigollot is the chef pâtissier of the 3-star restaurant Maison Pic in Valence. He followed a career that would make many of his colleagues envious. At the age of 15 he started at the Lenôtre boutique in Paris where he worked for 8 years. After that he became a chef-pâtissier at Le Pré Catalan. In 2005 he was part of the French National Pastry Team, under the guidance of Jacques Charette, and they became world champions. His philosophy: pure flavours. Don't mix too many flavours and textures together. Philippe is fond of fruits. When he develops a new creation, his first thought is a kind of fruit. Then he starts thinking techniques and presentation.

Exotic Fruits and Chocolate

For 8 people:

For the chocolate ganache: **200 g cream, 80 g milk, 200 g chocolate Manjari (Valrhona chocolate 64%), 20 g butter, 50 g eggs.**
For the lychee sorbet ice cream: **200 g lychee puree, 90 g water, 40 g sugar, 17 g glucose powder, 1 g stabilizer.**
For the passion fruit and banana cream: **100 g egg, 90 g sugar, 60 g passion fruit puree, 30 g banana puree, 20 g lime juice, 1 gelatin leaf, 150 g butter.**
For the pineapple-rum marmalade: **175 g pineapple, ½ vanilla bean, 25 g sugar, 3 g cornstarch, 10 g rum, 10 g raisins soaked in rum.**
For the rum Chantilly: **200 g cream, 20 g sugar, 5 g rum.**

For the ganache, heat cream and milk and pour over the chocolate and butter. Process to a smooth ganache and add the eggs. Pour in a cake form of 6 cm in diameter and bake for 4-5 minutes at 150°C / 300°F.
For the sorbet ice cream, make a syrup of water, sugar, glucose and the stabilizer. After boiling pour it on the lychee puree and spin in ice cream machine. Spread ice cream between metal rulers that are 1 cm thick and put in the freezer. Once frozen, cut rings of 6 cm in diameter and put back in freezer.
For the fruit cream beat eggs and sugar. Heat both purees with the lime juice, add to egg mixture and heat for a few minutes. Take off the heat and add the soaked gelatin till it reaches a temperature of 40°C / 105°F. Put in freezer. For the marmalade, peel the pineapple, cut in pieces, put in a pot with sugar and vanilla and let simmer on low heat. Mix cornstarch with the rum, combine with the pineapple and add raisins. Refrigerate. For the chantilly, combine all ingredients and beat to make a chantilly.
Place chocolate in a deep plate, put ganache tart in centre and pour chantilly around it. Put the ring of sorbet ice cream on the tart and a savarin of passion fruit and banana cream. Garnish the savarin with pineapple marmalade. Finish with a spiral of chocolate and gold leaves.

Rhubarb and Tarragon

For 8 people:

For the shortbread: **220 g butter, 100 g sugar, 35 g flour, 5 g dry yeast.**

For the rhubarb ice cream: **150 g rhubarb puree, 250 g vanilla ice cream.**

For the spice cracker: **100 g flour, 100 g water, 133 g brown sugar, 133 g sugar, 133 g butter, 8 g four-spice mix.**

For the tarragon crème: **375 g whole milk, 10 g spice cake, 50 g sugar, ¼ vanilla bean, 3 leaves of gelatin, 18 g fresh tarragon.**

For the spice cake: **250 g honey, 50 g sugar, 175 g whole milk, 1.5 eggs, 125 g rye flour, 20 g baking powder, 5 g four-spice mix, 50 g candied orange, 1 orange peel.**

For the rhubarb marmalade: **500 g rhubarb, 100 g sugar, 2.5 g lemon juice.**

For the sauce: **reduced rhubarb juice, neutral nappage (glaze), red colouring.**

For shortbread mix all ingredients and bake in the oven at 140°C / 285°F for 30 minutes. Crumble shortbread and set aside. Prepare vanilla ice cream and add the rhubarb puree. Pour in Pacojet or Frix machine and freeze. Mix water and both sugars for the cracker. Bring butter to room temperature and little by little add sugar-water to the butter. Next add flour and four-spice mix. Spread dough on a silpat and bake at 180°C / 355°F for 8 minutes. Cut squares of 21 x 4 cm and roll this around a ring of 6 cm in diameter.
For the crème heat milk and spice cake, mix together and add sugar and vanilla. Re-heat. Take off the heat and add the soaked gelatin and the fresh tarragon. Set aside in the cooler. Mix all ingredients for the spice cake, pour in a form and bake in the oven at 180°C / 355°F for 30 minutes. Cool and cut in small thin squares of 7 x 7 cm. Butter each square and bake in the oven at 160°C / 320°F for 10 minutes. For the marmalade, peel rhubarb, cut in pieces, mix with sugar and lemon juice, drain for 24 hours and cook like a compote. Mix the ingredients for the sauce to get a thick consistency and colour lightly with the red colouring. Put some shortbread crumble on the cracker and cover with tarragon crème and rhubarb marmalade. Top with a square of spice cake. Garnish with a quenelle of ice cream and a leaf of tarragon.

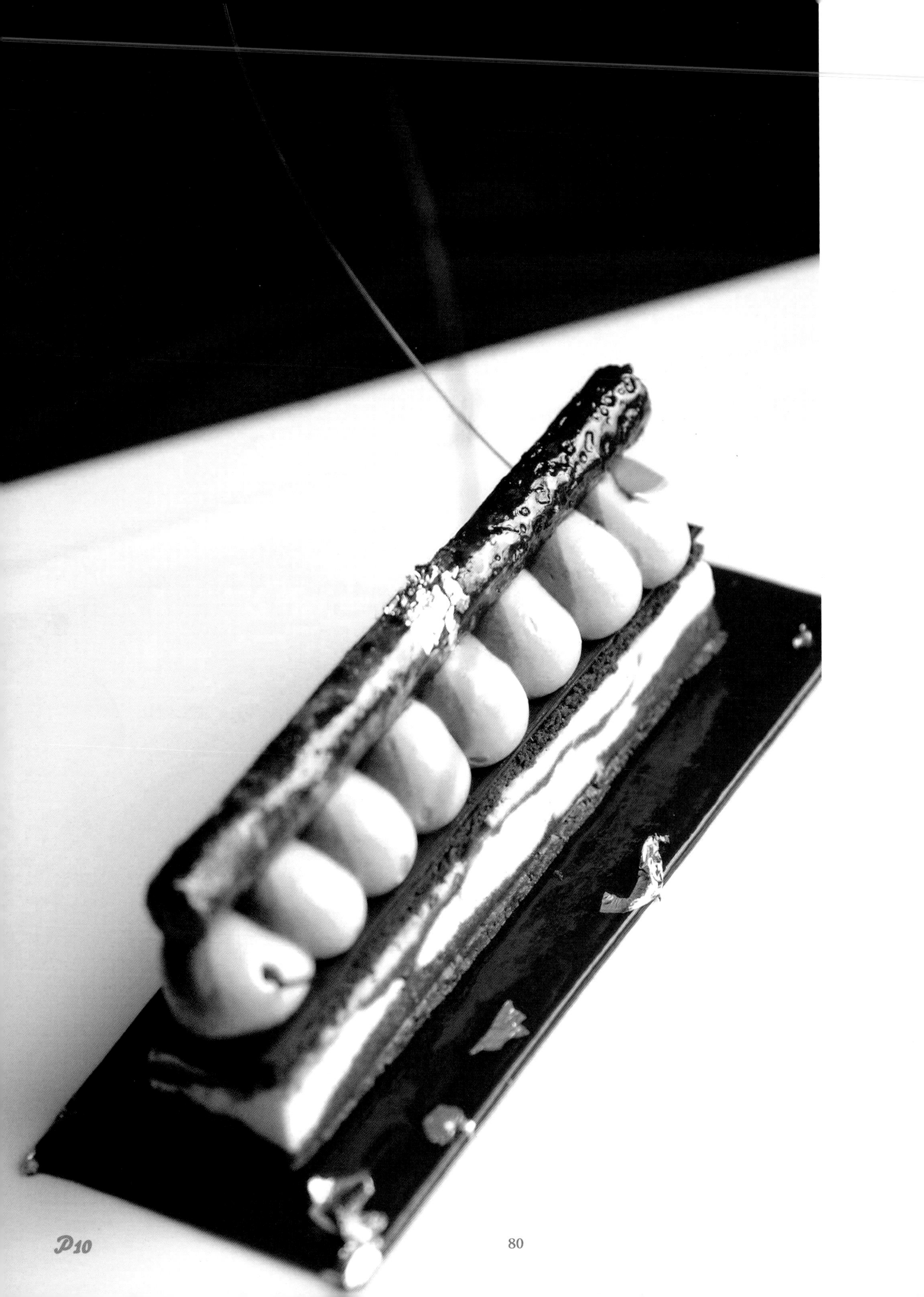

Raspberry and Paprika

This dessert made Philippe world champion in 2005

For 8 people:

For the crousti praliné: **50 g hazelnut praline 60%, 12 g hazelnut paste, 25 g Manjari chocolate (Valrhona 64%).**
For kirsch ice cream: **150 g milk, 10 g milk powder, 24 g butter, 8 g egg yolk, 16 g sugar, 9 g glucose powder, 1 g pink pectogel, ½ vanilla bean, 8 g kirsch.**
For the paprika-tarragon sorbet ice cream: **400 ml water, 5 g paprika juice, 40 g sugar, 12 g glucose powder, 0.5 g pink pectogel, 100 g raspberry puree.**
For the cocoa streusel: **100 g butter, 100 g light icing sugar, 100 g almond powder, 1 g salt, 75 g flour, 15 g cocoa powder.**
For the Manjari ganache: **90 g cream (35% fat), 10 g glucose, 10 g invert sugar, 80 g chocolate Manjari (64%), 180 g cold cream (35% fat).**
For the raspberry confit: **100 g frozen pieces of raspberry, 53 g sugar, 3 g pectin NH, 3 g lemon juice, 3 g kirsch.**
For the raspberry sauce: **100 g raspberry puree, 26 g sugar, 1 g pectin NH, 3 g lemon juice, 4 g kirsch.**

For the crousti, melt chocolate au bain-marie and using a spatula mix praliné and hazelnut paste. Spread out on parchment paper to get a 3mm thick layer. Put in cooler and cut in squares of 14 x 3 cm.
For the ice cream, heat milk, milk powder, butter and vanilla. Divide sugar in half; mix one part with the egg yolk and the other part with the glucose powder and pectogel. Cool milk to 40°C / 105°F and pour on the sugar and glucose. Pour that mixture on the egg yolk mix and heat to 85°C / 185°F, cool, sprinkle with kirsch and spin in an ice cream machine.
For the sorbet ice cream, make a syrup with sugar, glucose powder and paprika juice. After cooking add the raspberry puree and spin. Using both ice creams, create a "marble" and spread between metal rulers that are 12mm thick, put in the freezer.
For the streusel make a dough with all ingredients. Roll to 2 mm thickness and bake in the oven at 160°C / 320°F for 25 minutes.
Cut immediately in squares of 14 x 3 cm.
For the ganache melt chocolate au bain-marie. Cook cream and glucose, pour carefully on the ganache and process until smooth. Add the cooled cream and put in fridge for at least 12 hours. Whip ganache as for chantilly. For the confit, put all ingredients in a pot and simmer for 2 or 3 minutes. Take off the heat, add the lemon juice and kirsch and put in the fridge. Use the same method for the sauce as for the confit, pour on a plate and create a layer of 3 mm thickness, cut in rectangles of 17 x 7 cm and set aside in the freezer.
Arrange frozen raspberry sauce on a plate with a crousti on top. Garnish with the marbled ice cream and streusel. Using a piping bag, pipe ganache on the streusel. Put raspberry confit in a sugar dispenser to decorate the plate. Garnish with gold leaves and small sugar.

Apple and Champagne

For 4 people:

For the crumble: 50 g butter, 50 g egg yolks, 50 g flour.
For the champagne crème: 150 g cream, 175 g champagne, 60 g sugar, 4 g gelatin.
For poached apples: 4 cooking apples, 250 g apple juice, 25 g lemon juice, 3 g pectin NH, 15 g sugar.
For the sugar leaf: 40 g water, 100 g sugar, 40 g glucose.
For champagne-sorbet: 185 g champagne, 85 g water, 85 g sugar, 30 g glucose, juice and peel of ½ orange.
For the apple chips: 1 apple (granny smith), 100 g water, 100 g sugar, juice of ½ lemon.

For the crumble bring butter to room temperature, add sugar and mix well. Add egg yolk and then flour. Spread on a baking sheet and bake at 150°C / 300°F for 20-30 minutes. When done chop it coarsely and cool.
For the crème, whip the cream. Soak gelatin. Mix sugar with the champagne and dissolve gelatin in a bit of champagne. Then add rest of the champagne and the whipped cream. Cool in fridge.
Peel apples, cut in little balls with a melon baller and dip in water and a bit of lemon juice. Dehydrate the peels and remaining pieces of apple and heat apple juice with lemon juice. Mix sugar with pectin, add to the

juice and boil. Pour the warm juice over the little apple balls and put in the fridge. For the sugar leaf, heat water with glucose to 150°C / 300°F. Pour on parchment paper and cool. Then grind in Robot coupe, sprinkle on parchment paper and melt in the oven at 200°C / 390°F for 4-5 minutes. When melted, cover with another sheet of parchment paper and roll out into a very thin layer. Cut large rectangles and roll around a pipe. Before removing the paper, sugar should be totally cooled off.
For the sorbet, heat water, sugar, glucose, orange juice and orange peel. Add champagne, mix well, sieve and spin. For the chips, slice apples very thin. Boil water with sugar and lemon juice, dip apple slices in this syrup and refrigerate for 24 hours. Drain apple slices, put on parchment paper and dry in the oven at 50°C / 120°F for 3 hours.

Etoile of chocolate and peppermint

For the Caraïben gel: 300 g whole milk, 20 g sugar, 1.5 g pectin X58, 90 g chocolate Caraïbe (Valrhona 66%).
For the streusel: 100 g butter, 100 g light icing sugar, 100 g almond powder, 1 g salt, 75 g flour, 15 g cocoa powder.
For the peppermint-sorbet: 300 g water, 45 g invert sugar, 3 g stabilizer, 90 g sugar, 18 g lemon juice, 30 g peppermint leaves.
For the mint-espuma: 100 g whole milk, 6 g sugar, 1 g pectin X58, 20 g peppermint leaves.

For the gel, heat milk and add sugar-pectin mix. Bring to a boil, gradually add the chocolate and cool to 30°C / 85°F. Pour gel in chocolate rings and let crystallize in the cooler for 4 hours. For streusel, mix all ingredients to a dough, roll out to a 2 mm layer, bake in the oven at 140°C / 285°F for 25 minutes and cut in small squares of 1 cm. For sorbet, prepare syrup with water, the invert sugar, the stabilizer, the sugar and the lemon juice, cool and mix with peppermint leaves and spin in the machine. For the espuma, heat milk with sugar and pectin, add peppermint leaves and simmer for 10 minutes, cool and pour in a siphon, add two chargers and set in the fridge.
Using a template, create a star of chocolate and put on a plate.
Place chocolate ring filled with gel in the middle. Pierce a little hole in the gel and spoon in some sorbet ice cream. Sprinkle everything with streusel and cover with a chocolate star with a hole in the centre.
Fill with espuma. Roll a piece of streusel in gold powder and place that on the espuma.

Miniature flavours in your dessert

Koppert Cress

Last year we introduced you to the always innovative company Koppert Cress, a company that is famous all over the world for its miniature plants and specialties. In this edition of Pastry in Europe we will look at the applications of some of the products that are developed especially for pâtisserie.

Apple Blossom

This decorative heart and angel shaped small flower with a salmon colour has the distinctive taste of a green apple. It is very suitable for a variety of desserts and cocktails. Because of the colour, guests have a different taste association.

Pure Enjoyment with Pure Chocolate

by Wouter van Laarhoven

For 4 people: apple blossom
For the chocolate crumble dough: 450 g flour, 250 g butter, 250 g icing sugar, 200 g almond powder, 20 g cocoa powder, 40 g water.
For the chocolate brownie: 250 g butter, 155 g chocolate, 200 g eggs, 300 g sugar, 120 g flour, 10 g baking powder, 150 g chopped nuts.
For the caramelized cylinder of chocolate: 200 g glucose, 200 g sugar, 200 g dark chocolate.
For the chocolate mousse: 82.5 egg yolk, 62.5 egg, 187.5 g sugar, 100 g water, 375 g dark chocolate, 175 g milk, 9 g gelatin, 750 g cream.
For the sponge cake: 600 g egg white, 120 g almond powder, 120 g cocoa powder, 140 g sugar, 40 g flour.
For the chocolate crème: 500 g cream, 30 g water, 16 g gelatin, 120 g chocolate.

Using your hands, put all ingredients for the crumble dough together, divide on a silpat and bake in the oven at 140°C/285°F for 30 minutes. For the brownie, melt chocolate and in the meantime lightly whip the eggs and sugar till fluffy. Add chocolate, melted butter, flour, baking powder and chopped nuts. Grease a baking sheet and pour batter on the sheet, bake for 20 minutes at 165°C/330°F. Cool and cut in squares. For the cylinder, boil sugar and glucose to 108°C/225°F. Add the chocolate and heat further to 140°C/285°F. Pour on a silpat and roll into a very thin layer. Cut in strips and roll to create cylinders. For the chocolate mousse, heat sugar and water to 121°C/250°F. Beat egg yolk and egg and carefully combine with the sugar syrup while still beating until it is cold. Melt chocolate and boil the milk. Mix together and dissolve the soaked gelatin. Add milk mixture to the beaten egg and carefully add the whipped cream.
Pour mousse in half ball forms. For the sponge dough mix all ingredients into a smooth batter, pass through a fine mesh sieve and pour in a siphon. Attach three chargers and pipe in small plastic cups. Put cakes for 40 seconds in a microwave. Remove from cups and cut in coarse pieces.
For the crème, heat cream, water and chocolate, add the soaked gelatin and cool. Beat this mixture in a KitchenAid until it gets tough. Arrange all the different parts in a playful way on a plate and finish with freshly picked pieces of apple blossom.

Limon Cress

This is one of the 150 edible basil varieties. While the taste is lingering on, the lime comes to the surface, but in the back of the throat it tastes like pastis. This cress can easily be used in all kinds of desserts.

Cone-shaped dessert with coconut, raspberry, pistachio, and mascarpone

by Jurgen Koens

For 4 people: Limon Cress, Apple Blossom.
For the coconut mousse: 300 g coconut coulis, 150 g whipping cream, 7 g gelatin, 35 g Italian meringue.
For the raspberry crémeux: 80 g raspberry coulis, 10 g egg yolk, 20 g egg, 15 g sugar, 25 g mascarpone, ½ leaf gelatin.
For the pistachio crème: 135 g pistachio paste, 125 g whipping cream
For the dessert bottom: 180 g bastogne koek, 20 g cocoa powder, 15 g roasted almonds, 10 g milk chocolate.
For raspberry crunch: 100 g isomaltose, 20 g fondant, 20 g raspberry powder.
For raspberry jelly: 250 g raspberry juice, 3 g agar-agar, 100 g sugar, 1 g gellan.
For the lime mascarpone: 200 g mascarpone, 35 g icing sugar, 5 g finely cut Limon Cress, 100 g lime juice.
For the white chocolate spray: 100 g white chocolate, 80 g cocoa butter

For the coconut mousse, heat coulis and dissolve the soaked gelatin in it, cool to 28°C/82°F and carefully add the meringue. Then add the whipped cream. Set aside. For the crémeux mix egg yolk, egg, sugar and gelatin and in the meantime bring coulis to a boil. Pour hot coulis on the egg mixture and prepare as an anglaise. Let cool to 28°C/82°F and using a hand held blender mix with mascarpone until it becomes glossy.
For the jelly, mix the dry ingredients, heat juice and when it reaches 35°C/95°F add the mixed dry ingredients. Make a smooth batter with the hand blender and heat to 90°C/195°F. Cool and mix in the Thermomix until totally smooth. Let harden in the cooler. Fill a cone form with ¾ coconut mousse, pipe crèmeux on top and finish with raspberry jelly. Freeze, loose the forms and freeze again. Garnish softly with chocolate

spray and thaw. For the pistachio crème, put paste in Thermomix on #3 and slowly add the cream while processing. Let set slightly in the cooler. For the dessert bottom put all ingredients in a KitchenAid and process to powder. For the crunch, melt isomaltose, add the fondant until smooth, stirring firmly. Cool and process in Thermomix with the raspberry powder. Sprinkle powder on a silpat and melt in the oven at 150°C/300°F. Remove from the oven and let harden. Mix all ingredients for the lime mascarpone and serve cold. Spoon some of the bottom crust on a plate and place a cone in the centre. Drop some mascarpone and raspberry jelly along the side and add some crunch. Finish dessert with freshly picked Limon Cress and Apple Blossom.

Dushi Button

Mint and thyme-like flavour but much sweeter than sugar. It can be used anywhere to replace a drop of honey or another sweet enhancer. A small dot on a dessert gives a surprising flavour and goes extremely well with red fruit. It can also be hidden in a marshmallow or crumbled in part of a dessert.

Chocolate Covered Universe

by Hidde de Brabander

For the chocolate fudge: **950 g sugar, 500 g water, 500 g softened butter, 1350 g couverture, 1200 g eggs.**
For the black jelly: **965 g water, 1200 g sugar, 400 g cocoa powder, 1800 g cream, 40 g gelatin.**
For the chocolate mousse: **185 g chocolate couverture, 300 g pâte à bombe, 620 g lightly whipped cream, crumbled dushi buttons.**
For the crunchy chocolate: **500 g sugar, 500 g glucose syrup, 300 g dark chocolate.**
For the chocolate crème: **800 g whipping cream, 175 g egg yolk, 100 g sugar, 10 g leaves of gelatin, 100 g dark chocolate.**

For the chocolate fudge, bring water and sugar to a boil, put on the butter in pieces and mix thoroughly. Add the eggs and stir to a homogenous blend. Using a spatula mix it with the crumbled dushi buttons. Pour in desired forms and bake in the oven at 205°C/400°F.
For the black jelly, bring water, sugar, cocoa powder and cream to a boil and reduce on low heat for about 45 minutes. Dissolve soaked gelatin in it and set aside. For the mousse mix the melted couverture with part of the lightly whipped cream, add the pâte à bombe and the rest of the cream. For the crunchy chocolate, caramelize the sugar and glucose syrup lightly. Immediately add the couverture and pour on a silpat. When hardened process to a very fine powder and using a shablon (template) sprinkle a thin layer on a silpat. Melt in the oven at 180°C/355°F and cool. To prevent it from getting soft, pipe couverture on each side. For the crème, combine cream, egg yolk and sugar, pour in the Thermomix and process for 5 minutes at 80°C/175°F. Add the soaked gelatin and mix for another minute. Pass through a fine mesh sieve. Using a cake form create layers with the different parts and let set. Remove from the form, heat the jelly slightly and glaze the cake. Garnish with some dushi buttons, some coloured powder and a crunchy cylinder.

Atsina Cress

This has a very aromatic sweet flavour like licorice. Endless combinations with desserts are possible. It beats the peppermint leaf, not only in presentation, but also in digestion. This is THE dessert herb for the future.

Chocolate crémeux and cherry mousse wrapped in thin layers of feuillantine and chocolate sablé

by Peter Remmelzwaal

For 4 people: Atsina cress, crumbled chocolate biscuit, melted chocolate, spiced cherry compôte.
For the Breton chocolate: 200 g butter, 160 g light brown sugar, 6 g lemon juice, 2 g salt, 25 g egg, 12 g baking powder, 315 g flour, 15 g cocoa powder, 15 g finely ground cocoa nibs.
For the chocolate crémeux: 240 g milk, 360 g cream, 96 g egg yolk, 54 g sugar, 7 g gelatin, 75 g cream cheese, 180 g manjari chocolate (Valrhona).
For the cherry mousse: 200 g Moscato d'Asti, 300 g cherry puree, 60 g lemon puree, 600 g unsweetened whipping cream, 125 g sugar, 12 g egg white powder, 18 g gelatin, cherry liqueur.
For the cherry jelly: 100 g water, 300 g strained cherry puree, 400 g sugar, 200 g glucose, 6 g pectin X58, 6 g pectin NH, 3 g lemon acid.
For the feuillantine: 2 parts of manjari chocolate, 1 part praline, 1 part crêpes dentelles (small crispy biscuits)

For the Breton chocolate stir to soften the butter and sugar, salt and lemon juice. Combine with egg and slowly add flour, baking powder and cocoa powder. Finally add the ground nibs. Roll this dough to 2 mm thickness and cut in slices of 2.5 x 9 cm. Bake in the oven 170°C/340°F. For the cremeux heat milk and cream. Whisk egg yolk and sugar and carefully add to the hot milk. Prepare further as an anglaise and take off the heat. Slowly mix with the cream cheese, soaked gelatin and chocolate. Spread cremeux in a rectangle form and sprinkle with crumbled chocolate biscuits. Freeze and cut in strips of 2 x 8 cm. For the cherry mousse mix sugar and egg white powder and 100 g cherry puree of 30°C/85°F and beat in KitchenAid until stiff. Heat part of the rest of the cherry puree to 80°C/175°F, dissolve soaked gelatin in it and mix with the last part of cherry and lemon puree. Spoon the obtained foam through with a spatula and add the Moscato and cherry liqueur, finishing with the whipped cream. Pipe mousse in small tubes of 2 cm in diameter and freeze. Remove from their forms and cut in 9 cm length, glaze with cherry jelly. To make the jelly, mix both pectins with 100 g sugar and water. Heat cherry puree with sugar and glucose to 70°C/160°F, add pectin and bring to a boil. Add the lemon acid, let rest for a bit and remove the foam. For the feuillantine, mix all ingredients, roll out thinly and cut in strips of 2.5 x 9 cm. Spread some melted chocolate on a plastic sheet of 9 x 12 cm and go over it with a serrated comb. Cover a small plastic tube and roll chocolate around it.
Let harden and remove the plastic. Place a slice of Breton chocolate on a plate with cremeux and finish with feuillantine. Put chocolate spiral on top and fill with cherry mousse. Garnish with Atsina Cress and spiced cherry compôte.

Director and creative brain behind Koppert Cress Rob Baan

Koppert Cress Europe
De Poel 1 – Monster (The Netherlands)
Phone: + 31 174 24 28 19

Koppert Cress USA LLC
22425 Middle Road / Route 48
Cutchogue NY 11935
Phone: + 1 516 437 57 00

www.koppertcress.com

Spices in Pâtisserie

Five years ago we introduced the use of spices in pâtisserie in our European magazine Pâtisserie & Desserts. This we did, and still do, in collaboration with the well-known spice company Verstegen. This initiative led to widespread acceptance and spices have now become commonplace in the pâtisserie and chocolaterie of restaurants.

Small apples and red cabbage

For 4 people: **2 apples, sugar, 1 tbsp cinnamon, thin strips of apple.**
For the red cabbage: **1 red cabbage, some water, 400 g sugar, 4 pieces star anise, 2 cinnamon sticks.**
For the cannelloni: **600 g cooked red cabbage without spices, 4.8 g gellan.**
For star anise sauce: **700 ml cream, 300 ml milk, 5 pieces star anise, 50 g sugar, 10 g sugar, 10 egg yolks.**

Finely slice red cabbage on a slicer and cook with cinnamon, star anise, water and sugar until done. Cool and puree 600 g, pass through a sieve and catch the juice. Cook 250 g of the juice with the gellan. Pour a very thin layer on a flat surface and slice gel in wide strips. Roll the red cabbage in the clear gel. For the sauce bring cream, milk, star anise and sugar to a boil. Beat egg yolks with the rest of the sugar until foamy. Pour boiling mixture on the egg yolks and prepare as an anglaise. Core apples in different sizes. Fry apples in a dry pan with some sugar until golden. Serve cannelloni on the plate with fried apples and star anise sauce. Garnish apples with red cabbage and the cannelloni with some apple strips.

Carrot Parfait

For four people: **4 small shaped carrots, 1 carrot, sugar water 1:1, sugar, 4 thin round biscuits.**
For the parfait: **2 carrots, 2 cm fresh ginger, 3 pieces star anise, 3 eggs, 120 g sugar, 40 g ouzo, 300 g cream.**

Using a slicer, slice thin strips of carrot; dip in sugar water and dry in the oven at 120°C/250°F until totally dry; cut in long straight strips. For the parfait cook the carrots in water with ginger and star anise until done. Remove spices, puree the carrots and pass through a sieve. Whip cream lightly and beat eggs au bain-marie with sugar and ouzo. Beat until cold and add 200 g carrot puree. Mix whipped cream with the egg mixture; pour parfait in small round forms and freeze. Cook the small shaped carrots till done, dip in sugar water and roll through sugar. Wrap the dried carrot strips around the sugar carrots. Serve on a piece of biscuit and garnish with a small carrot.

Bloody Mary ice creams

***For about 10 small ice creams:* 200 ml vodka, 200 ml tomato juice, juice of 1 lime, 6 drops of Worcestershire sauce, 4 drops of Tabasco, salt, ground maniguette (African pepper).**
***For the celery:* 3 stalks of celery, 500 ml sugar water 1:1.**

Peel the celery and finely dice as a brunoise. Preserve celery in sugar water. For the ice cream mix all ingredients and use maniguette to taste. Divide celery in long small bags and add the Bloody Mary. Vacuum pack and freeze.

Spiced candy bar

***For 3 candy bars:* 400 g bitter chocolate 64%, 1 tbsp maniguette, ground in a mortar, 150 roasted almonds, 6 dried prunes, 200 ml caramel sauce.**

Polish bonbon forms with paper towel and chop the almonds and prunes. Melt chocolate and temper it. Line forms with chocolate and let harden. Divide the almonds, prunes, maniguette and sauce over the forms and cover with tempered chocolate. Let harden and loosen the bonbons.

Elvis' poppy seed bread with peanut butter and banana.

***For 4 people:* 1 banana, caramelized chopped peanuts.**
***For the brioche bread:* 1 kg flour, 700 g butter, 30 g fresh yeast, 30 g salt, 140 g milk, 12 eggs, 60 g sugar, 3 tbsp poppy seed.**
***For the peanut butter crème:* 150 g butter, 5 tbsp peanut butter, 100 g crème anglaise.**

For the brioche whip butter lightly. Heat the milk and make a paste with the yeast. Add to the eggs, sugar and flour. Mix this mixture slowly with the butter and knead for 5 minutes. Let dough rise and fold. Divide the dough on greased and floured baking sheets. Let rest in the fridge for 24 hours. Then let rise again. Bake brioche in the oven at 180°C/355°F for 45 minutes. For the crème, beat butter and peanut butter till white and add the crème anglaise. Once bread is cool, cut straight slices and pipe a layer of peanut crème on it, cover with slices of banana. Sprinkle some caramelized peanut pieces on top.

Pastry
in europe
BAR

VOLUME
6 7 8
BIEM/GEMA
ELVIS PRESLEY
ON STAGE

Liers Vlaaike

Under the smoke of the harbour of Antwerp lies a very old city called Lier. Some parts of the city are reminiscent of the beauty of Bruges or Gent. Judging by the many neo-renaissance and baroque facades, it was probably once a very rich city. On the other hand this city is also a village with its own known "vlaaike" (small flan). This is one of the oldest known local pastries in Belgium.

Although this "vlaaike" has existed for centuries, it was not until 1722 that someone wrote about it for the first time, maybe because it is such a simple pastry. The vlaaike has simply a pastry bottom and a filling. The bottom is made from flour, butter and water and has hardly changed over the centuries. The dough doesn't have to be sweet; the filling takes care of that. The dough is rolled out and pressed in small wooden forms of 6 cm in diameter. Then the bottoms are taken out of the forms, still unbaked, and dried. This was done until 1960 when small metal forms were introduced. The filling is simple but ingenious. Most of it is light syrup mixed with milk, spices, flour and breadcrumbs. After it is mixed it looks more like porridge than filling. It takes about three hours for the flour and breadcrumbs to absorb most of the liquids. It then becomes a piping bag filling. Cinnamon, ground coriander and nutmeg provide the extra flavour. In the old days these spices could change a lot but thanks to a special Order of the Liers Vlaaike, is it now mostly the same.
It is important that part of an earlier filling mixture is added to the fresh one, the same as how sourdough bread uses a starter to be added to fresh dough. New mixtures will always contain enzymes of past products.
The bakers use light syrup because the darker syrup becomes bitter when baked. As soon as the filling is put on the pastry bottom it is baked. Typically the pastry will have a crack because the filling shrinks after it is cooled off. The bakers sell it as individual pastries or ten in a box.
The Vlaaike is more than a delicacy: the sugar content gives a hint about the weather according to baker Ceulemans: "The sugars draw humidity. When the filling is sticky and greasy there is a lot of humidity in the air so we know it is going to rain."

The Order of the Liers Vlaaike

It goes without saying that all bakers in Lier like to show off this sweet delicacy. In the past every baker had his own secret recipe that was whispered from father to son. Of course everyone thought that his own recipe was better than his neighbour's. This eventually resulted in so many different varieties that its stature as a recognizable tradition was in jeopardy. Rigid measures had to be taken. Baker Hendrickx led the way. During a meeting with the Bakers Guild, Hendrickx disclosed all his recipes and told them the time had come to make one rule.

Hendrickx: "Because everyone just did what he pleased, the public got very confused and didn't know anymore what a real Liers Vlaaike was. We were getting vlaaikes with sour cherries and apple filling." And it wasn't just the recipes that created controversy. When his Majesty the King visited Lier, one of the bakers offered him a vlaaike, which the King thoroughly enjoyed. The day after the King's visit, this baker put a big sign on this shop saying "Hofleverancier" meaning "I deliver to the Royal Family!" The rest of the bakers went nuts. Rules and regulation became the order of the day, so during the meeting with the Bakers' Guild Hendrickx garnered support from the other bakers. It was decided to compare recipes with each other and come up with one recipe only that became the recipe of all the members of the Guild. Calm had returned to Lier, for a while. Despite the rules, some bakers started to use different packaging and promote lower prices, but that has changed. The Liers Vlaaike has now one kind of packaging and one price. In the meantime the Liers Vlaaike has gotten official recognition and protection from the European Union. You can also bake your own but cannot call it Liers Vlaaike, as this belongs solely to Lier.

Liers Vlaaike

For 400 Liers Vlaaikes: 1 litre water, 500 g butter, 1700 g flour. *Filling:* 2200 g breadcrumbs, 750 mls light syrup, 4 litres milk, 400 g flour, 200 g four-spice powder, starting dough from the previous batch.

In the mixer combine butter, flour and water to make a dough. Let rest and roll out to 2.5 mm thickness. Press in little forms and let rest again for 15 minutes pressing it a bit more. Mix milk and syrup and stir well. Add the rest of the ingredients. Leave the filling for at least 3 hours; then put in a piping bag to fill the bottoms. Pre-heat oven to 190°C / 375°F. Bake until brown, let cool and invert.

Berlin

It is quite amazing to see old churches and stark office buildings right next to each other. When we are in Berlin the weather is glorious; that of course makes any city more beautiful. But we imagine it can also look pretty gloomy on a bleak winter day. We cannot complain about pâtisserie here as there is something for everyone. It is a must to visit the old fashioned konditoreis (pastry shops).

Albrecht Pâtisserie

Not far from Kollwitzplatz in North Berlin is the Rykerstrasse. Here we met one of the most famous pâtissiers of Berlin: Stephanie Albrecht. There are three shops in Berlin, but we visit the oldest and largest one. It has a nice ambience with a little side café so patrons can also enjoy the pastries outside. The shop, located in a nice neighbourhood, is doing well. There is a line up of customers. We couldn't find Chef Albrecht in there, but find her a few blocks down the street in her production kitchen. She is busy making ice cream as summer is just around the corner. Fortunately she takes some time to talk to us: "My grandfather was a baker and I like working with my hands. I have been working in pâtisserie for the past eleven years. I got my experience in a number of pâtisserie shops in Berlin or so called konditoreis. These shops were not famous but I learned the basics. Why I chose pâtisserie I don't know. It could have been bread making or even woodcarving. Before I started my own business I worked six months in Paris at pâtisserie Dossemont. France really is the foundation of pâtisserie." After her adventure abroad, she wanted to get her Masters in pâtisserie, which she finished in two months. Then it became time to start for herself. "Many people were skeptical about my pâtisserie ambitions. I do not make pompous cakes or heavy meringue tarts. One thing led to another and now we have three shops, so there is a market for my style." She has a total of nine employees. It is too bad there are few young people in Berlin starting in pâtisserie. "The rent in Berlin is much higher than anywhere else, and

you can't live from pastry alone." Stephanie has no plans for the future. "I do hope to find some time to work with a colleague in France, even if it is just for a few days. I am not planning a fourth shop yet. We are busy enough and we want to keep delivering quality."
Next to Stephanie's shop we found a small chocolate store called Choco Finesse and the name says it all. Here we find about thirty different kinds of chocolate from all over the world and a small selection of truffles and bonbons. It is managed by Stephan Hähnel and his mother Angela. Should you decide to visit the Albrecht Pâtisserie then don't forget to visit this store as well.

Wiener Conditorei

Wiener Conditorei & Coffeehaus am Roseneck

We travel from one classic pâtisserie shop to another, because it is only a thirteen minute drive to our next destination. We arrive at a large café that is filled with customers sitting outside. There, Berliners are chatting away with a cup of coffee and a piece of an unmistakable German pastry that you can find inside behind the beautifully displayed window.
We also see beers coming by so it is obvious people are enjoying themselves. We have an appointment with Manfred Otte who is a man of stature in Berlin. Otte was born in 1939 and has been in the baking business since 1955. He was involved with the world exposition in Brussels and also as a pâtissier on the Holland America Line, which gave him the opportunity to visit 58 countries. After that he worked in Yokohama in Japan and so on and so on. When we see a silver Mercedes AMG parked in front we know the owner is there. We also see the staff suddenly all perked up and standing straight. Herr Otte warmly greets everyone and tells us about his business. "My father was a pastry baker; we had a shop close to the Olympic stadium. After my traveling adventures I took over my father's business. It turned out to be too small for me very soon." Herr Otte is now owner of many cafés, cocktail bars and even an opera building. We are getting a tour in the Viennese konditorei, a classic one with the posh atmosphere of pastry shops we have gotten to know in Vienna. There is a separate section for specialty cakes, like wedding cakes. Many of these cakes have been made for years and they are all still bestsellers. We enter the bakery where fourteen pâtissiers and ten students are at work. If one notices the owner, the radio is immediately shut off. It is not fear, just respect. Herr Otte snaps his fingers and within two minutes the counter is full with twenty cakes. We ask Otte to describe the German pâtisserie, because if there is any expert here it is him. "The German pâtisserie is known for its large and filled cakes. As Germans we love our chocolate and also have many cakes with cream cheese as a base. Personally I prefer strudels." Herr Otte let us taste several cakes and indeed these do not fit in a calorie conscious diet. To be polite we did our best to taste them all. It is not easy to be a journalist sometimes.

Other cultures

As in other big cities there are warehouses that are ten storeys high. The department of pâtisserie in these warehouses is reminiscent of Paris and London. The business located on the Wittenbergplatz became the symbol of success of West Berlin after the war. French companies like Lenôtre are unbelievably successful here as well as several German chocolatiers. We see a sign that it is strictly prohibited to take photographs, so our photographer takes a risk going to jail or worse.
Another well known name in the pâtisserie of Berlin is Harry Genenz. His shop with the same name is on the Brandenburgische Strasse. It is a modern shop with dense little cakes. While we are visiting there is a constant line of customers. The owner is not active anymore; he has left it to 35 year old Frenchman Jean Christophe Duc, who did the famous apprenticeship "Tour de France", where he got a lot of experience in ten different companies. He picked up more experience in France and abroad. Why would a French pâtissier go to Germany? "That's a good question. I met Mr. Genenz ten years ago during a trade show. He told me that he wanted to make a change in the heavy German pâtisserie and asked if I wanted to work for him. My task was to bring in some French influence without insulting the German customers. Germans have a lot of pride. For example, I make a tart on the basis of the famous Baumkuchen. People in Berlin used to be happy with what they had, but now the city has become more open minded and gastronomy and pâtisserie have become much better."
As a foreigner in Germany, Jean had a vision that changed the classic pâtisserie in this country. "Many successful businesses have been pushed out by ruthless large industry. The number of skilled pâtissiers has become very small and the new generation is hard to find; there is no feedback." Jean likes to teach people what he has learned and therefore shares one of his recipes.

Sensation

For 2 round cakes of 15 cm: **sweet pastry dough, caramelized nuts**
For the chocolate ganache: **600 g cream, 200 g maracuja puree (passion fruit), 400 g dark chocolate, 120 g milk chocolate, 140 g egg yolks, 140 g sugar, 1 small minced chili pepper, 8 g ginger.**
For the chocolate biscuit: **300 g egg white, 250 g sugar, 240 g egg yolk, 160 g dark chocolate.**
For the chocolate glaze: **750 g milk chocolate, 250 g dark chocolate, 500 g cream, 50 g trimoline, 4 leaves of gelatin.**

Line the forms with the rolled out dough and pre-bake in oven at 180°C / 355°F until golden. For the ganache, bring chili pepper, ginger and cream to a boil and simmer a few minutes. Pass through a sieve and mix with the puree. Beat egg yolks with sugar, heat the puree and prepare as an anglaise. Mix the warm cream with the chocolates and pour on the pre-baked bottom. For the biscuit, beat egg whites and sugar until stiff, separately beat egg yolks and mix both with the melted chocolate. Prepare as a biscuit: spread thinly on a baking sheet and bake in the oven at 220°C / 355°F for 12 minutes. Cut two rounds out of the biscuit and press in the ganache. For the glaze, heat trimoline and cream and pour on the chocolates. Mix to a smooth consistency and add the soaked gelatin. Pour the glaze over the cakes and garnish with caramelized nuts.

Sucré

We have only been in Berlin for one week and have traveled from one end to another through the city. In every neighbourhood we try to discover what is happening in pâtisserie. We are looking for the famous Berlin balls. Unfortunately, nobody is interested in this winter treat at this time of the year. What about the Laugenbrezln? This cookie, resembling a pretzel, is not made in Berlin. Pâtissier owner Otte tells us that all brezln is delivered frozen and is a specialty of Beieren in Germany. "Fortunately we still have the Baumkuchen."
Our next destination is Kreuzberg, which reminds us of the problem neighbourhoods we were once told about. What we experience here we will never forget. It is proof that Berlin has become an amalgamation of different cultures. We stop at Barcellos-Salon Sucré but they are closed, understandable as we are too early. However, we do hear music coming from inside. No German Umpapa music, no Rammstein, but classical music by Frans Schubert. When we start knocking really hard on the door, it opens upon a strange combination: Erik Muller and his wife Katia Barcellos are the owners of a pâtisserie shop and a hairdressing salon. A cheerful smile, a firm handshake, a cup of tea and a perfectly baked croissant welcome us. Customers who notice that Erik is open a bit earlier than normal spontaneously help and put tables and chairs outside. A Turkish boy greets the owner with a well-meant "Bonjour".
It takes no time to have the sidewalk café opened and full of customers. The little shop is very cozy and small, divided in two sections. Katie runs the hairdressing salon and Erik is in charge of the small pâtisserie shop. The woman of the house is originally from Rio but decided to establish herself in Berlin. After she met Erik they joined the two businesses together as one store. Why did they decide on Kreuzberg? "We like the neighbourhood, to us this is the real Berlin. The people here are normal, down to earth and there are lots of cultures. Nobody hides behind masks of fashion and the latest trends." Erik is busy filling his display windows with beautiful French pâtisserie. He has a rigid life schedule. During the four days they are open, he gets up at 4:00 am and together with colleague Andreas he prepares all the dough. He goes to bed exactly at 9:00 pm on his working days. The chef is a philosopher who loves to talk about the enjoyment of his work. His motivation? The chirping birds that wake him up each morning. It doesn't seem important to him to make money. "As soon as people start to make money they want more and they lose the focus of quality. I am an artist and would rather have a small bakery where everything is made fresh. Our customer pays a bit more than somewhere else, but the quality is a lot better. For the money of two commercially produced croissants, here you get one!" Do we detect a bit of French arrogance? After tasting some more viennoiserie we leave that thought immediately. Without a doubt his products are divine. Each bite of his millefeuille is a small culinary orgasm. Erik gives us his vision: "A good pâtissier is somebody who prepares all his own dough with the

best butter and best flour available. It is somebody who works with love and passion. Not just the worker, but also the dough should have no stress." He has no rules, just makes what he likes every day. His assortments range from viennoiserie to beautiful fruit tarts.

Chocolate

As mentioned before, Germans love their chocolate. In Berlin you will find famous commercial stores, like Fassbender & Rausch in the Charlottenstrasse, well-known for their chocolate desserts. We also visit some unknown gems. We received a tip to go to THE German pâtissier talent, Guido Fuhrmann. His pâtisserie-chocolatier is called Werkstatt der Stube and has just been open for a few weeks. When we go inside our mouth drops in amazement; a rather small counter shows beautiful bonbons and pastries. Our eyes catch the ornamental display behind a large glass wall. Guido gives us more explanation: "In Germany pâtisserie was seen far too long as a step child. That is one of the reasons why I put the Werkstatt (workshop) in my store. When people see that we work with passion and detail on a small pastry or petit four, they are willing to pay for quality rather than mass production." Guido was also chef pâtissier in several hotels and restaurants; some of these were the Ritz Carlton Hotel, the Schloss Hotel and several Michelin-starred restaurants. His style is hip and fancy and he is playful with his pastry moulds. For example, he puts a dripping pastry on its side, which gives it a different look. We feel that his prices are rather low. "We can't be expensive. First I have to prove myself and I like my store to be accessible to everyone. Young and old should be able to enjoy my pastry and bonbons. In the few weeks I have been open, the reactions have been overwhelming. We are already making products for restaurants and hotels. I don't think my store should be any bigger." He has a bookcase with books from different chefs. "It is always a joy to look through a book from Pierre Hermé and also Pastry in Europe is one of my favourites. It inspires me to see and taste pâtisserie of my colleagues. I also like to follow the seasons, something that everyone should do. I change my assortment every two months." One of Guido's specialties is Chococrisp, made with puff pastry on the bottom, combined with a honey-chocolate mousse. He also shares another specialty with us.

Carré of blood orange with pistachio financier

For 15 carrés: **chocolate (melted) for piping, 15 sugar pearls, 15 small orange peels, 30 white chocolate gallettes.**
For the pistachio financier: **65 g icing sugar, 70 g egg white, 40 g ground almonds, 40 g white flour, 2 g baking powder, 25 g pistachio paté, 5 g trimoline, 40 g browned butter.**
For the blood orange jelly: **250 g blood orange coulis, 6 leaves of gelatin, 25 g sugar.**
For the mousse: **1 egg, 1 egg yolk, 3 leaves of gelatin, 10 ml Grand Marnier, 600 g lightly whipped cream, 300 g white chocolate.**

For the financier, mix icing sugar, ground almonds, flour and baking powder together. Beat egg whites and combine with flour mixture. Add the cooled browned butter, pistachio paté and the trimoline. Let the batter rest for one night in the fridge and bake a thin layer on a baking sheet at 200°C/390°F for 9 minutes. Cut in squares of 45 x 45 mm. For the jelly, bring part of the coulis and sugar to a boil, dissolve the soaked gelatin in it and add the rest of the coulis. Pour the jelly on a sheet, let set and cut squares of 40 x 40 mm. Beat egg and egg yolk au bain marie till foamy and beat until cool. Heat liquor and dissolve the soaked gelatin in it. Using a spatula combine Grand Marnier with the egg mixture and add the melted chocolate. Blend to a smooth consistency and stir in the cream. Build the pastry upside down in the carrés, starting with the mousse, then the jelly and finish with the financier. Pipe white chocolate on top and garnish with a sugar pearl, a small orange peel and a chocolate gallette.

In 't Veld

We are back in Berlin, in Prenzlauerberg, a nice new area with lots of sidewalk cafés. There are many trendy shops and the way we are dressed in our suits doesn't match with the skaters. We stop at a small shop called In 't Veld. The name sounds Dutch so we inquire. Indeed the father of the owner Holger in 't Veld was a Dutch captain who sailed the world oceans on luxurious ships under the Franco-Italian flag. His son went the other way and became a journalist for a pop magazine. However, his other passion was chocolate and he decided to build on that. We talk with Ronald Hermann, once a customer here but now an employee. "In this shop you can find lots of chocolate; we have about seventy kinds from different countries. Our goal is discovering unknown chocolate products. In 2006 we started with our own brand, since we were not happy with the flavours we received. We now produce eight different kinds, varying from 80% Criollo from Indonesia to a chocolate with a bit of chili." We taste some pieces and although strange flavours can turn disastrous, they seem to have found the right balance. The chocolaterie is not far from the shop and Ronald is proud to show it to us. Once in the shop, we cannot get enough of it. We see something that we have never seen before. A music record made of chocolate that actually can be played! Our German friend is changing some electric plugs and after a few minutes we hear the scratching sounds from Trude Herr, a German music Queen, born in 1927. The song's title is quite appropriate: "Ich will keine Schokolade." (I don't want chocolate). This is about a lady who likes to trade her chocolate for a handsome man. The record can only be played a few times and then has to be eaten....quite unique!

Fischers Fritz

Berlin has several top restaurants with a Michelin star. One restaurant has two stars and that is Fischers Fritz. In the kitchen we find the friendly chef Christian Lohse. His culinary talent is top class. In the pâtisserie we meet 28 year old Franka Segebrecht, who has been working in the Regent Hotel, where the restaurant is established for the last eight years. Five years ago she became the chef pâtissier. She studied visual art, which was a very suitable skill for her: "A dessert on a plate is like a painting. Flavours, colours and textures have to be in harmony. In pâtisserie it is good to have freedom working with different flavours. I am fond of sweets and that is why I like to work with Asian fruit that I combine with European influences." Franka gets a lot of inspiration from books of Hermé, Conticini, Adriá and the German chef Juan Amador.

Basil-lime sorbet with buttermilk foam

For 4 people: **lime chips, gold leaves.**
For the basil-lime sorbet: **500 g sugar, 600 ml water, zest of 1 lime, 400 ml fresh lime juice, 30 leaves basil, 2 Granny Smith apples (peeled and cut in pieces).**
For the tamarillo jelly and sauce: **10 peeled tamarillos, 100 ml water, marrow of 1 vanilla bean, brown sugar, 1-½ leaves of gelatin.**
For the buttermilk foam: **1 litre buttermilk, 200 g sour cream, 300 ml lime juice, 300 g sugar, 7 leaves of gelatin.**

For the sorbet, bring water, sugar and zest to a boil. Take off the heat and add the lime juice, the basil and the apple pieces. Marinate overnight, pass through a sieve and spin in turbo mixer. For the jelly, mix tamarillos with water and vanilla, add sugar to taste, heat the mixture and dissolve the gelatin in it. Pour on a plate to gel and cut in pieces. Prepare sauce the same way but without gelatin. For the buttermilk foam, bring lime juice and sugar to a boil, add the soaked gelatin, cool and add the sour cream and buttermilk. Let mixture cool, pour in a siphon and insert two chargers. Spoon the sorbet in a thin tall glass and pipe foam on top, press the lime chips in the foam. Serve with tamarillo jelly and some gold leaves.

Orange chocolate cream with mousse and chocochilli sorbet

For 4 people: orange powder, orange chips, gold leaves, edible pansies, mint.
For the crème: 2 litres cream, 600 g sugar, 100 g cocoa powder, 1 tbs cornstarch, 850 g orange chocolate from Valrhona, 12 leaves gelatin.
For the cocoa syrup: 100 g glucose, 40 g water, 1 tsp cocoa kernels, 1 tsp piment d'espellette (chili pepper), 1 tsp brown sugar, 1 tsp minced pistachios.
For the chocolate mousse: 120 g egg yolks, 1 egg, 100 g sugar, 50 g water, 1 leaf gelatin, 130 g dark chocolate, 130 g milk chocolate, 400 g lightly whipped cream, cocoa kernels.
For the sorbet: 250 g water, 30 g sugar, 30 g trimoline, 110 g bitter chocolate, 1 chili pepper.
For the tuille: 100 g glucose, 100 g milk, 250 g butter, 300 g sugar, 4 g pectin, 250 g cocoa kernels.

For the crème, heat cream, sugar and cocoa powder. Combine cornstarch with water and add to the mix to get a light smooth consistency. Then add the melted chocolate and the soaked gelatin. Pour the crème in small pastry molds and cool in the refrigerator. After they are set, take out of the molds and put through orange powder. For the syrup mix all required ingredients. For the mousse beat egg yolks and egg to a foam; boil water and sugar to 130°C / 265°F. Prepare like a pâte a bombe and while you are whisking it together add the soaked gelatin. Mix a small part of the crème with the melted chocolate till smooth and add the pâté a bombe. Using a spatula, carefully add the rest of the crème into the mix. Pour the mousse on a plate and sprinkle with cocoa kernels. Once the mousse has set cut in small squares. Garnish with gold leaf and a pansy. For the sorbet heat water and sugar, trimoline and chili pepper, add chocolate and blend to a smooth mixture. Pass through a sieve, cool and spin in a turbo mixer. For the tuille heat the glucose, milk and butter. Add sugar and pectin and cook at a temperature of 106°C / 220°F. Mix cocoa kernels with the mixture and pour on a sheet lined with parchment paper. Put another sheet of parchment paper on top and roll out into a paper-thin layer. Freeze and then bake the tuille in the oven for 7 minutes at 175°C / 350°F. Put the three layers (crème, mousse and sorbet) on a plate, garnish with crème and half an orange chip and serve with a small sprig of mint on the tuille.

Salad of Thai mango and coconut foam

For 4 people: 1 mango, coriander.
For the peach jelly: 10 peaches, sugar, 1 litre water, 5 leaves gelatin.
For the salad: 1 Thai mango, 10 lychees, 2 limes, 2 tsp peach jelly, chiffonade of green coriander leaves.
For the coconut foam: 1 litre coconut puree, 200 ml cream, brown sugar, juice of 1 lime, 7 leaves of gelatin.
For the coriander caramel: 130 g fondant, 75 g glucose, 1 tbs coriander seeds.

For the jelly, cut the peaches in pieces. Caramelize some sugar and add the peaches. Boil the water and deglaze the caramelized peaches. Mix and put through a sieve. Heat 500 ml of this juice and dissolve the soaked gelatin in it. For the salad peel mango and finely dice it as well as the lychees. Peel the lime and cut in small pieces. Add to the salad. Mix salad with the cooled peach jelly and coriander to taste.
For the foam cook puree and the cream, mix with the lime juice and add brown sugar to taste. Dissolve soaked gelatin in this mixture. Cool and pour in a siphon with two chargers. Caramelize the fondant and glucose and pour on a silpat. Roast the coriander seeds and put in a blender together with the cooled caramel to get a fine powder. Sieve this powder over round stencils and bake in the oven at 170°C / 350°F for one minute to get another caramel. Peel the mango, cut in slices and roll them up. Fill these with the foam and garnish with coriander.
Spoon salad in a tall round glass and place the rolls of mango around it. Garnish the foam with coriander and the rounds of caramel.

Marshmallows

Who hasn't indulged themselves as a child with bags full of marshmallows? This very well-known diamond-shaped candy in Europe gave all of us sweet sticky hands. The popularity of this candy is still growing strong.

The history of marshmallows is more interesting than it seems. Who would think of a small plant when we talk about these candies? But the herb Althaea officinalis has a lot to do with this. The English name for this plant is actually Marsh Mallow. Time to get a biology lesson. This little plant comes from the same family as herbs used for cheeses and can grow 100-150 cm high. The fleshy and wooden stalks have nice soft velvety leaves. The flowers are pale soft pink. Originally this plant grew on brackish soil; now the plant is grown on uncultivated land. The root of this plant is the basis for the candy. This root releases a sticky juice that acts like starch. The root pulp used to be boiled with sugar to process the thickening, then passed through a sieve and cooled. There is proof that the Egyptians mixed marshmallow with honey and grains to bake cakes. This delicacy was only served to the Gods and Pharaohs. The marshmallow we eat today was discovered in 1850 in France and was then called paté de guimauve. The confectionaries used the root juice as a thickener with sugar syrup and water. This mixture was beaten lightly, heated and poured in baking forms that were coated with cornstarch. In those days volume was unimportant. That started in 1900 in America when a new machine came on the market that hastened the process. This was the so-called Starch Mogul.

Campfire

In 1955 we had 35 manufacturers of marshmallows in the United States. At the same time the production method was patented and the marshmallow could be produced within 60 minutes. This method is still used today. The marshmallow is not just a candy for children; the roasting of a marshmallow over a campfire is still a social event. Sometimes a warm marshmallow is served on a graham cracker that has a traditional piece of Hershey chocolate on top. During a visit to the Bernardus Lodge in the Carmel Valley, Ben Spungin gave us his vision on Campfire S'More. The Americans also melt little marshmallows in warm chocolate milk, the same way Europeans do with coffee cookies. There are two recipes for marshmallows, one with a base of cornstarch syrup, the other one with meringue. The one based on egg white is widely used in Europe.

It is a small step from the American marshmallow to the Dutch "spekje"; only the structure is a bit different. Traditionally marshmallows are white, the Dutch "spekjes" are nice pastel colours. They come in numerous shapes from a classic diamond shape to a spiral form. It is not difficult to make your own spekjes or marshmallows. There is a difference using fresh or pasteurized egg whites. Fresh egg whites give a stronger and better consistency.

Method 1

***Ingredients:* 10 gelatin leaves, 120 ml water, 400 g sugar, 160 ml cornstarch syrup or glucose syrup, 60 ml water, 1.5 g salt, marrow of 1 vanilla bean.**
***For the powder:* 200 g icing sugar, 200 g potato starch.**

Soak gelatin in 120 ml water and in the meantime bring sugar with syrup and the rest of the water to a boil. Cook at 121°C / 250°F. Start mixing it slowly in the KitchenAid and gradually increase speed. Add the pre-soaked gelatin and when mixture forms soft peaks add salt and vanilla bean marrow. Beat further at high speed until mixture is quite fluffy. Pour on a baking sheet covered with parchment paper. For the powder, mix all ingredients and sprinkle lightly over the marshmallow.
Let harden gradually and sufficiently. Cut in desired shapes and roll through the powder before using.

Method 2

***Ingredients:* 120 g egg white, 500 g sugar, 150 g glucose, 150 g water, 3 tbs sugar, 10 gelatin leaves.**
***For the powder:* 200 g icing sugar, 200 g potato starch.**

Cook water and 500 g sugar to 100°C / 210°F and add the glucose. Keep going till you reach a temperature of 140°C / 285°F. In another (fat-free) bowl beat egg whites and add rest of the sugar in stages. Add the warm syrup. Dissolve the gelatin and add while beating. Make sure the foam has cooled off a bit. The gelatin can also be dissolved in a colouring agent. Beat until mixture is cool. Pour on a baking sheet covered with parchment paper. For the powder, mix all ingredients and sprinkle lightly over the marshmallow. Let harden for at least one night. Cut in desired shapes and roll again through the powder. Use fine sugar for traditional "spekjes".

New Method

There are other new methods to make "spekjes" that don't have much in common with the traditional preparation, but the structure is the same as the classic candy. It is a light product that feels soft in the mouth. You can really use anything and it doesn't have to be sweet. Believe it or not, marshmallows have entered the savoury world. One of the new methods is invented by Ferran Adriá of Restaurant El Bulli in Spain. The recipe and the preparation are simple.

***Ingredients:* 400 ml liquid, 4 gelatin leaves.**

Cool 300 ml liquid at 0°C / 32°F; make sure it doesn't freeze. Dissolve gelatin in the remaining liquid and beat in the KitchenAid until foamy, but before it starts to gel. Add the cold liquid slowly to the foam. The foam will fill the whole bowl. Pour on a sheet covered with foil or paper. Let gel and cut in pieces. It is also possible to pour the mixture in a silicon form and freeze. This will thaw after you take it out. Needless to say, you can add any flavour or colour.

Almost all bread in Europe has been proofing before it goes into the oven. This is because most bread is baked with yeast or sourdough but the classic Irish bread uses bicarbonate instead, creating a special bread.

Irish
Soda Bread

Proud Irish Bread

We are getting a lesson in Irish bread from Jimmy Griffin, whose bakery, named after him, is in Galway on the west coast of Ireland. Jimmy is not just a baker. He is a judge at international competitions and while captain of the Irish Bakers' team, he brought home all sorts of medals from competitions around Europe's most important event, "Europain". We assume that most of our readers will know him from his global demonstrations as he makes sure that Irish bread is known all over the world. The bakery of Family Griffin is very special to say the least. The building dates back to the 15th century and is one of the oldest in the city but fortunately has kept many of the elements of that time. Jimmy is the fifth generation in his family who became a baker and he also shows a passion for renovations. The interior of the whole building is stripped and will be rebuilt with a show room bakery and several tea-salons. Jimmy: "If everything is ready we will have five tea salons and an open bakery where our customers will be introduced to our trade. I also hope that we can show the techniques of Irish baking to our colleagues."

Soda and basics

The history of Irish soda bread goes back to the time of the Romans. As they slowly took over Europe all the different cultures were influenced by the habits and techniques of their rulers. Fortunately they never got to Ireland and that's why the bakers never learned to work with yeast for proofing bread. It was the Normans (Vikings) who conquered Ireland

in the 12th century and who tried to indoctrinate their rules and techniques to the Irish. However, since they were not welcome guests, the bakers kept baking in their own way. The fibre rich food that the Irish have eaten for centuries is rolled oats and usually in the form of porridge. Legend has it that the first bread was created with hardened porridge and baked on a grill above the fire. Over the years they slowly added barley and even wheat to the porridge and the "bread". Because of the addition of buttermilk and soda, the bread, as we know it today, was slowly developed. In spite of the unique taste and structure of soda bread, it is actually very simple to make and only takes a few minutes of work. The ingredients only have to be mixed, then formed and baked. Yeast is not used and there is no fermentation process whatsoever. The bread becomes light and airy because of the chemical reaction of buttermilk and a basis of bicarbonate. The proportion is very important, as you don't want to taste the soda after it is baked. Although the recipe is very simple, each bread tastes different from each baker. "It seems simple, but there are a few issues you have to take into consideration. You only get ONE chance for the bread to get volume and that is in the oven, so the proportions have to be perfect.

The dough should be mixed very fast to avoid gluten content. When working with it the dough looks more like a cake batter or porridge than bread dough; a constant dusting of flour is the only way to work well with the dough. It is too weak to make rounds of it so we press it with the palm of our hands into a round form and divide it in four parts so it looks like a catholic cross. Because of the quantity of starch, the bread will set fast while absorbing moisture. It is crucial to work quickly and let it rest for only twenty minutes before it goes in a pre-heated oven. And last but not least it is important to work with an oven with a heated floor, no convection oven. Make sure the ventilation is off or the bread will not rise. Also leave the oven damper open so the steam can escape." Traditionally the Irish eat this bread with butter or marmalade, or if they want it fancier, they eat it with Irish salmon. An authentic bread consists of flour, buttermilk, salt and bicarbonate. However, you will find more and more varieties in the Irish bakeries, like bread with dried fruit, olives, dried tomatoes, spices and cheese. Jimmy gives us his recipe of the real classic, so no special effects here!

Irish Soda Bread

Ingredients: **720 g whole grain flour, 840 g pastry flour, 120 g cracked whole wheat (soaked in buttermilk), 30 g sugar, 45 g bicarbonate, 45 g sugar, 90 g butter, 1800 g buttermilk at room temperature, enough mixed whole grain flour and wheat flour for dusting.**

Mix flour, pastry flour and soaked wheat with salt, sugar, and butter in a dough mixer with flat beater. Make sure all ingredients are cool otherwise the fermentation starts too early. Add buttermilk and mix for 4 minutes at low speed, beat one more minute at fast speed and in the meantime dust working area with flour mix. Divide dough in portions of 700 g each and make balls with the palm of your hands. Dust generously with flour mix, put on a baking sheet and cut a cross in the bread. Let rest for 20 minutes and put in a non-convection oven at 250°C/480°F. Make sure the ventilator is off and the damper is open. Turn temperature down to 225°C/435°F and bake bread for another 30-35 minutes.

Chocolate and Spices

The use of spices in chocolate has really taken off in the past few years. We tasted some excellent combinations with Kristoff Derykere, chef chocolatier at De Sukerbuyc in the old city of Bruges, Belgium.

Most of the pralines (bonbons) made by Kristoff start from a classic base. These recipes have had enough consistency over the years that it has become easier to create variations. For almost twenty years, Kristoff has been working at De Sukerbuye and for him chocolate and spices are a logical combination. "Although I don't have extreme flavours in my assortment, the addition of that one spice can just give the all important edge. For a chocolatier extreme flavours are fun to use and of course fun to sell." Competition in Bruges is huge, partially owing to a large number of tourists. As in gastronomy, chocolatiers in Bruges work with the seasons. In the first months of the year the theme is Easter, the months of May and June are called the Japanese season and a few months later they are already working for Christmas. The longest period is the Japanese season. Japanese tourists are so important that many sales staff have taken up a bit of the Japanese language. A praline with teas was the logical result.

A real boost

Kristoff shows us a number of pralines with spices and starts with the combination of apple and cinnamon. "This praline has a familiar taste. Almost all of my products come from this kitchen; for fruit flavours I use compounds (juice extracts), as they are consistent in taste. Of course apple goes well with cinnamon. In this case I use cinnamon powder as it is easier to adjust the flavour." Our next praline is one with peach, coconut and anise. "Not everyone likes anise. If you chew on anise you get a strong sensation. If you don't chew on it, you will still get a light

taste of anise and the rest of the filling." Our next example is a praline with speculaas (Dutch crusty and spiced cookie, made with pepper, cinnamon, ginger, cloves, cardamom and nutmeg). He uses the spices as well as crumbled speculaas cookies, which besides enhancing the flavour gives it the extra crunch.
Now comes the strongest flavour we have ever tasted, a praline with cumin and cloves, pretty risky, wouldn't you think? However this gives a real boost to the flavour. Of course one has to be careful not to go overboard on these spices, as it would take away from the rest of the filling, which would lose its effect. By total coincidence the chef discovered something much appreciated and liked by his English customers; it is almost too simple for words: candied ginger, strained, dipped in sugar and then dipped in chocolate. Only three flavours, but in perfect harmony with each other.

Praline with apple and cinnamon

For three sheets of pralines: **tempered milk chocolate.**
For the filling: **1600 g icing sugar, 160 g unsalted butter, 80 g trimoline, 150 g apple extract, 1 tsp cinnamon powder, 25 ml alcohol 96%**

Mix butter and sugar until smooth, add the rest of the ingredients and check to taste. Line the praline moulds with tempered chocolate and let harden. Fill the forms and let the filling set a bit before finishing the pralines. Let harden and invert the forms.

Peach-coconut praline with anise

***For 3 praline moulds:* tempered pure chocolate.**
***For the filling:* 250 g butter, 250 g icing sugar, 125 g trimoline, 200 g coconut oil, 128 g peach extract, 175 g white chocolate, 2 tbs anise seeds.**

Mix butter and sugar till smooth. Add the trimoline, coconut oil and the peach extract. Fold in the white chocolate and anise seeds.

Speculaas praline

***For one baking frame of 5 mm high:* tempered milk chocolate.**
***For the filling:* 1 kg praliné, 600 g tempered chocolate, 50 g speculaas cookies and speculaas spices.**

Put cookies in the blender and mix with the praliné. Fold the milk chocolate through the filling and season to taste with the spices.
Pour the filling in the baking frame. Let harden and cut small squares using a special kitchen tool, called a guitar. Dip squares in milk chocolate and again let harden.

Truffle with cumin and cloves

***For about 100 truffles:* tempered pure chocolate, cocoa powder.**
***For the filling:* 500 g cream, 700 g milk chocolate, 500 g white chocolate, 150 g honey, 50 g unsalted butter, 2 tbs cumin powder, 1 tsp ground cloves.**

Bring cream, sugar and spices to a boil, melt chocolate in this mixture and add honey and unsalted butter. Mix well and cool. Pipe the truffles, dip them in tempered chocolate and then in cocoa powder. Let harden.

Ginger and pure chocolate

1 small jar of candied ginger, 1 kg fine crystal sugar, tempered pure chocolate.

Drain ginger, mix with sugar and let harden overnight. Remove excess sugar, dip squares of ginger in tempered chocolate and let harden.

Dobla

Innovation in Chocolate

In 1955, the family business Dobla started when the parents of the previous owner, Arthur Dontje, merged the two names of the founders, Dontje and Blank. This business started small as a supplier of baking goods including chocolate decorations, which later became their main focus. More than 50 years later, the business has grown as a world market leader in chocolate decorations with deliveries to pastry shops, hotels, restaurants, airlines, caterers, cruiselines, wholefoods etc..

Although decorations for a cake or tart sound simple, we can now find a lot more on the market than the familiar garniture on the whipping cream cake. Today, chocolate decorations can be seen as an edible art. With its creative and challenging chocolate decorations, Dobla has become a leader in captivating the market for years. The scale of products is large and is recognized for easy applications and spectacular forms. We visit the head office in the Dutch village of Heerhugowaard. A worldwide market has led to offices in Belgium and the USA, each with their own production and distribution Centers. Dobla likes to be approachable and that starts in their office where you'll hardly find any dividing walls. One can see the entire office from the very back all the way to the Innovation Center.

Manual labour

Looking at the production it is clear that this world leader has not lost its craftsmanship. Every chocolate produced is checked and manually wrapped to meet with the high quality specifications, considered to be more than 200%. They only use Belgian chocolate; no artificial materials are used and the level of hygiene is extremely high. The business has a kosher and Halal certification. Starting this year, the business will only use chocolate that is certified sustainable by the UTZ 'Good Inside' program. Using UTZ chocolate means Dobla is making an investment in helping farmers achieve a good quality cacao bean while ensuring they receive a good price for their product in a stable business environment. One can divide Dobla products in different categories: decoration, cups, toppings, logos, seasonal garnishes and the Chef's Collection. This last signature category is known for its exclusive forms and very luxurious content. It's quite an exception that they allow us to see even a small part of the production process of the Chef's Collection; it is mainly traditional and manual work. The delicate and fragile artworks are wrapped in such a way that they're not susceptible to outside elements.

Innovation Center

The beating heart of Dobla's business is the brand new Innovation Center. This space is about 250 square metres and equipped with every comfort and technique. Rik Prins is the person responsible for the Center and together with a product manager they constantly develop new ideas. Rik Prins tells us about the goal of the Innovation Center: "Dobla is a business that wants to be the leader in the world with innovative decorations to enhancing the development of pastry.
You can read numerous books or sit behind a computer every day but that doesn't work in our business. We have to practice. Our Center is a source of inspiration, where we can brainstorm and put our ideas into practice right away. Our intention is to make chocolate creations that give the pastry chef the idea that he created them himself.
We don't develop everything ourselves. We invite national and international craftsmen to come for a "Jamming Session" with us, just like jazz. You put some artists together and give them the instruments. After 10 minutes we have the most beautiful music. Really, anything a pastry chef needs we have at the Innovation Center."
All worktables are identical, so nobody feels lost. "The layout of space is well thought out which makes working very convenient. Besides that the Center has a welcoming and open style; the chefs can almost feel at home. To be able to create spectacular products, we consider it essential that the environment and atmosphere are optimum." Rik has seen many colleagues come to his Innovation Center and he plans to continue that even more in the future. It's also a great way to connect national and international professionals. "This was the reason why we were able to publish our first book, called The Recipes with help of chefs like Johnny Chan, Kenny Kong, Olivier Bajard, Ramon Morató and Keegan Gerhard. This book shows how you can apply our products in a creative way."

Don't think that only pastry chefs are inspiring. Inspirations can also be found in the art world, architecture, and nature. Being a trendsetter, Dobla is open to anything. What will the trend be in the next few years? "I believe we will see more and more three dimensional forms that will inspire a pastry chef in the development of his own desserts and cakes. The artistry will always be there, even stronger. In our business we will concentrate on that even more and refine the applications." A good example is the Collar sheet (see the picture above). This will enable a pastry chef to give his cake an exclusive look in ten seconds. Since Dobla exists all over the world we wonder how different cultures will fit in. Rik: "Asians love their bright colours and minuscule details. Great-Britain is very traditional. But for example in Dubai nothing can be too extreme. For us the most important priority is our unique style and quality and keeping a good eye and ear to the market."

Higher Level

While we are at the Center, CEO Eric Kakebeen drops in. For many years this practical Dutch man has put his heart and soul into the business and has seen Dobla growing immensely. This growing trend will undoubtedly continue, as Eric's plans are still ambitious. In short he tells us how he sees the future of Dobla: "We are now at a certain level but this is just the start. A few years ago we started to take a new direction and have raised the bar since. Because of our contacts with chefs and pastry chefs from different cultures we are forced to think differently." Dobla is prepared for future winners, as they are sponsoring a number of important competitions like Coupe du Monde de la Pâtisserie and the World Pastry Team Championship. Eric: "We like to contribute by bringing pastry to a much higher level. In the future we will surprise this industry with our products, but don't worry we will make sure that everything we produce is affordable."

If you would like to know more about Dobla and see their complete assortment, please go to *www.dobla.com*

Dobla Head Office – The Netherlands
Galileïstraat 26
1704 SE Heerhugowaard, The Netherlands
Phone: +31 72 576 07 77

Dobla Belgium Productions
Lindekensbaan 91a
2560 Kessel Statie, Belgium
Phone: +32 3 491 93 33

Dobla USA Manufacturing
1775 Breckinridge Parkway
Suite 600 Duluth GA, 30096
Phone: +1 770-887 0201

Tomatoes
of Michel Troisgros

The restaurant of the family Troisgros in the French Roanne district has been tops in the world for decades. More than forty years ago, Jean and Pierre Troisgros knew how to achieve three Michelin stars; today these stars are still displayed on the front of their restaurant. The current owner and chef Michel Troisgros respects the classics of his father and uncle, but is not afraid of modern and global trends. He was one of the first to adjust his style of pastry techniques in the savoury kitchen. As an example, you will find his world famous tomato recipe below.

Chinois of tomatoes

Ingredients: 20 cherry tomatoes, 100 g breadcrumbs from white bread, 200 g beignet batter, 150 g sugar, 1 tsp white sesame seeds.
For the syrup: 100 g sugar, 100 ml water, 50 ml vinegar, 5 g ginger, 5 coriander seeds, 1 star anise, 1 bruised clove, the peel of one orange and one lemon.
For the beignet batter: 100 g flour, 100 g cornstarch, 150 ml beer, 100 g water, 15 g dried yeast, 1 egg yolk, dash of salt.

Make beignet batter, cover with foil and set aside for a few hours in a cool spot. Whisk batter slightly before use. One can use two types of yeast. Dried yeast gives an airy dough that gets crunchy when fried. Fresh yeast will give a softer and more "fleshy" result.
For the syrup, heat water and sugar, add spices and peels and stew for 20 minutes. Prepare the tomatoes and marinate in the syrup for 2 hours. Drain well and roll through breadcrumbs and then through the beignet batter. Deep fry about five at a time in vegetable oil at 160°C/320°F. Once they are crunchy, drain on paper towels. In the meantime prepare a bowl of water with ice cubes. Heat sugar in a frying pan to make caramel and dip tomatoes in it. Sprinkle with sesame seed and move the pan around so the tomatoes are covered with caramel. Take tomatoes, one by one out the caramel and immerse them in ice water for a few seconds. Drain and serve immediately, preferably on shaved ice.

Firenze | Florence

Firenze, also called Florence, is an old city with hundreds of thousands of monuments. The city was originally established by Julius Caesar in 59BC. You can taste the culture everywhere as the whole city exhales art, architecture and ancient history. How does pâtisserie fit in with all this culture? When we walked through the city we found the answer.

Pâtisserie in Firenze is quite diverse. There is an incredible number of so-called pasticcerias where the locals go for tarts or a piece of coffee cake. This often is accompanied by a ristretto, a very strong little coffee. In the morning, on the way to work, people will get a brioche, a kind of croissant filled with crème pâtissère. But during the day they treat themselves also to pastries, profiteroles, cookies, etc. After lunch, around 4:00 pm, it's time for a bombolini. This kind of donut that has no hole is mostly eaten by children and can be filled with some delicious crème. Sometimes people eat ice cream around this hour too. A walk through the city is a pastry delight.

Our adventure starts at the corner of Via Della Spado and Via de Torbabuon. It's an unusual place but it gives you a good sense of this city. At the store of top designer Roberto Cavalli the coats in the window are as expensive as an average car. But it is apparent that Roberto has taste, because in his store is a small coffee shop with a pâtisserie corner. Here, the divas eat their pastry or plate of cookies after they have maxed out their credit cards. A pâtisserie shop in a fashion store is not a common sight. We are told that there was a pasticceria here before Cavalli came into the picture. He was the one who wanted to keep the pasticceria going as he felt that so many of these had been lost over the years.

In 2000 he decided to incorporate these in his fashion boutiques and took everything over. The pasticceria started in 1820, the staff of Giacosa is still there but now dressed in designer suits.

Street pâtisserie

It is extremely busy on the street with chatty Italians wearing sunglasses even if there is no sunshine. But these sunglasses are drawn to the windows of the numerous fashion houses. It is good for business. Fortunately we also spy other things, like a chestnut roaster. Behind a little cart, with the name Caldarroste on it, we meet a very old Italian. His name is Lucco and together with his wife he roasts the chestnuts that they have been gathering for 24 years. One portion of chestnuts cost only 3 euros. He was not to keen to get his picture taken, as he is too modest for that.
For the early birds there is an early market and there are a few of these in Firenze. We head for a small market on the Piazza Lorenzo Ghiberti. Next to the many stands outside, there is a covered hall where you can find just about anything edible. Paola, who is trying to sell her bread, manages one stand named Panificio. Some of these breads are organic and baked in Tuscany. It is a fun market where old ladies are buying their fruit while feeling and judging it, all accompanied with lively discussions. Go and have a look at the fantastic grapes of Francesca or the pears of Lucia. They don't speak a word of English but that makes it so much more fun.

La Bottega del Cioccollato

Not far from the early market is Via de Macci. Here you'll find the most modern chocolatier of Firenze. La Bottega del Cioccolato is a small shop, owned by Andrea Bianchini. He is no stranger to chocolate experts as he participated in the Pastry Coupe du Monde in 2005. We notice more diplomas and awards in his work area. The praline shop has an austere interior, but Andrea is less serious. He started his career 20 years ago. "It all started in a small pâtisserie called Codecasa. In those days pâtisserie was not as trendy as today. You just had a few chocolates and that was it. It was a traditional shop where I learned the basics, but after five years I had enough of it. I wanted more so I built up my experience and worked as an apprentice." This brought him to Lucca Mannori in Prato. "He was very inspirational and advised me to visit more colleagues. I broadened my knowledge further by taking courses from Pierre Hermé, who at that time worked as a chef at Fauchon. After all these courses I took a year to study at Chocovic in Barcelona. I learned a lot and became an apprentice in many establishments, each time for three months."
Andrea doesn't like traditional flavours and works only with fresh products except for the violet flavour when he uses aromatic oil.
The fruits come from different parts of Italy, but he prefers to get these

locally. He has one praline with caramel and balsamic vinegar. He gets this vinegar from his friend Maglia Bechi in exchanges for pralines. Andrea's pralines are many combinations of aroma and flavor, such as orange-fennel or apricot-lavender. Each of his twenty-five kinds is special. Next to his bonbons we notice five different kinds of cookies, cakes and pastries. His specialty is the Biscotto de'Macci, a deviation of the well-known cantuccini, but made with cocoa powder, chocolate, almonds and hazelnuts instead of just almonds. The bonbons look very inviting. The small pralines are mostly coated bonbons weighing only 8 to 10 g and that is done deliberately. "I love small tasting explosions, people tend to buy more when the pralines are small," he chuckles. Andrea is happy to share some of his secrets with us.

Olive oil praline

For about 110 pralines: 200 g cream, marrow of 1 vanilla bean, 550 g white chocolate, 250 g high quality olive oil, 100 g glucose, tempered dark chocolate.

For the ganache heat cream, vanilla and glucose. Mix this with the white chocolate and add warm olive oil at 35°C / 95°F. Coat praline forms with tempered chocolate, let harden and pour the ganache in the forms. Once it has all set finish the pralines.

Caramel-balsamico praline

For about 100 pralines: 400 g sugar, 150 g glucose 250 g cream, 100 g butter, 55 g aceto balsamico (preferably Maglia Bechi), tempered dark chocolate.

For the ganache caramelize the sugar and glucose, add the butter and cream and cook a bit longer. Add the balsamico, re-heat for 2 minutes and check for taste.
Coat praline forms with tempered chocolate, let harden and pour in the ganache. Once it has all set, finish the pralines.

Szechuan-passion praline

Use a baking sheet of 30 x 30 cm: 175 g passion fruit coulis, 75 g cream, 60 g glucose, 250 g milk chocolate, 200 g dark chocolate, 75 g butter, 20 g Passoa (passion fruit liquor), 20 g szechuan pepper, tempered dark chocolate.

For the ganache bring the coulis, cream, glucose and pepper to a boil. Pass through a sieve and mix with the butter and alcohol. Pour ganache on a deep baking sheet, let harden and cut into small squares. Take these through the tempered chocolate and finish.

Dolci & Dolcezze

Although Firenze looks like a big city, the centre is more like a village. People seem to know each other and most tourists only have to walk one kilometre from the well- known Ponte Vecchio to the Duomo Baptism. We go outside the tourist area and arrive at Dolci & Dolcezze, which means nothing less than Pâtisserie & Desserts. The shop is very small but cozy. The outside windows lure you inside and the interior reminds us of a classic English teahouse with soft green colours. We meet Ilaria Balatresi. A beautiful story but somewhat tragic. Twenty years ago she and her husband Giulio Corti decided to make a drastic change in their careers. She was a secretary and he was a photographer. Giulio had a passion for anything sweet and decided to start baking pastry. Although both had no culinary background, soon they were selling cakes to restaurants. This was all done from their home but after five years the kitchen became too small. Since they wanted more people to enjoy their pastry, they opened Dolci & Dolcezze. It was a great success until Giulio died three years ago. Ilaria decided to continue her husband's work. Even with two children at home, she gets up every morning at 3:30 to make her pastries. Her only two employees start one hour later. Although she had to sacrifice a lot she loves what she does, but is secretly looking for a successor. Her pâtisserie, as she calls it, is feminine, seductive and above all delicious. Quality is number one, which is obvious in the taste but also in the price. According to our chef, quality is not just in the cake but also in the presentation. Her specialty is the chocolate cake, delicious but quite rich. The recipe is a secret, but we are not going home empty handed because she wanted to share her recipe for chestnut tart (Mont Blanc is the name of the highest mountain in Europe). It is a simple recipe and according to Ilaria has more to do with feelings than the recipe.

The Mont Blanc tart

For 2 tarts: 600 g chestnuts, 1 litre milk, 100 g cocoa powder, 200 g butter, 1 litre whipping cream, 200 g sugar, purple bows or little sugar dipped flowers.

Peel chestnuts and cook them in milk, cocoa powder and butter for 30 minutes. Leave the chestnuts in the fridge for one day. Put them through a passe-vite (food mill) and add some sugar if necessary. Spoon about 370 g on a cake carton and mold into a bombe. Pipe little dots of whipped sweetened cream all over the tart until it looks totally white. Garnish with purple bows or sugary flowers. This tart is not sliced in triangles but served with a spoon.

Folk pâtisserie

In Firenze we wanted to see all kinds of pâtisserie and find out where the general population buys their pastries. One of the common pâtisseries is Cosi. The shop is named after Patricio Cosi, who retired one year ago. He sold his business to Ricardo Camoresi who is now at the helm.
The shop has a long shaped interior and it always seems busy. One of the specialties is the Nonnina alla crèma. We can describe it as a large cookie, made with hard Vienna dough filled with pastry cream. It is baked for 5 minutes at 300°C / 570°F. The store has a 12 metre long glass showcase with all kinds of cookies and delicacies and we ask Ricardo where we can find the famous Florentines. He tells us that these are only made around Christmas time, the same as Panettone, so obviously we are too early (or too late). A bit disappointed we try the Nonnina and forget the Florentine.
Besides sweet things, bread is all important in Italy; in the evening the dinner table is not complete without a basket of bread. Most Italian bread doesn't contain much salt. We ask Ricardo why. His answer is simple but to the point: "In Italy bread is made to fill the stomach and to be part of dinner. Bread should not take away the taste of the main meal. Maybe I am wrong but it has been a long kept tradition. Who knows, maybe Firenze didn't have much salt in the old days." After leaving Cosi, we feel that next to diva-pâtisserie or street-pâtisserie his products would classify as folk patisserie.

Ice-Cream

Of course we cannot forget the ice cream parlours, or as they are called in Italy gelaterias. Each city has hundreds of them; we picked two that were definitely worth a visit. The first one is Vivoli, located on the Via Isole delle Stinche. It is a busy ice-cream parlour with many tourists. We stop here because of the quality and the history. We are introduced to Silvana, the third generation of ice cream makers in the Vivoli family. It started with Raffaello Vivoli who was looking for work between the two World Wars. Together with his brother he started a small coffee shop in Firenze where he sold more than coffee; there were also buns and cigarettes for sale and sometimes even ice cream. In those days there were no luxury ice-cream machines; water, salt and snow from the mountains were his ingredients. It was a challenge to make ice-cream during the war as it was considered a luxury, but Raffaello knew how to get sugar and milk on the black market. The business took off and was eventually taken over by his son Piero Vivoli. In the seventies things got better and Italy started to prosper. The business was booming and growing like crazy. It has been successful ever since. Today we have Silvana and brother-in-law Simone Gori as ice cream makers and mama Vivoli as the lady sitting behind the cash register. Their secret is consistency in the quality of their products using the best cream and the best eggs.

At Vivoli you will never see coulis in the freezer. Only pistachios and hazelnuts come in as a paste, otherwise an ice cream of these ingredients would be far too expensive for their customers. One of their specialties is the crèma ice cream. It's an ice cream with lots of egg yolks and has a distinctive flavour, the locals love it. Quickly we take another spoon of ice cream and head for the next store, Il Sorriso, meaning "the smile".

No grandeur or opulence, no rich messy details, but a small ice-cream parlour on the outskirts. We feel relieved not to find any tourists here, but wonder why. Many believe that this ice cream is superior to others. Il Sorriso has been in existence for 12 years. Owner Beatrice Viti learned ice-cream making from her grandfather. The locals know where to find this place; within 15 minutes of our arrival they have sold 85 Euros worth of product and today is just an ordinary weekday in the fall. An ice cream here costs almost half less the price than downtown and you really get your money's worth. An ice cream with two flavours weighs about 300 grams and cost only €2.20. We are forced to taste some and who are we to refuse? We taste the Buon Talenti, a typical flavour for Firenze and made with mascarpone and honey. It is a perfect combination for some people. One highlight is the pine nut ice-cream. We notice that we don't see vanilla ice cream anywhere. Beatrice explains that people prefer the already mentioned crèma ice cream. Vanilla is quite expensive here and Il Sorriso has not enough storage space to let the composition ripen. In summer they sell three hundred litres of ice cream per week. Should you be tempted to visit them in the future, you might find another Il Sorriso. They are in the process of re-building as their kitchen was far too small.

Giorgio

About fifteen minutes from the city centre and close to Il Sorriso, is, according to many, the best pasticceria of Firenze. The name reminds us of the fashion brand Giorgio, and it is a classic Italian family business. The eldest son Andrea Bernacchioni runs the business, the younger brother Maximo works in the kitchen, mama sits as many mamas behind the cash register and papa, Giorgio Bernacchioni, is, and will remain, the big boss. You probably can imagine the atmosphere, busy, hectic and lots of talking, so very Italian! When Giorgio was fourteen he learned the trade in the centre of Firenze when he walked one hour to work every day. He started at Pasticceria Robiglio, a shop we will visit later. In 1972, after he had learned the trade, he decided to start for himself, not in the centre but in the outskirts where he was born. The business was first managed by the family only but now they have a staff of twenty-five people. Although Giorgio was born in 1924, he is still actively involved and works in the kitchen. He wants to keep the family secret, a dough of Schiacciata Fiorentina, a flat cake with icing sugar. Papa and son Maximo are the only ones who know the recipe. Without any form of modesty we are told that Giorgio makes the best Schiacciata in Italy. He was even invited to come on TV and since then the shop receives orders from as far as 60 kilometres away. We have the nerve to ask the boss if we can write down his secret recipe and suddenly everything comes to a standstill! Giorgio looks at us in disbelief. Then everyone realizes it was a joke and life continues as usual.

During our visit we see some dishes appear on the table, first one plate and then another and another. You'll understand that soon the table is full with sweet delicacies. Giorgio insists that we should try everything and we politely taste small bites. Another specialty is the Millefoglie, a kind of vanilla slice with crème Suisse and perfect crunchy puff pastry. Let the truth be said, it was divine. We ask the master the secret of his business. It is the consistency of quality that has been the key for years. Artificial flavours or aromas are never used. When we say goodbye we are proud that we might be the first foreign journalists ever to write about Giorgio, but being as proud as Giorgio is of his pâtisserie is almost not possible.

The secret little door

On the advice of Giorgio we visit his first learning institution, Pasticceria Robiglio. It is a small store downtown, Via de Servi 112 to be exact, not far from Dolci & Dolcezze. The store has a seventies interior, but opened in 1928 with Pietro Robiglio and is about the oldest pâtisserie in Firenze. Over the years the number of stores has increased and they are now owned by the 3rd generation. Make sure you taste the Fruttodoro or the Torto Campagnola. We walk on and pass many little streets full of tourist shops. In one of the alleys, close to Palazzo Medici, we come to our next

destination, a place full of young talent. Our first impression of Dolcissima is of a classic Viennese pâtisserie with lots of mirrors and gold details. On the shelves around these mirrors we see glass goblets with different candies. It is not a large shop but has a nice atmosphere. Behind a secret little door you can get a cup of coffee. Why? Dolcissima has no licence to serve coffee. Again we are treated to a large assortment of delicacies from small pralines to large cakes. Should you decide to visit Dolcissima you will get a totally different experience because they change their assortments constantly.

Tortapistocchi

We have almost finished our visit to this beautiful city, the capital of renaissance, when we get a tip from one of our guides to meet the man of chocolate cakes. In each pasticceria we have tasted a chocolate cake and they were all delicious, so we're very curious as to why the cake of Claudio Pistocchi would be so special. We travel a bit outside the centre to Via Ponte di Mezzo. The new atelier of Claudio is somewhat hidden, so don't expect a pasticceria, it's just a working area. His story is exceptional so we want to share it with you. The chef tells the story: "I was born a chef and now I work every day in a black jacket making chocolate. After having worked at several restaurants, I started a small shop with wine, cheese and other delicacies. Actually it was a restaurant without chairs. Together with my old colleague pâtissier Michele Mezzasoma, who I met in one of the restaurants, we developed our chocolate cake.
The cake became a success and we started getting orders from restaurants. We were able to handle it until we started getting orders from outside Firenze. We decided to vacuum pack the cakes before we send them away. Of course we tested everything making sure the quality didn't suffer. One day a journalist tried the cake. When he started to write about it, pandemonium set in! We got an invitation to come to a chocolate trade show in Perugia, especially for our cakes. It was a huge step for us even though we didn't have to pay for the booth. We sold three hundred cakes in one weekend. All at once the cake became known everywhere. We got orders from Milan and Pisa and now we make 65,000 cakes per year. All by hand!" We peek in the kitchen and we only find three other workers. These are the parents and the sister of Claudio. It is clean and quiet here. Only one thing is produced and it's the cake. They let us taste it and we like it. Compare it to a perfect ganache but thicker. Claudio uses different kinds of chocolate in his recipe. In total he uses six flavours: chili, cherries, citrus fruit, coffee, pear and of course the original version. The chef has a passion for his work and that comes through in his cakes.
This finishes our trip to Firenze, or Florence, whatever you prefer. It's a city well worth visiting and not just for its art and architecture from the past. Make sure you go with an empty stomach and upon your return home, sign up for a fitness class! Those proud Italians love to make you taste all of their goods.

Meringues

This very light processing of egg whites and sugar was discovered in 1720 by the Swiss Pâtissier Gasparini, after which the French and Italians came up with their own, so we now have three versions. These are easy to make unless you don't follow the rules.

The name is derived from the small Swiss village of Meringen, where Gasparini was born. There are basically three kinds of meringue: French, Italian and Swiss (sometimes called German), but we can divide them in two groups. The soft meringue that is used for toppings on cakes, and the hard meringue that is baked in the oven and becomes crispy and crunchy.

Beating Method

A meringue can be beaten in a machine or by hand. If you do it by hand using a whisk it is better to use one with thin wires. These are more flexible and lighter. Make sure that the bowl doesn't contain any traces of fat or egg yolks, as the meringue would definitely fail. Egg whites should also be room temperature. Start beating slowly and then add salt if you want. More about salt later. When the egg whites have increased three times their volume with a machine, you can slowly start adding parts of sugar. If you do it manually you will have to wait for more volume before adding the sugar. Keep beating until stiff peaks form; with the machine it is done at the highest speed, but manually you need a lot more patience. Once stiff peaks have been formed, don't beat much longer as it can cause the egg whites to curdle or separate. Some meringues need to be piped and baked immediately but that is not necessary for all of them. One method that doesn't need beating is using a siphon, a new technique from Spain.

Pasteurized or fresh egg whites

Anyone who tells you that pasteurized egg whites have the same qualities as fresh egg whites is a liar. Pasteurizing will damage the enzymes that are important for making meringues and will make the foam weak and cause it to collapse faster. The best result is achieved with fresh egg whites, unless you are worried about health issues in which case you had better use the pasteurized eggs.

Adding other substances

There are a few things that can enhance the meringue. Salt gives more taste but will reduce the strength of foam and you will have to beat a bit longer. Adding acids (i.e. lime juice or cream of tartar) will not reduce the volume but will stabilize the foam and give it a nice shine. And you only need a little bit otherwise it will taste sour.
You can add flavours or colours to a meringue. When making Italian meringue you can boil the syrup with some liqueur and a coulis.

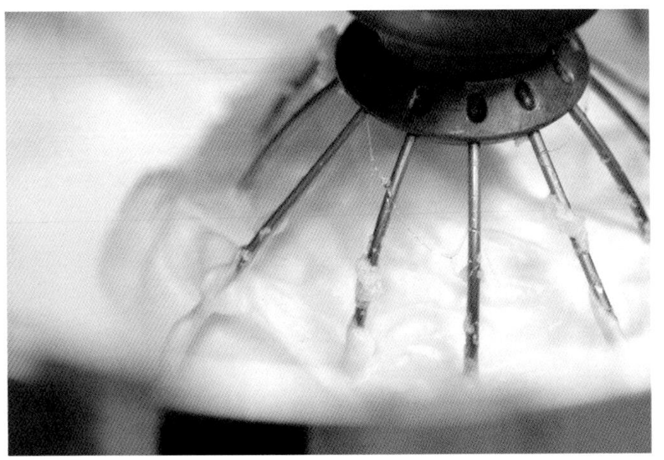

The coulis can be replaced with a colour enhancer but that is less professional. One can add flavour with herbs, spices, etc. These can be infused in the syrup but also added to the beaten egg whites.

The right bowl

Choosing the right bowl is very important. Plastic can contain microscopic fat residues and aluminum can cause a grey colour. In the old days people used copper bowls. When Henri-Paul Pellaprat wrote about this in 1936, copper had already been in use for a long time. Why should copper be so much better? Egg white contains six proteins. One is conalbumin, a component that bonds with metal ions such as the ones found in copper, resulting in a yellower foam with a stronger structure. Much research into this topic is still going on so we will stick with just using stainless steel bowls.

Temperature

Temperature plays a major factor in making meringues. The higher the temperature of the sugar syrup, the tougher the foam. A temperature of 121°C / 250°F keeps the syrup clear and gives a nice structure to the foam. Temperature can be different in the oven but this relates in general to the baking time. Escoffier used to call it drying at 90°C / 195°F instead of baking. Alain Ducasse would dry his French foam for two hours at 120°C / 250°F, not higher or the egg whites will become a soufflé. The drying or baking time is related to the quantity and thickness of the meringue and can take hours. The meringue will bake evenly at a low temperature and will also stay white. However, sometimes the temperature has to be higher, for instance with Pavlova, where the foam should be crunchy on the outside but soft on the inside. You can also poach foam as with Oeufs à la neige. The poaching is done in milk, sugar and vanilla. At the World Team Pastry Championship in 2003, the Belgian team made this award-winning dish in flexi pans and it was poached in a combi-steamer. One separated the snow eggs by pouring warm syrup over it that created floating foam balls. Beautiful and innovative!

Meringues can be used in many ways and are a basis for a wide variety of dishes. One example is Omelet Sibérienne, where the soft foam is meant to isolate the ice cream underneath. A derivation of the French foam is the Japanese meringue.

Storing Meringue

Freshly beaten meringue should be processed immediately. Italian meringue can wait a bit longer. Baked meringue should be kept in a dry and warm spot where there is no humidity. You can even place some silica gel next to the meringue.

French Meringue

Ingredients: 160 g egg white, 3 drops lime juice, 200 g fine crystal sugar.

Clean bowl and beater with lime juice and beat at high speeds until it has increased four times in volume. Add sugar in parts. Keep beating until stiff peaks have formed. Immediately pipe meringue in a baking form and bake at 99°C / 210°F so the meringue will be nicely dry and hard on top and bottom.

Italian Meringue

Ingredients: 200 g egg white, 3 drops lime juice, 75 g icing sugar, 325 g crystal sugar, 85 g water.

Clean bowl and beater with lime juice and boil water with 325 g crystal sugar to a syrup of 121°C / 250°F. Beat egg whites at high speed and add icing sugar. While beating gradually add the syrup and try to pour it in a running stream so it is absorbed right away. Beat until the foam is cold and stiff peaks have formed.

Swiss Meringue

Ingredients: 160 g egg white, 3 drops lime juice, 250 g icing sugar.

Clean bowl and beater with lime juice. Add sugar in parts and beat au bain-marie. When sugar has totally dissolved beat until it is cold and peaks have formed. Immediately process this tough foam.

Japanese Meringue

Ingredients: 240 ml egg white, 3 drops lime juice, 310 g fine crystal sugar, 225 g ground almonds.

Prepare as a French meringue, but add ground almonds last.

Modern Spanish Meringue

Ingredients: 1 litre pasteurized egg white, 250 g or 400 g crystal sugar, dash of salt, siphon, 2 chargers.

Mix egg white and sugar and make sure it is all dissolved. Pour in a siphon, add the charges and let rest for one hour. The quantity of the sugar depends on the dessert. 250 g will make it less sweet but it will collapse faster. 400 g sugar keeps the meringue stronger, but of course it will be very sweet. Try to use something in between.

Le Gâteau Battu

France is a country full of traditions and regional products. We visit the region of Picardie, in the northwest.

There have been many assumptions made on the origin of regional pâtisserie. The first time anything was written on the subject goes back to the sixteenth century in the village of Lambercourt in the Vimeau region, a tableland between the Brei and Somme valley. At that time, the Duke of the county had the privilege to receive a delicious cake every year from his servants. But the first gastronomic text is found in the book Pâtissier François in 1653, which mentions egg bread. In 1900 the gâteau battu was officially recognized as a regional specialty. In the old days it was made to get rid of the abundance of eggs and butter; it became a tradition to serve this cake at weddings, baptisms and village festivals. When we ask Picardie pâtissier Guilhain Pichon what a gâteau battu really is, his response is: "Eggs, eggs, and more eggs. It's a kind of brioche, but richer and moister. Much harder to make." To honour this bread, they created a confrérie (a brotherhood), which is very common in France. When you see a group of people walking in a parade, dressed like a strawberry with even a green crown on their head, it's likely the strawberry-confrérie. In Picardië they might walk with a cake form on their heads, or rather with a hat in the shape of a gâteau battu. It is a bit like a fluted brioche form, but less wide and much taller. It looks more like a chef's hat. They believe that the pastry will fail should you use a different form.

Some tricks

Why is it so difficult to make? We explored the different methods of several pâtissiers. First of all, the preparation should be in a humid and warm environment with absolutely no air circulating, as this would hinder the proofing. The ingredients should all have the same temperature. Another trick is to always make dough for at least four breads, never for one. Some pâtissiers put a rusted nail in the dough to enhance the colour of the egg yolks. When the pâtissier sees our disbelief, he says: "A rusted nail is more natural than synthetic colouring." However we think that synthetic colouring is government regulated, not a rusted nail! A gâteau battu consists of egg yolks, flour, yeast, butter, and alcohol like rum, cognac or kirsch, depending on personal taste. There are two versions. One is made with soft butter and mixed with flour, sugar, salt, egg yolks and yeast and kneaded by hand to obtain elasticity. Then alcohol is added. One third of the dough is put into each of three greased forms until it has risen to the edge. Then it goes into the oven. The oven is of utmost importance. Ideally it should be a baker's oven or a brick oven with even temperature. To find out how important the oven temperature is, lock yourself in a room, close the doors, turn up the heat and put on the humidifier...

Confrérie recipe

For 2 kg dough of 3 pieces of Gâteau Battu: 1 kg flour, 24 g salt, 12 eggs, 40 g yeast, 200 g sugar, 800 g butter, some milk.

Put flour in a bowl and add the yeast dissolved in milk. Add the eggs and salt and mix while slowly adding the sugar. Knead dough for 15 minutes by hand and add the soft butter. Knead dough again for another 15 minutes and put in the fridge overnight. Fill forms with 1/3 of the dough to proof under a wet cloth. Bake for 30 minutes in the oven at 200°C / 390°F. One more hint, the gateau will taste better the next day when it has lost the yeast taste.

Wedding Cakes

Everything should be perfect on the BIG day; the wedding dress, a flock of white doves and a luxurious car! But all of that glamour is set aside when the wedding cake is presented. The oohs and aahs from the guests are the ultimate reward for the pâtissier.

When we visited an old fashioned baker who was selling off all his collections, we discovered his bookcases were filled with literature on the making and decorating of cakes. So, we expanded our library accordingly with this enormous collection. Decorating cakes is an art, but let's start at the beginning. An inspiration for this story came from the book Spectacular Cakes by Mich Turner. We met her in London when we were doing a city profile and visited her Little Venice Cake Company. We very highly recommend this book to any pâtissier.

The Filling

To make a cake from A to Z can take days of work. The filling is most important. Cakes filled with butter cream are not suitable for a warm summer day; neither is a bavarois cake. It's often safer to make a fruit cake, in any size or form. The delicious flavours are kept longer by filling it with lots of candied fruit and alcohol. The Little Venice Cake Company gives its clients a choice of five flavours; three are based on butter cream, the other two are carrot cake and a rich fruitcake.

Carrot Cake

For a 10-inch cake: 75 ml dark rum, 300 g raisins, 525 g flour, 6 tsp cinnamon powder, 3 tsp ground nutmeg, 3 tsp baking powder, 450 ml sunflower oil, 225 g sugar, 225 g brown icing sugar, 6 eggs (whisked), 3 lemon zests, 3 orange zests, 525 g grated carrot, 150 g shredded coconut, 150 g chopped walnuts, marrow of 2 vanilla beans.
For the citrus syrup: 150 g brown sugar, juice of 2 lemons, juice of 2 oranges.

Soak raisins in rum for 1 hour. Sieve flour with the cinnamon, nutmeg and baking powder. Beat oil, sugars and eggs to a smooth batter. Put flour in the KitchenAid with the flat beater and mix with the zests, the carrots, coconut, walnuts, vanilla and the soaked raisins. Mix the oil mixture with the rest of the ingredients. Pour batter in baking form lined with parchment paper and bake the cake for 2 hours and 30 minutes in the oven at 150°C / 300°F. For the syrup dissolve brown sugar in the fruit juices. When the cake comes out of the oven prick some little holes in the cake with a saté stick. Pour syrup over the cake and loosen the cake from the form after it has cooled off.

The Rich Fruit Cake

For a 10" cake: 375 g red berries (also called red currants), 300 g raisins, 300 g California raisins, 115 g halved dried plums, 115 g halved dried apricots, 115 g chopped dried dates. 150 g chopped candied cherries, 225 ml brandy, zest and juice of 3 lemons, zest and juice of 3 oranges, 525 g flour, 3 tsp ground ginger, 3 tsp ground cardamom, 1 tsp ground nutmeg, 375 g unsalted butter, 375 light icing sugar, 6 eggs (whisked), 11/2 tsp dark molasses, 75 g chopped almonds.

Mix all fruit with brandy, the zests and the juice and marinate, preferably 72 hours. Sieve flour with spices. Beat sugar and butter till fluffy. Add eggs one bit at a time and mix gradually with the flour. Stir molasses through the mixture and add fruits and almonds. Reserve the marinade. Spoon the mixture into a parchment lined baking form and bake for 5 hours in the oven at 150°C / 300°F. Let the cake cool and spread the remaining marinades over the top. Wrap the cake in parchment paper with another layer of aluminum foil.

The Lining

Some of the fruit may have pushed out of the batter as it baked, so roll the cake flat again with a rolling pin. The sponge cake will be filled with either crème or mousse. The cakes are smoothed with jelly (mostly apricot jelly) to form a coat of stickiness for the next layer: the marzipan. Roll marzipan out to 3 mm thick. Create a bottom of marzipan and put the cake on top. Roll another layer of marzipan, 3 mm thick to cover the fruitcake. The cake is straightened with a palette knife, a flattening tool or smoother. Marzipan can come in different kinds. The marzipan used for covering fruitcakes (Mich Turner works with the high quality Lubeca) is 1:3 or 1:2, the latter giving a stronger almond taste. Another layer to be added is fondant, a somewhat magical substance, as it rolls out easily, gives a clean finish and is a perfect basis for the garnish.
A good fondant becomes hard but is still easy to cut. There are many very good finished fondant products available on the market.
Put the marzipan-covered cake in a cake box of the same size. Later it is put on a 3 mm thick board covered with foil and should be larger than the cake. This becomes the baseboard. Use cold boiled water to coat the baseboard. Knead the fondant and roll out to 3 mm thick. Put on the baseboard, smooth out, cut edges off and let rest for one night. Cover the marzipan cake with liquor. This is used as a flavourful protection but also as a sticky layer for the fondant. Roll fondant to 5 mm thick and

P10

make sure that it is large enough to cover the whole cake. Smooth the top and sides with both hands carefully so the fondant doesn't break. Use a palette knife to smooth and straighten the cake; small air pockets can be pierced with a needle. Put cake on a plateau and cut the excessive sides off. Finish nicely and put cake on the baseboard.

Royal Icing

Once the covering of the cake has been done, the decoration can start. This is probably the nicest but also the most finicky work on a wedding cake. The classic method for decorating is garnishing with royal icing. Many different types of ready-to-use icing are also available on the market. It is very easy to make the icing yourself with fresh egg whites or egg white powder. The advantage of egg white powder is that it is clean and it keeps longer. To make icing:

10 g of egg white powder, 60 ml cooled boiled water and 300 to 500 g sugar.

Put part of the icing sugar with egg white powder in a bowl and while beating slowly add the water gradually. Once stiff peaks form, the icing should be done. For firmer icing add icing sugar, for thinner icing add some lemon juice or water. You can create some 3-D effects with icing that is runny.

Piping

There are endless kinds of piping bag tips available. In many cases simple paper cornets are used with piping tips inside. Garnishing can then start. For a complicated motif one usually makes a drawing on paper first. This is put around the cake and marked with pins to make the decorating easier. Take note that good piping skills take years of experience. Many patterns are symmetric so they must have the same form and piping thickness. In England we noticed that cakes with a straight-line design could also be garnished with different colours. This gradually builds up the wedding cake. The number of layers depends on the number of guests.

Just like fashion, wedding cakes have certain trends. Instead of delicate decorations it is also possible to use pliable chocolate. England is now working with fresh colours that make the cakes cheerful and summery, even in a different season. At The Little Venice Company we saw black and white being used to give the cake a chic and distinguished character.

Styles

It is believed that the original wedding cake tradition began in England. A baker from London had a view on Bride's Church from his bathroom. This church narrowed to its snow-white steeple and was five storeys high. Now, the traditional wedding cake is tiered from large to smaller layers. It is often garnished with white or pink marzipan roses. Everything has a special meaning. The colour white means prosperity, almonds in the marzipan stand for happiness in marriage, roses symbolize eternal love.

The American wedding cake is more like a showpiece. The cake is often much sweeter than we appreciate in Europe and filled with sweet butter cream. The major difference is the look of the cake. Instead of white layers, here we see a large flat cake with lots of colours.

And then comes the moment of cutting the cake. The bride holds the knife. The groom puts his hand over his wife's as a sign of their communion. The groom serves the first piece to the bride.

Yogurt structures

There is no other discipline where changes in modern techniques are made as fast as in Pâtisserie. Playing with new ideas and designs has been very common for years. The sweet part of a restaurant kitchen with its modern techniques makes this more and more interesting. Some methods are simple and easily understood. Other techniques demand high accuracy and the recipes can be detailed to one-tenth of a gram. For this chapter all techniques have been tested and where possible improved and corrected.

Yogurt structures

Yogurt is a dairy product that is extremely popular today and has good exposure. It is easily digested, good for the intestines, adds a fresh flavour to sweet and savoury dishes and tastes natural. Classic recipes will never disappear, but for this book we looked for new techniques and tasty combinations.

Foam made of Greek yogurt

Ingredients: 300 g Greek yogurt, 200 ml whipping cream, 50 g sugar water.

Mix Greek yogurt with whipping cream and sugar water. Pour in a siphon. Add a charger and cool in the fridge for several hours.
Pipe immediately on a chosen dessert; red-coloured fruit or a salad of mango and honey, for instance. See some serving suggestions below.

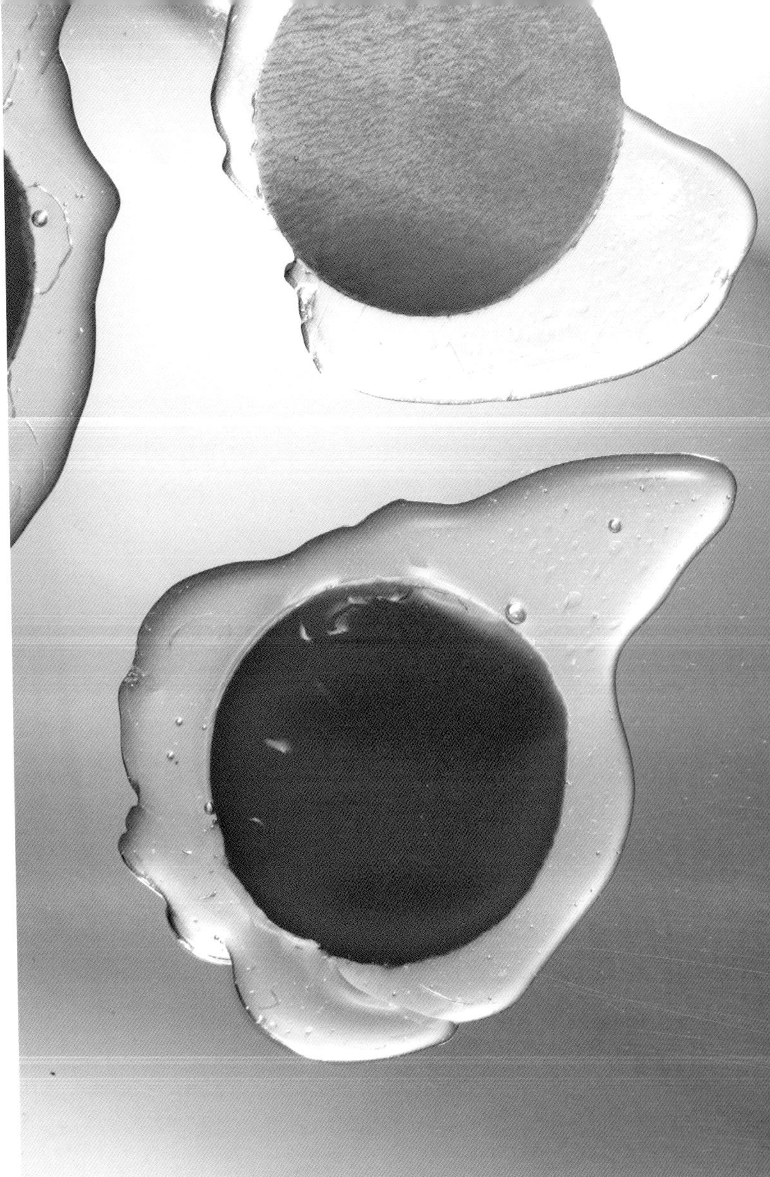

Taco of crunchy yogurt and foam made of Greek yogurt

Ingredients: 150 g fondant, 75 g glucose, 75 g isomaltose, 60 g yogurt powder, foam of Greek yogurt.

Cook glucose, fondant and isomaltose to 160°C / 320°F, let cool to 130°C / 265°F and stir firmly with the yogurt powder. Pour mixture on a plate and let semi cool. Cut in pieces and cool further. Grind pieces very finely in an electric coffee grinder or in the Thermomix. Keep powder in a tightly closed container with silicon grains. Using a small semi round sieve, sprinkle some powder on a silpat and put in oven for 2 minutes at 160°C / 320°F. Cool and take tacos off of the silpat. Cool further and keep in closed container with silica grains. Fill tacos with yogurt foam and serve immediately.

Yogurt streusel

Ingredients: 125 g flour, 125 g soft butter, 125 g icing sugar, 75 g yogurt powder.

Put all ingredients in a bowl and mix loosely by hand. Rub, like crumbly dough, between your hands to get crumbles. Let rest for 2 hours at room temperature and bake in the oven at 120°C / 250°F. Keep in tightly closed container.

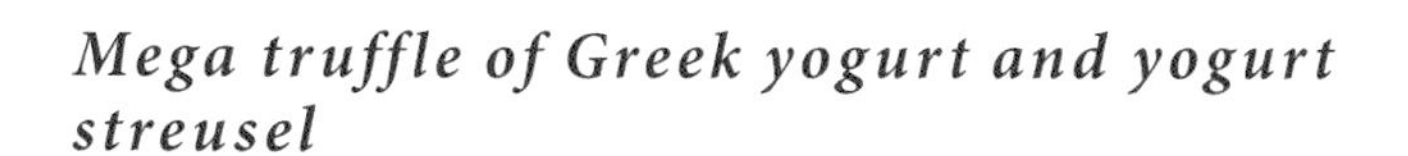

Mega truffle of Greek yogurt and yogurt streusel

Ingredients: foam of Greek yogurt (see recipe) to which 1 gelatin leaf is added, and yogurt streusel (see recipe).

Put a small layer of streusel on the working counter and pipe some foam on top. Carefully spoon the foam through the streusel so it is totally covered. The crunchy streusel and the soft foam create a wonderful sensation in your mouth. This truffle is ideal as part of a dessert.

Truffles of white chocolate and yogurt

Ingredients: 185 g Greek yogurt, 300 g white chocolate, yogurt streusel or almond powder mixed with yogurt.

Heat yogurt (preferably au bain-marie) and chocolate at 35°C / 95°F and pour in a proper bowl. Let thicken in the fridge. Pipe little balls and roll them through streusel or powder. Serve as part of a dessert or friandise.

Egg, sunny side up: mango and clear yogurt jelly

Ingredients: 200 ml drained yogurt, 50 g sugar water 1:1, 2.5 g kappa carrageen, 1 mango.

Mix drained yogurt and sugar water with kappa and bring to a boil. Keep liquid warm. Cut mango in thin slices and from these cut little rounds. Divide the rounds on a baking sheet and pour one spoon of the warm liquid over each piece of mango. Make sure that the liquid will pour over the edges. Let set and serve with a mango dessert or as a dessert amuse.

Powder of almonds and yogurt

Ingredients: 60 g sugar, 20 g water, 100 g bitter almonds, 60 g yogurt powder.

Heat sugar and water and cook to 177°C / 350°F. Add the almonds and stir so they are all coated with the caramel. Set aside to cool. Grind mix with yogurt powder in a food processor or Thermomix. This is the powder that can be used with the yogurt truffle and the white chocolate.

Yogurt snow

Ingredients: 600 g Greek yogurt, 100 g sugar water 1:1.

Mix yogurt with sugar water and pour in a Frix or Paco beaker. Freeze for at least 24 hours and grind to a powder.

Egg yolk with crunchy honey caramel

For the yolks: 400 g yogurt, 100 g unsweetened whipping cream, 1 gelatin leaf, 50 g sugar water 1:1.
For the alginate bath: 5 g algin, 1 litre water.
For the honey caramel: 150 g glucose, 150 g fondant, 100 g honey.

A modern variety of the Greek classic yogurt with honey. For the yolks, dissolve pre-soaked gelatin in 50 g heated cream. Add the rest of the cream, sugar water and yogurt. Mix water and algin with a hand held blender. Let stabilize for a few hours to get rid of any air bubbles.
For the caramel, mix the glucose, fondant and honey and cook to exactly 165°C / 330°F. Pour on a silpat and slice or break in pieces. Keep in a tight container with silica grains until ready to use. Just before serving heat a piece of caramel between two silpats in the oven at 160°C / 320°F. Remove from the oven and roll as thin as possible with a rolling pin and break in small pieces. Hold a deep serving spoon (15 ml) with the yogurt mix and dip very close to the surface of the alginate bath then flip spoon in one quick movement. This way you get a yolk without strings. Let sit for one minute and rinse carefully in a bowl of cold water. These yolks can be prepared ahead. Immediate put a piece of caramel on the yolk and let melt under a salamander or heat with a small torch. This way the caramel will melt over the yolk and become very crunchy again.

Dutch sausage roll

More than bread, less than sausage

In a time when everything is about new technology, it's always exciting to find a classic. Every region in Europe has its own classics, including a sausage roll in the Dutch province of Brabant.

One would expect that books have been written on this historical piece of pastry, but this is definitely not the case. We did a lot of research and approached the right people but nobody seemed to know its history. However, the name of the sausage roll appeared in Dutch dictionaries around the 19th century. It was described as bread filled with sausage meat or a sausage. We assume that the sausage roll as a delicacy was associated with the Catholic religion, as many people from the province of Brabant still eat these as a tradition after attending midnight mass at Christmas. Further research led us to discover that there is a lot more to the Brabants Worstebrood than just a bread roll with a sausage inside.

The champion

Nobody would be better suited to visit and learn about the process of this specialty of Brabant than this baker we discovered in Tilburg (Brabant), Theo Pastoor. He has had his bakery for over twelve years and has become a specialist in making this authentic sausage roll. So much so that he has won the national championship four times in the past five years. We meet the baker and his six employees early in the morning, which is actually late for them on a normal working day. After they have finished their regular duties, they make the sausage rolls. At first, it seems like a simple procedure, but it is a lot more complicated than that. We watch what Theo is doing and learn the details: "Everything starts with finding the right ingredients, which means finding a top quality butcher. We work with 100 per cent pork, which has more fat content than regular sausage meat. The meat consists of 20 per cent pig's head and the rest is from the lean part of the shoulder. The meat must be juicy. When squeezed it should release pure juice, no fat. We use basic spices in our ground meat, which means salt, pepper and mace. Per kilo of ground meat we add two eggs and our home made breadcrumbs." Theo jumps quickly from one subject to another, without missing a beat as production continued all around us. It is quite normal to produce more than 1500 rolls on a Friday. "The process has been refined since I started this bakery. You can see that in the oven temperatures. The meat is done in 8 or 9 minutes, while the bread requires a few minutes longer. If you bake it too long the meat will shrink, therefore you have to find the right combination for both." Because we are visiting a baker we wanted to know more about the dough, a basic white flour to which vegetable oil, salt, yeast, milk products and half amount of water is added: "After the ingredients have been mixed to a flexible dough, the proofing becomes the most important part. We take at least three to four hours for this,

while others just take one hour. The proofing process gives it acidity that enhances the flavour." After the dough has been formed in big round balls, it is left to proof again and formed in new balls; then it is time to proof once again. "The dough becomes more and more flexible which will strengthen the gluten in the dough. If the proofing is too short, the dough will be stiff. If the rolling of the dough is easy you have a good dough."

Little balls are rolled out on a laminoir (sheeter) to 2 mm thickness and a surface a little larger than the sausage. The ground meat is rolled by hand and placed on the dough. You sense that the employees get on well when soon another cart is full of sausage rolls. "It is pure relaxation for us. When we are busy we share funny jokes and baker's talk. You can see that we do everything by hand. There are lots of people who work with one slab of dough or use a machine that does everything. We prefer authenticity without any waste and give it the attention it deserves."

The sausage rolls are sprayed with egg wash and then proofed again at 30°C / 86°F. "We used to put egg wash on with a brush, but spraying gives a better and smooth result. Another very important part that I haven't mentioned is the temperatures. The dough should always be 26°C / 78°F. A cold sausage put on that dough would create a shock and you will not be able to proof again. Therefore the meat should be 20°C / 68°F before you roll it on the dough." Finally we are ready to bake the rolls in the oven at 220°C / 430°F and we are set to taste. Theo cuts one of the sausage rolls and says enthusiastically: "You have to taste the sausage right away and see its structure. The first bite should easily cut the sausage, you don't want the dough loosely wrapped around the sausage. The roll itself should be shiny and golden brown."

The titles that Theo has been awarded over the years have been very beneficial for his business. "When we started, we didn't sell more than 30 sausage rolls per day. Now, 300 are quite normal. We baked almost 40,000 rolls last December. The customer likes to buy something special; they want to tell their guests that this is a champion's sausage roll.

It affects everything; I have more staff now and the profits have greatly increased." Are the sausage rolls at a competition different than the ones we tasted today? "No, they are exactly the same. Of course, at a competition, you make sure they are perfect. It's the same as when you are selling a car, you would give it some extra polish. But another engine, no, you won't do that."

Bern is the capital of Switzerland, but Zürich is the largest city and the center for the Financial District and gold. The towers of the imposing Grossmünster and the Sint Peterskirche churches on the river Limmat give you an impressive view of the city. It's the area where trading is active and it's here where we find pâtisserie.

Our trip from Belgium to Switzerland was easy as we drove through Belgium, Luxembourg and Germany in just five hours. To get a real flavour of Switzerland we should have driven into the high Alps, but unfortunately we didn't have time for that. Zürich doesn't really look like an inviting city. There are not many impressive buildings or monuments and with its stark bank buildings and many offices the city looks almost square. However, behind this façade, we discover some very friendly and modest people. The old centre, where lots of activity takes place, is all within easy walking distance. There are plenty of trams should you not want to walk. Our first impression of pâtisserie is that the Swiss are still quite classical, with some exceptions.

Fabian Rimann

Our trip starts at one of the most beautiful hotels of the city, Baur au Lac. Chef pâtissier is Fabian Rimann, a young guy with a lot of potential. At the age of twelve he got his first minor job at a local bakery. He liked making delicacies and decided to develop that further. Fabian is now 27 and in spite of his young age he has participated in many competitions. One of the highlights was winning the bronze medal at the World Team Pastry championships in Nashville. Although the 5-star hotel looks very classic, Fabian's pâtisserie style is quite new. "Desserts can be trendy but not crazy; it's the modern combinations. If I come up with a new idea or suggestion, I sit around the table with my four pâtissiers and try to refine the idea. Each season we have a new menu, but the winter is my preference. It gives us a chance to work with warm flavours like cinnamon and dark chocolate." This chef has a passion for chocolate but bitter chocolates are his favourite. "These have a fuller flavour and more bouquet." The chef runs into the kitchen to make some of his specialties. "For me, the most delicious dessert is a crème brulee, simple but delicious. Or the traditional carrot cake." The latter looks very classical but: "This cake has earned its marks; it has no flour, but has put Switzerland on the map. The cake might look old fashioned but the taste is superb."

Baila Meringue

Cake, ice cream and vermicelli of chestnuts

For 10 desserts: chestnut puree, raspberries, raspberry coulis, chocolate garnish, fresh peppermint.
For the chestnut ice-cream: 500 g milk, 333 g cream, 250 g egg yolks, 150 g sugar, 500 g chestnut puree, 20 g kirsch.
For the honeyhüppe: 300 g icing sugar, 60 g melted butter, 90 g honey, 130 g flour, 30 g rum.
For the chestnut cake: 360 g egg yolk, 720 g icing sugar, 60 g vanilla sugar, 1200 g chestnut puree, 600 g melted butter, 900 g ground hazelnuts, 480 g egg white, 180 g sugar, Vienna dough, apricot marmalade.
For the meringue: 300 g egg white, 120 g sugar.
For the chestnut mousse: 280 g egg white, 52 g sugar, 200 g Alaska 666 (substitution for gelatin), 185 g water, 60 g kirsch, 375 g vanilla crème anglaise, 375 g chestnut puree, 840 g lightly whipped cream.

For the ice cream bring milk and cream to a boil. Beat egg yolks with sugar till foamy; mix with the boiling cream and prepare like an anglaise. Pass through a sieve and blend with puree and kirsch. Pour mixture in Paco or Frix beakers, freeze and spin. For the honeyhüppe combine ingredients to a smooth batter. Let thicken in the fridge and pour little heaps on a baking sheet. Bake cookies in the oven for 14 minutes at 180°C / 350°F or until golden-brown. For the cake whip egg yolks and icing sugar until foamy, and with a spatula blend in the chestnut puree and melted butter. In another bowl beat egg whites with the remaining sugar until stiff and mix with the egg yolk mixture. Carefully blend with the ground hazelnuts. Roll this Vienna dough on a baking sheet, spread with marmalade and pour cake batter over top. Bake cake in the oven for 20 minutes at 200°C / 390°F. Cool and cut in slices of 2 x 7 cm. For the meringue make a foam with the ingredients and bake in the oven for 24 hours at 70°C / 160°F. With a serrated knife cut squares of 5 x 5 cm and serve with honeyhüppe and a quenelle of ice cream. For the mousse, beat egg whites and sugar till stiff. Heat 1/3 of the water with the Alaska 666 and add the rest of the water. Mix puree with the anglaise and kirsch and process until smooth with the Alaska mix. Combine with the egg whites and the cream. Pour mousse in flexi moulds and set aside to gel. Put a small amount of chestnut purée on the mousse and garnish with chocolate and a raspberry. Sprinkle cake with icing sugar. Create a little tower of meringue, honeyhüppe and ice cream and garnish with mint. Pipe some raspberry coulis on the plate.

Plumplemplem

Trio of plums

For 4 people: peppermint, 4 chocolate curls.
For Breton dough: 208 g butter, 208 g icing sugar, 104 g egg yolk, 293 g flour, 20 g baking powder.
For the chocolate crème: 110 g cream, 30 g glucose, 120 g milk chocolate, 80 g dark chocolate, 250 g cream.
For the hazelnut brownie: 135 g egg yolk, 115 g sugar, 45 g melted butter, 370 g ground hazelnuts, 13 g lemon juice, 5 g baking powder, 135 g egg white, 115 g sugar.
For ice cream of sour cream: 400 g sugar, 200 g water, 1300 g sour cream, 20 g honey, 20 lemon zests.
For the plum ice cream: 1000 g plum puree, 83 g glucose powder, 33 g invert sugar, 193 g sugar, 350 g water.
For the poached plums: 8 plums, 500 ml red wine, 200 g sugar, marrow of 1 vanilla bean, 2 cinnamon sticks, 1 star anise.

For the dough whip butter and sugar until white and slowly add the egg yolks bit by bit. Mix with the flour and baking powder and let rest in the fridge overnight. Roll out to 4mm thick and bake in the oven at 180°C / 355°F or until it is golden-brown. For the crème, heat 110 g cream with glucose. Add carefully to the chocolate and stir to make a smooth batter.

Whisk the rest of the cream through the cooled mixture and let rest in the fridge for one night. Before using whip the crème lightly.
For the ice cream, heat water and sugar. Mix with the rest of the ingredients, pour in Pacojet or Frix beakers and freeze. Spin. For the plum ice cream, bring water, sugar, glucose powder and invert sugar to a boil and pour that on the frozen coulis. Process until smooth and pour in Pacojet or Frix beakers and freeze. Spin. For the poached plums heat everything except the fruit. Cut plums in quarters and poach them. Pipe both ice creams in a little glass and garnish with a chocolate curl. Cut brownie in a rectangle and pipe a dot of crème on it. Garnish with some poached plums. Put in the centre of a plate and garnish with mint.

Burnout

Crème brulee of caramel

For 10 people: **1500 g cream, 500 g pasteurized milk, 360 g sugar, 480 g egg yolk, cane sugar, peppermint and sugar pieces.**

Heat cream and milk, caramelize the sugar and deglaze with the boiling cream. Heat again, beat egg yolks and prepare further like an anglaise. Pour mixture in small ramekins, cover well with baking foil and bake in a combi-steamer at 96°C / 205°F with 30% steam. Sprinkle the cooled cream with cane sugar and burn to crunch. Garnish with a sugar piece and mint.

Café Felix

Crossing the street from our hotel over the Quai Bridge, we arrive at Café Felix. This café hasn't been open for long and is already the place to be in Zürich. The interior is baroque and busy; kitsch might be a better word. The ambiance is cozy, the café is alive. At this café you can be seen in a suit or shorts, it doesn't matter. It is full of people from all walks of life, young and old. The baked goods are done by House Teuscher. Not really a coincidence, because Mr.Teuscher was the manager for the previous owner of Café Felix, then called Schober Café, at a different location. The café is cozy and warm and the Gugelhopf cake is highly recommended by their staff. It is a fresh piece of cake full of raisins, actually quite a large piece as they don't believe in small portions.

Sprüngli and the Luxemburgeli

The most important street in Zürich is the Bahnhofstrasse. Here you will find large stores and the well-known banks with trams moving back and forth. On the corner of the Bahnhofstrasse and the famous Paradeplatz is a gorgeous building: Confiserie Sprüngli. The store is divided in two parts. One is an eating area that is especially busy in the morning. Business people as well as locals enjoy their coffee and croissant here. The second area is a pâtisserie shop with twelve sales ladies to help you. This shop is square with glass display counters along the walls and in the center. Everything is available here. Sprüngli is an institution in Zürich; everyone knows them because they have been in existence for more than a century. The first steps were made in 1836 by David Sprüngli. In 1859

he opened this building on the Bahnhofstrasse. It didn't stop there because this chain is now run by the 6th generation. Today, there are 18 stores in Switzerland, most of them in Zürich. We are introduced to Luxemburgeli and the minute we get this delicacy we think of a Macaron de Paris. But we are reprimanded, because we attacked the pride of Zürich: "The Luxemburgeli is NOT a Macaron de Paris!" Fortunately we had the difference explained to us. When Mr. Sprüngli went to Luxembourg as a young pâtissier, he noticed these typical cookies and took the recipe to Zürich. When the war broke out, the recipe was forgotten. But in 1958 an apprentice visited Mr. Sprüngli from Luxembourg. The now quite older Mr. Sprüngli remembered the cookie and asked his apprentice to make it. In honour of the apprentice they named it Luxemburgeli. It became a hit and it is still as popular as ever. We are still wondering what the difference is between that and the Macaron de Paris. In a friendly fashion we were clearly told it is a secret. Later we find out that there are differences. The Luxemburgeli is made with Italian foam, whereas the French macaron is made with regular foam. The Swiss cookie has more almonds and is thinner. Another main difference is that the Luxemburgeli is made fresh each day. All in all small differences and to us they don't affect the taste. We see 12 different kinds in their display units. Besides the familiar flavours like coffee or chocolate, there are also other hip flavours like Bailey's or jasmine. For the 50th anniversary of the store, they made a special Champagne-Luxemburgeli. Next to this delicacy we also find other sweet treats like Zuckerguss. These are small squares of cakes filled with buttercream and covered with marzipan. The whole store is full of chocolates because Sprüngli played a major role in the history of Swiss chocolate.

At the Market

From Sprüngli it's only a few minutes walk to Bürkliplatz where you'll find a market every Tuesday and Friday morning. Next to lots of flowers we see many local delicacies. We come by the baker's stand of Elisabeth Stoutman and Marie Louise Ast. It is difficult to get a few minutes to talk to them; it is not the language barrier but the many customers. Fortunately the ladies take time to get their picture taken with the breads. Another booth we visit at the market is Paul Ströbels' stand with Swiss cheeses. To mention a few: Simmentaler, a raw cow's milk cheese or the Sbirnz, a three-year-old cow's milk cheese. Paul is very happy to let us taste his cheeses. He explains: "Because Switzerland exists of several cantons(states), there is great diversity in cheeses. For example, the Appenzeller comes from the German region in the country." Between all the professional market stands we see a small table with a very sweet old lady behind it. It is 80 year old Ada Santelli. She is Italian and has been coming to the market for more than 20 years. She only sells five items but all home made: nuss gipfeli (rolled up puff pastry with nuts) and keks (cake with filling), jars with confiture, cookies and dried apples. Ada is an authentic part of the market.

The Alststadt

The centre of Zürich is split in two by the river Limmat that runs into the Zürichsee. The medieval heart of the city is also called Alststadt. We have arrived at the east part of the downtown area with its landmark the Grossmünster, the big Dome with the two steeples that stand tall over the city. Around there is a labyrinth of small streets and many small shops. Although in some cities you are inundated with souvenir shops, in Zürich there are almost none. Apparently the visiting businessmen don't need cowbells, cuckoo clocks or snow globes. We cross the Rathaus Brücke and arrive at Martgasse 9 where we find a little shop called Chocomotion, owned by Franziska Goesser. It has a concept that we have seen before but is not less attractive. There is an assortment of chocolate here from 8 different countries. The shop has only been open for one year and besides chocolate bars they also sell sandwiches and other products with cocoa, like body paint and cosmetics.
Next to the chocolate shop is Bärenland owned by Christian Schmidt. This shop has about 120 kinds of gummy bears and Christian would love it if we tried all of them. Besides the familiar flavours, he also sells gummy bears that are made without gelatin or sugar and some are even

organic. All gums that Christian sells are made without any artificial colour, aromas or flavour. His favorites are strawberry-raspberry gum and the buckthorn gum with extra Vitamin C. Further down at Munstergasse 19 we discover a charming little shop called Schwarzenbach. It is a grocery store going back to 1864. We are lured inside by the appealing and tasty looking dried and sugary fruits. Once inside we find about fifteen kinds and also some creative cake decorations. Nothing seems to have changed over the years as we can see from the pictures on the wall. The lady behind the counter is not the friendliest, but the rest of the little shop made up for that. We became quite excited when we saw the Lolipop shop. It is a candy shop specialized in confiserie from all over the world. Alexandra Bisaz is one of the founders of this shop. It hasn't always been easy for her, as she tells us: "We opened the first Lolipop store in 1998 in Davos. Unfortunately this became a big flop. We had no back-up financing and could hardly pay the rent. We had to make a decision and said farewell to Davos. We didn't want to give up our concept and decided to try a new title: Lolipop 1st Candy Shop in Zürich. We found a small building and furnished it with our own furniture. We promised ourselves to go back to Davos if Zurich proved to be a success." The ladies worked extremely hard from morning to night and it paid off because the store became a great success. After 10 years there are 26 stores all through Switzerland. Alexandra takes us through the shop and points out special items. We see NASA ice powder, jellybeans and a large sugar ball called a jawbreaker. It is all too much to mention but we highly recommend it if you don't want ordinary candy. The address of the Lolipop shop we visited is Stüssihofstatt 10. A well-known pâtisserie in Zürich is Teuscher. Maybe not necessarily for their specialties, which are excellent, but more for the interior of their stores. The interiors are really kitschy and that is an understatement. The shop is decorated with flowers and as you can guess they are all artificial. This thanks to the interior designer for Teuscher, Mr. Felix Daetwylers. He is also the man behind the name Café Felix. The specialty of the house is the champagne truffle. There is also a Teuscher at Bahnhofstrasse 46. Don't worry, you can't miss it!

Honold and the Pain de Gênes

If you want to visit classic pâtisserie houses then go to Honold in Zürich. Behind the counter are six ladies politely waiting to serve the clients. The interior looks a bit old fashioned, but the shop and the tea-salon are very busy. We have an appointment with Mrs. Lotti Honold; she is the 3rd generation after the founder Fritz Honold. When she meets us she is pretty stern but soon she starts to relax. "We have many specialties and one is the famous Pain de Gênes. My grandfather travelled a lot and found this recipe in Genua. You best describe this cake as an almond cake without flour. Opa introduced the cake in Zürich and it became a great success." It seems it doesn't matter which patisserie we visit in Zürich, they always talk about their shops respectfully. We asked her to describe her style in the business: "Contrary to the old days, the pâtisserie has changed and is now more modern. We only use top ingredients, like real butter and delicious cream. We are working with trendy flavours, like chili or other spices. I used to travel a lot and that is where I got to know and learned the use of different flavours. We have a few classic items here that we don't want to change. One is the Züri-läckerli, these are small marzipan bites." It is obvious that Mrs. Honold has been very involved in this business. We are curious to know the difference between then and now. "Zürich is not a large city. We didn't have big shopping centres forty years ago. There was a small bakery or konditorei on every corner. Some have grown, others have disappeared. It is too bad but that's the way the world is. Our business doesn't grow any more; our building is too small and I don't mind being small. Take our sandwiches, they are always fresh. When you grow too much the quality suffers sometimes." We get a tour around the chocolate area with Chef-chocolatier Ivo Jud and he let us taste some special pralines. We love the absinthe bonbon, but don't eat that on an empty stomach.

Warehouses

Like any other city, Zurich has some large warehouses. There are two that are worth mentioning: Jemoli and Globus. The last one is affiliated with a Swiss bakery chain called Fleischli. Here we find typical Swiss products. Behind the counter we find two very helpful Swiss ladies, Yvonne and Elizabeth. First we are introduced to authentic Swiss bread, called Walliserbrot that originated in the area of Wallis located in the Alps. It is a very dense bread based on rye and sourdough. Zopf is white sugarless bread and is usually eaten on Sundays during brunch. Laugenbrötli is a soft white bread mostly used for sandwiches. The last bread we taste is the Tournette, baked in a variety of ways. It's a long shaped bread, crunchy outside and soft inside. We also find some sweet Swiss specialties. The Lägere Hupfi are small almond cakes. Another one is the Bündner-Nusstorte; this little tart originated in the mountains and is made of nuts, honey, cream and almonds. Yvonne enthusiastically gives us a bag of Thurgauer Öpfleringl. "Everyone loves these, they are dried apple slices with a layer of chocolate." Finally we taste the Bündner Birnbrot, a heavy bread consisting of two parts. A thin crust of ordinary bread that is filled with a heavy dark bread made of pears, figs, walnuts, orange and lemon peel and flavoured with cinnamon and coriander powder.

After we leave the department store we head back to Bahnhofstrasse and at #106 we find pâtisserie Merkur, a store that sells a great assortment of chocolates and pralines. But what really catches our eyes is the large demonstration area in the back of the store where we meet Adrian Müller, a chocolatier who works for the Swiss chocolate brand Läderach. In his life he didn't always deal with sweet stuff. Adrian: "This is my second career. I used to be an interior designer. I always liked to be a chocolatier, so when I decided to change professions, I started to work at different bakeries and chocolate shops. Now I educate and demonstrate chocolate to the public. It took me a while to adapt but it is fun and here I get more appreciation for my profession."

Franz Ziegler

Our visit to Zürich gives us the opportunity to meet another great professional: Franz Ziegler. In order to meet him we have to travel about sixty kilometres to the small town of Schwyz. It is a great trip weaving through little hilltop villages and cute little houses that have loads of character. We are personally invited by Franz as he wanted to share his knowledge of Swiss chocolate and the Swiss pâtisserie. When we met him for the first time, he was very excited as he had just been named Pastry Chef of the Year in Nashville. Franz was born in the village of Landquart, about 100 kilometres from Zürich. As a child of a baker's family he had two dreams: becoming a football player or becoming a pâtissier but in the end he chose the latter. It was his brother Alois who became a baker first to follow his father in the bakery. Franz studied to become a chef, but never gave up his love to be a pâtissier so decided to specialize in pâtisserie. "I loved the profession but not the low salary. In those days there were not as many opportunities as today, long hours, and I often thought of quitting. One day I was really fed up and I realized that to become somebody you have to reach for the top. In 1990 I got my certificate of Meister Konditor, the Swiss Master degree in Pâtisserie. I graduated with a very respectable final result of 5.8 out of 6 points. After that I contacted Felchin, the Swiss chocolate brand. There I became chef pâtissier and traveled the world. At that time I started to write my first book titled Magic Chocolate. It was a great success and translated into three languages. The book was so popular that I was convinced it would give me the name I was after. In 1996 I left Felchin since I had a chance to buy a chocolaterie. However, that adventure went down the drain. Now I am a consultant and teacher." More books were written and the chef kept in contact with Felchin. Just like the Belgians, the Swiss are very proud of their chocolate. We asked about his secrets regarding Swiss chocolate. "The difference is in the quality of the ingredients.

The Swiss are very conservative and won't compromise quality in products. Just like our watches, we like to tempt people with quality and strength. A good example is the choice of cocoa beans. Switzerland has always played a major role in chocolate, just look at the invention of the concheer (conching) machine by Rudolph Lindt."
Franz takes us through the chocolate factory of Felchin. Here he explains the making of chocolate and it is obvious that this is where his heart lies. We enter the last stage of the tour where we see the chocolate processing with the already mentioned conching machines. Conching chocolate was nothing new, but Lindt invented a machine that gave chocolate a more beautiful emulsion. The machine reminds us of wheels of a locomotive. Franz: "Large companies replaced the old machines with new ones but we didn't. We have chocolates here that go through a conching process for 72 hours." Later we taste the difference between chocolate that has been processed sixty and forty hours in the conching machine and the difference is obvious. The longest process gives the chocolate a more subtle taste. "It is a combination of everything. The milk powder we use comes from Swiss cows. If you see those animals grazing in the mountains you know they are healthy." Franz is a man with experience and knows exactly what goes on in the pâtisserie world. We are curious as to what he thinks of Swiss pâtisserie. He smiles: "How strange this might seem, but there is hardly any progress. Of course there are people with an open mind, but these are few and they work on an international level. The basics are here, but nothing happens. As said before, we as Swiss are very conservative. Maybe some weird ideas will come on the market but then you have to take a risk. We don't have real pioneers here. If there is one it would be Fabian Rimann. France, Spain and Japan understand these things better. They realize the demand; another example is Austria. They have a very classic pâtisserie culture but know how to work with it."
How does he see pâtisserie in the future? "We have reached a very high level. I think we are close to the big bang! Pâtisserie and economy always go hand in hand. Everyone wants to exceed the other, but what happens when you are already at the top? I will give you an example. Recently I saw a French chef making sushi that he garnished with gold leaves. Too strange for words? A sushi, as perfect as can be, is garnished with the most expensive material on earth. This you eat and secrete! This makes no sense. If you have made something that is absolutely perfect in taste, why would you tamper with it by adding gold leaves? It's the same with pâtisserie; it will always be there because it is delicious. I believe that we will go back to the basics in the future. No expensive packaging, as it is too costly for people. In short, just delicious real pâtisserie and forget the bullshit around it."

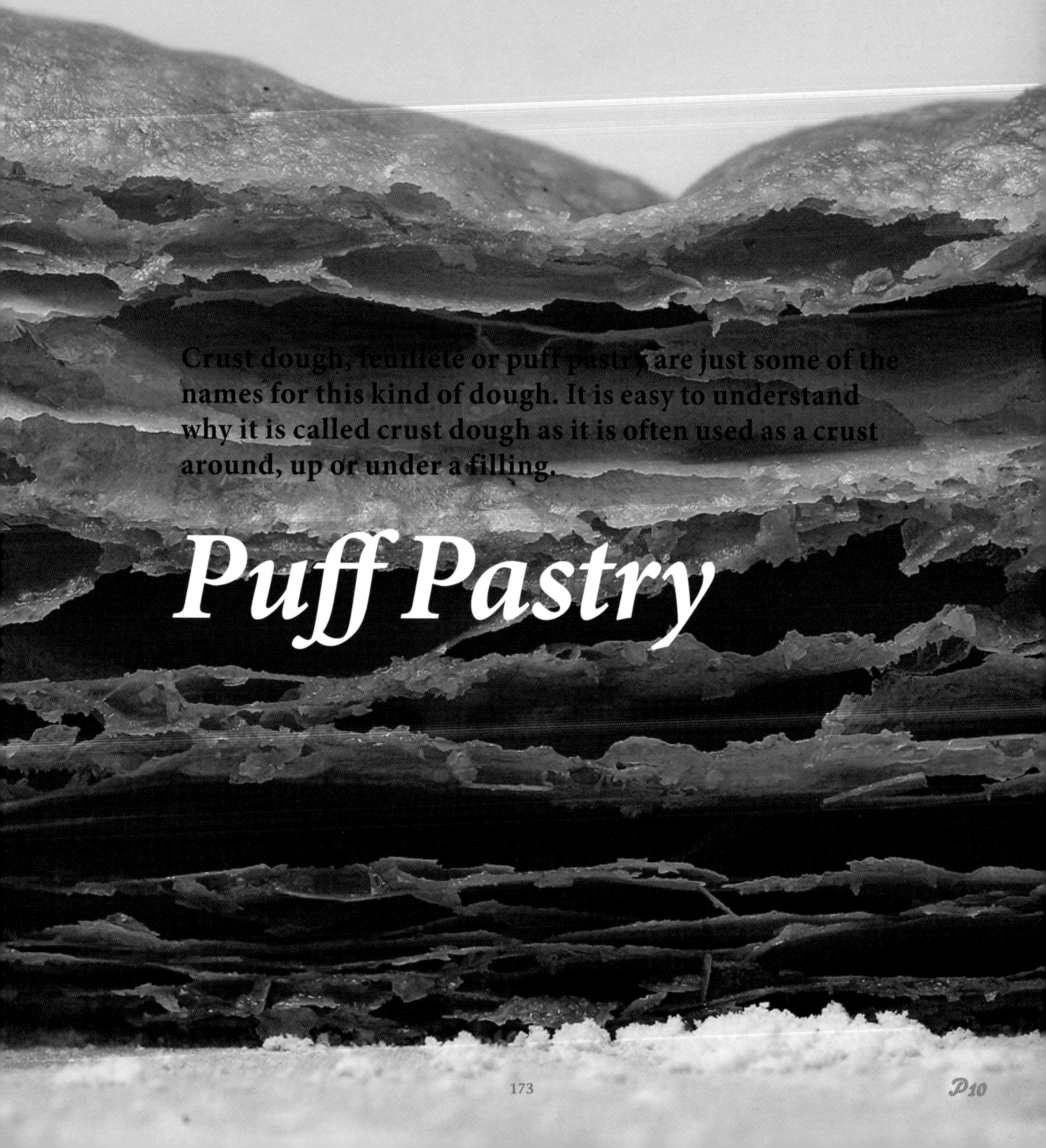

Crust dough, feuilleté or puff pastry are just some of the names for this kind of dough. It is easy to understand why it is called crust dough as it is often used as a crust around, up or under a filling.

Puff Pastry

All over Europe you can find varieties of this dough; almost every country uses its own methods. Don't confuse German puff pastry with French millefeuille. They only have one thing in common: it is a very flaky and crusty dough. This is because the dough consists of tens to hundreds of layers. The basic ingredients are simple: flour, water and butter. The folding, rolling and turning are what make the dough so complex and interesting. Butter is added to the dough of water and flour. Every time the dough is rolled and folded many layers are created, called lamination.

The basic ingredients

To understand the working and the possible wrong doings of puff pastry it is important to know the role of the different ingredients. As mentioned before, the three main ingredients are water, flour and fat content. Besides that, one can add salt, milk powder, egg yolks, soya flour and starch, all to create a better or different result. The only flour suitable for puff pastry is wheat flour because it is rich in gluten. The gluten is water absorbent and has the ability to make pliable dough. Wheat protein absorbs water best and gives the dough the elasticity and the stretching ability. The absorbency of flour is not always the same. Good flour protein can take about 200% of its weight in water. Different kinds of flour from various flourmills can make a huge difference. This depends on how the wheat has been grown. Today large factories know how to make a good standard finished product with a minimum of dissimilarities. What is the role of starch? The starch used has to have a strong binding power, which means that it should absorb sufficient water in the baking process. The flour used for puff pastry contains about 68% starch. The starch granules swell, enlarge and create a full structure during baking. The binding process happens between 65°C / 150°F and 85°C / 185°F. Some kinds of flour very suitable for puff pastry are the American patent flour, top patent flour (made with a certain ratio between soft and hard wheat), unbleached American patent flour and the French flour type 55.

Fat content

The fat content is not put in the dough, but between layers of dough through kneading. This creates different layers of dough and fat that don't stick together. The type of fat used must also be pliable and stretchable. Don't use olive oil as nothing would happen. Unsalted butter is the best natural ingredient as it has elasticity and stretching capabilities. The quality is reproduced by manufacturers who call their product crust margarine. The butter that is incorporated in the layers melts during the baking process and makes the layers loose enough to lie on top of each other. The force of the steam that exists between the layers pushes the layers apart. If the butter is evenly divided the dough will rise equally.

The layers of dough (containing starch and protein) will absorb the fat during and after the baking and because butter transports flavours well the result will be even better. Fats can also give a flaky effect depending on the quantity. If there is not enough butter added, the end product will be harder. It is important that the structure stays intact during the baking process. Because of its natural flavour, unsalted butter is by far the favourite above any other fats, but has also disadvantages. In a warm environment it is harder to work with than margarine or lard. Another

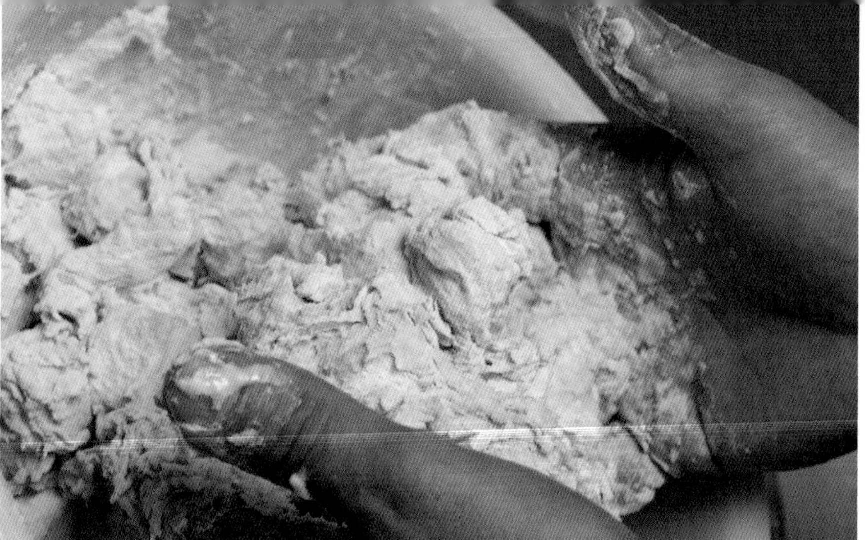

problem with butter can be the melting point; it is shorter and has a shorter sustainability. To firm up unsalted butter you can add part of the flour (about10%) to the butter. Another disadvantage is the high content of fat acidity for baking. The acidity stimulates shrinking and that makes the dough tougher. Crust margarine is another option. The fat contents are specially produced in factories for working with puff pastry.
Of course in this case many artificial flavours are used and that is an insult to puff pastry. The similarity between butter and margarine is the fat-water ratio that is decided by law. Both ingredients contain at least 80% fat and maximum 16% water. Another option: lard that doesn't contain any water. In that case, 80% of regular quantity butter has to be used. This is the same as the quantity of fat in butter. Lard and margarine, manufactured in factories, are produced in a way to maximize the toughness of the dough and have a much higher melting point than butter.

Water

When water in the oven changes to steam, it will increase its original volume more than a thousand times. The same principle was used in making steam engines and steam locomotives. This principle is of enormous influence in the baking of puff pastry. It takes care of the thin layers of dough becoming separated. The higher the temperature of the oven, the faster it creates steam that forms the crust also faster. It is interesting to note that the steam increases by 10% if the oven temperature is increased by 27°C / 80°F. If the oven is saturated by steam it makes the process of laminating much easier. If the oven is too low the steam will develop less. This will mean that the protein is curdled and the starch hardened before the steam has done its work. If the baking temperature is too high the steam becomes too strong and we will get an uneven, undesirable product with fast colouring. We call that "wild baking".

Optional ingredients

There are a few ingredients that are used to improve the dough.
Salt: The normal percentage of salt used is 2% of the total weight of flour. This is to increase the flavour.
Milk powder: About 1% of skim milk powder is added when lard or margarine is used. Milk protein or milk sugar, both colour enhancing, are not present in lard. Therefore, milk powder is used to improve the colour of the dough.
Egg yolks: It is not common to use egg yolks in puff pastry. It does give the product a fuller flavour and a better colour; the lecithin present in eggs gives it a thicker cell structure and improves the baking quality. However, the product won't keep as long.
Soya flour: The maximum amount of soya flour to be added should be 2%. It gives the dough a better colour and the protein of soya keeps the flavour longer. The soya lecithin also delays the fat oxidation process.
Starch: The crispiness of the puff pastry products is influenced by the gluten content. If the gluten is too strong you can add 10% starch, but that means using 10% less flour. The dough will be less tough and is easier to handle without sacrificing the layer effect. The puff pastry will also be flakier since it has less crunchy baked gluten.

Rolling and folding

When we learn about puff pastry, the most well known methods are the French, the Dutch and the fastest method. In all three it is important to provide the flour and water with layers of fat content. By rolling and folding the dough many times, one creates a very fine distribution of fat and layers. Rolling and folding is the most important preparation of puff pastry. The number of times the rolling and folding is done and the way the dough is folded is different for each method. In practice, impressions are made in the dough with fingertips. The amount of impressions is the same as the number of rolling and folding. Why is this so important? After just ONE folding and rolling, a diagram of the dough would show two layers of dough with a butter layer in between, but not yet suitable to bake. If you would start baking this, part of the flour would mix with the dough and the rest runs out. It then becomes rather dense dough that doesn't resemble puff pastry.
After several times of rolling and folding, the fat content becomes so delicate that it is totally absorbed by the dough and the cells are covered with a thin film of fat. The fat ensures that there is no correlation in the structure of the dough so the layers can be pushed away from each other. It is obvious that the folding and rolling should be done neatly and controlled or the dough will have an uneven layering. Proof will be in the baking. To obtain the desired result it is important that the dough is rolled in more than one direction so that the gluten will be equally stretched and the dough will not shrink to one side. Of course one can fold and roll too much in which case the cell structure and fat membranes are mixed together and the layer effect will be very small.

Rolling and resting

It must be obvious by now that making puff pastry is not easy. The rolling of puff pastry dough has to be taken seriously and should be done in an environment of about 15°C / 18°C. It has to be done in stages or the structure will be damaged. In a bakery where one works with machines, there is a fixed schedule. As mentioned the dough should be rolled in different directions by turning it 45 degrees each time. Attention should be paid to dusting with flour. If too little is used, the top layer will get sticky and break. Too much will damage the dough, it will be stiffer and not easy to bake. To avoid confusion fold the dough always towards you. The resting of dough will let the gluten relax so the dough will not shrink.

The baking

The oven and the temperature are extremely important for baking puff pastry. Frequently the set temperature is not exactly the same as inside the oven. And there is often a difference between the top and bottom of an oven. There are some oven manufacturers who take extreme care to ensure that the oven temperature is as accurate as possible and that makes baking a lot more pleasant. The kind of oven is also important. Certain products can be baked at 200°C / 390°F in a convection oven, but have to be baked at 220°C / 430°F in a regular oven.
During the baking process the incorporated fat will melt, separating the layers of dough. Because of the heat, water becomes steam; this steam establishes itself between the cells and is held together by the gluten. Strong gluten can carry steam pressure easily and that creates the layering of the fat-dough cell structure. You can see the layers when you cut the dough. The dough works itself to the top whereby the temperature rises to 60°C / 80°C or 140°F / 175°F. The binding of the starch in the flour will prevent the rising dough from collapsing. Because of the heat the starch has a stronger binding effect with the fluids. One part of this will be water, but the other part is the fluid that releases itself through the binding process of the protein.

Never open the oven during the baking. We have just seen that it is water that creates the layers of dough. Besides the starch, the protein (like albumin and gluten) also prevent the dough from collapsing. This point is reached when the steam pressure is at its highest. If somebody opens the door at that moment, most of the steam would be lost. The pressure will be gone and the layers that were separated to give the baking a crunchy crust will then stick together and the damage is done.
Time and temperature must be totally connected. Note that the layering takes place at the start of the baking. The oven has to be at the right temperature but the temperature also depends on other factors like the thickness of the dough.

The French method

Ingredients: 500 g flour, 75 g fat content, 300 g water, 5 g salt, 375 g fat content

Mix all ingredients to a basic dough except the 375 g fat. Make sure the dough doesn't get tough and let it rest another 10 minutes. Make the rest of the butter flexible and pliable and ready to roll out; the dough and the fat content should have the same consistency. Roll the dough in a ball, make a cross in it and fold the points out. Roll out evenly so it looks like a cross with the centre of the dough a bit bigger and thicker than the sides. Put the rolled out butter in the middle and fold points of dough to the center so it covers the fat content. You will now have a square. To fold and roll adequately, the dough should not be thicker than 4 cm. Roll out the dough in stages to 1 cm thickness. The length has to be three times longer than the width. Make a tri-fold of the dough, turn it 45 degrees and again roll out in stages to create a rectangle. Repeat four times and let rest for 20-30 minutes. It is then ready for further processing.

The Dutch method

Ingredients: 500 g flour, 500 g butter at room temperature, 300 g water, 10 g salt.

Cut butter in small cubes of 2 x 2 x 2 cm and divide evenly in the flour. Add water and salt and knead the dough in a machine. Roll out to a rectangle of 1 cm thickness. The length of the dough should be four times the width. Roll and fold three times, always fold in a square.
Turn the dough 45 degrees half way of each folding and rolling. Let rest for about 30 minutes after one full set of rolling and folding. Make sure you don't knead too long as the butter should be enclosed by the dough. Too much kneading will flatten the butter, so maybe it is better to mix than to knead.

The Fast method

This method is fast because the resting time is shorter and sometime there is no resting at all. The folding and rolling is also less. Margarine producers play into this by bringing pre-produced margarine into the market. These kinds of margarine, sold in sticks or balls, have a coating that prevents the fat from sticking.

Ingredients: 500 g flour, 450 g fat content, 5 g salt, 280 g water.

Mix the ingredients in a way that doesn't show any fat content.
Roll the dough to a layer of 1 cm thickness with the length of the dough four times longer than the width. Fold the dough three times in five layers, turn it 45 degrees after rolling and folding and bake without resting the dough.

Soft Friandises

by pastrychef Jacques van Bragt

Soft Caramel

Ingredients: 900 g sugar, 1 kg light syrup, 400 g butter, 1200 g whipping cream, 1 vanilla bean, sliced in half.

Bring sugar and syrup to a boil and separately cook whipping cream, butter and sliced vanilla bean. While the syrup is cooking, Jacques uses a wet brush to moisten the edges of the pan to prevent crystallization. Cook the caramel to 91°R or 175°C / 345°F. Remove the vanilla bean from the cream mixture and deglaze the caramel with the hot cream. To prevent burning, the caramel should be stirred constantly. Pour the hot caramel in a baking frame and let cool. After it has cooled, the caramel can be cut in any shape you wish. In his shop, Jacques makes bonbons of the caramel by dipping them through crunchy nuts and covering them with chocolate.

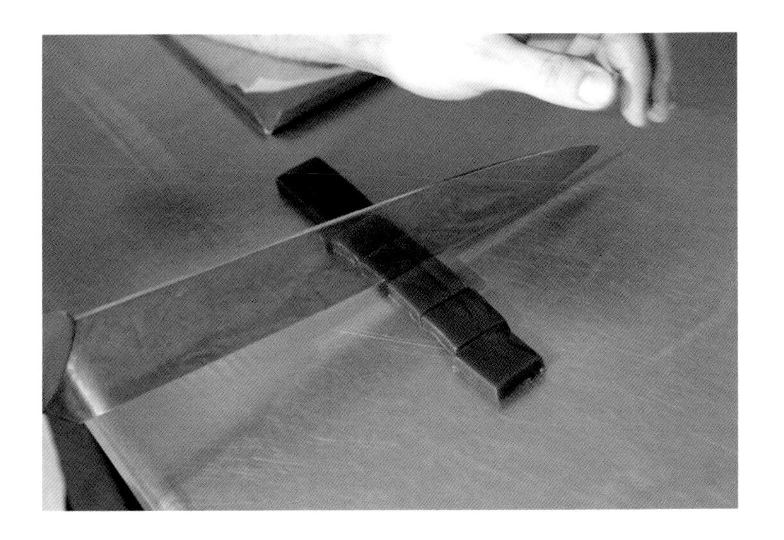

Pâte de Fruit

Ingredients: juice of 2 lemons, 1200 g raspberry puree, 2 kg sugar, 40 g pectin or 250 g pecca, 25 g citric acid.

This friandise can contain many flavours; the recipe depends on the content of citric acid in the fruit that is used. Jacques' choice is a pre-made clear raspberry puree from Boiron that doesn't have any seeds or other residues.

Cook the puree with the lemon juice. This gives a fresh flavour that makes the pectin work better. Add the pectin and sugar and cook thoroughly. Add the citric acid and cook again until everything is dissolved. It is a matter of feeling to get the pâte the right thickness. The pectin has to be adjusted if it is made with lemon or other sour fruits. When the thick mixture starts to gel lightly pour into a shallow form and sprinkle with crystal sugar. Cut the pâte in small little cubes and dip in crystal sugar.

Soft Nougat

Ingredients: 550 g water, 1650 g light syrup, 1925 g sugar, 220 g egg whites, 220 g crystal sugar, 220 g icing sugar, 500 g whole almonds (skin removed), 550 g hazelnut (skin removed), 200 g pistachios, all nuts roasted.

Bring water, light syrup and 1925 g sugar to a boil and cook to 98° Reamur. In a non greased bowl, beat egg whites at 94° Reamur and add the crystal sugar in stages. When syrup has reached the right temperature, slowly add it to the egg whites. Beat slightly, replace the metal beater with a plastic beater and add the icing sugar.
Jacques: "The egg whites get so tough that it can destroy the beater. Besides that I don't want the nougat to be too airy. That's why we change the beaters." Beat the mixture for another 8 minutes at the lowest level and add the toasted nuts at a temperature of 60°C / 140°F. The nuts cannot be too cold, as it will cool the egg whites too fast. Beat it once again but be careful that the nuts don't break. Scoop the foam on a baking sheet lined with sugar, pressing with your hands that you have lightly covered with sugar. Press a bit more with a rolling pin, let dry overnight and cut in squares. This is a soft nougat. The well-known Montelimar is much harder.

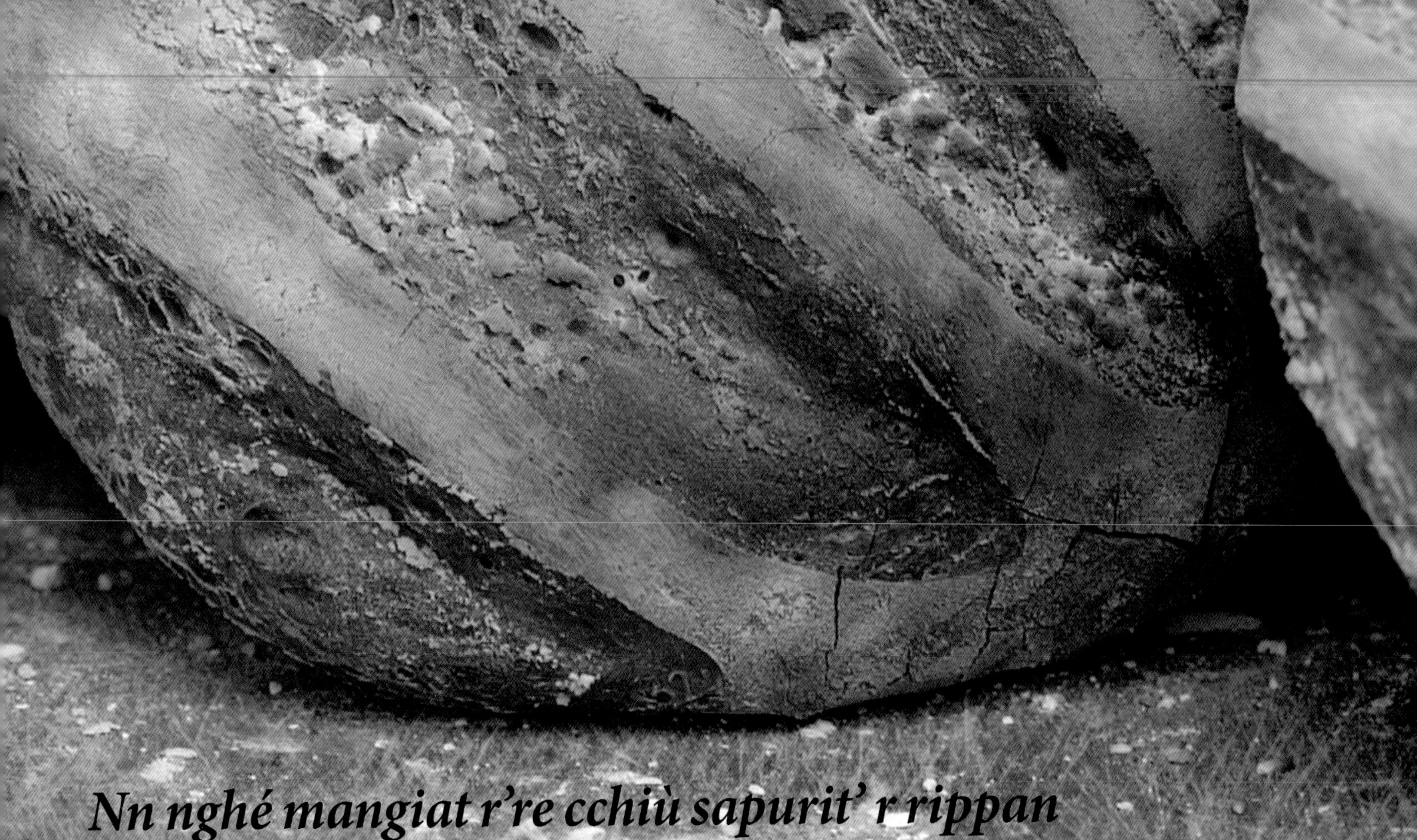

Nn nghé mangiat r're cchiù sapurit' r rippan

(nothing is more royal than bread)

Italian bread

Bread in Italy is the most important part of the meal. Although we are inclined to think it is pasta, nothing is further from the truth. Bread is essential to each meal, while pasta in any way or form is just one part of one meal. Surely everything is different now than in the past. The warm sensation of the smell of homemade bread is almost nostalgic now. The bakery used to be in the centre of each Italian village with often the only oven in the village. Not only to bake bread, but the village people brought their home-prepared food and the baker would put those in the oven as well. While the oven was baking the food, the wonderful smells combined with crackling wood kept the village people busy bringing each other up to date on the stories of the village.

Nostalgia, rituals and superstition

Especially in Calabria, one of the poorest regions in Italy, the inhabitants are much attached to the products that grow from the land in adverse conditions. Whatever they can grow is extremely valuable to them and handled with loving care. Not even that long ago baking and working with bread was a matter of life and death in some areas. One could not afford the baking to fail and therefore it was left to the real bakers to do the work. Baking was a fun and social event and yet taken quite seriously. In the early mornings, the women would bring the yeast dough left over from the day before to work it again with lukewarm water. In the meantime, kindling and wood was put in the oven, fired up and spread out so that the oven would get an even temperature. Once it was really

hot the oven was cleaned with iron bars and wet rags. The women in the village would slowly approach. Their dough would be put in wooden bowls and covered with wet towels so the dough could rise. While they were waiting, the women muttered secret phrases, made some interesting gestures and mumbled little prayers that brought together pagan habits, Christian rituals and the necessary superstition. Everyone who entered the space had to pray to Saint Martinus for help. Also the uncovering of the bowls was accompanied by aphorisms and three crosses were cut in the risen dough. Finally the bread went into the oven, together with smaller kinds of bread, braided wreaths and sometimes pita bread. The baked wreaths filled with ricotta were eaten warm at the spot.

Great variety

Italy was divided in many different Kingdoms, Republics and Duchies before Unification. Each region had its own culture that is seen today in different culinary customs. Over time bread baking became very experimental, which made for an enormous assortment of breads. Thanks to the baking industry Italian breads became well known all over Europe. Bread (pane) in Italy is made mostly with very refined flour, the 00 flour (doppio zero). If the flour is heavier it becomes whole grain bread.
In the south of Italy wheat flour is added to get firmer bread.
For digestive reasons, other flours like rye and corn flour are used, also to get a better texture, a typical flavour and a nicer colour.

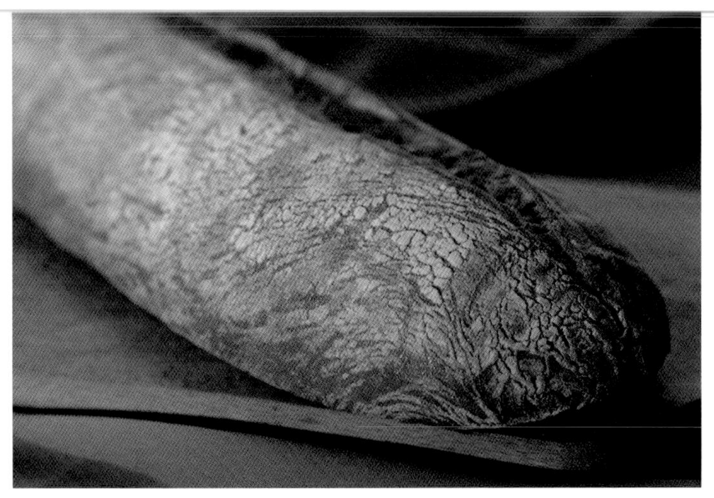

Large Ciabatta

Focaccia

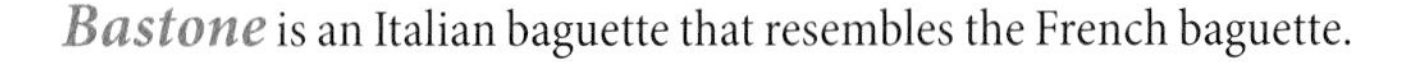

Bastone is an Italian baguette that resembles the French baguette.

Biova, Biovetta is bread from Piedmont, made with hard flour (dura) and consumed mostly in Northern Italy. This dough doesn't rise but is kneaded well to make it softer and to remove air. When baked this bread gets a crisp crust and is available in all imaginable shapes.

Biscotto is a bread that originally was baked twice to gain dryness for better preservation. To eat it one would add milk or water. It is a reminder of the medieval sea biscuits. Today biscotto looks more like a rusk. It is made with eggs, flour, sugar, honey, yeast and special add-ons like almonds or chocolate. Derived from the biscotti are *Taralli* (savoury) and *Amaretti* (sweet).

Bruschetta are slices of toasted bread with oil and garlic and eaten as a hors d'oeuvre. It is not seen as a special kind of bread but it is consumed everywhere. In Abruzzo and Lazio, one puts olive oil, tomato and basil on it. In Tuscany it is called *fettuna* or *panunto*, which means greased slice of bread. For this, one uses unsalted bread: pane sciocco.

Buccellato Lucchese is somewhere in the middle of bread and pastry and is a specialty of Lucca and Tuscany. In Sicily one adds eggs and sucade (candied peel); it is eaten as a dessert or dipped in milk for breakfast.

Calzone we know as stuffed pizza. In Italy anything that is stuffed in dough is called calzone. It is prepared with bread dough as well as pizza dough.

Carsenta Lunigianese is bread from Lunigiana that is baked on chestnut leaves especially to honour Good Friday.

Carta da Musica or *Pane Carasu* is bread that looks like old music sheets, hence the name. It is extremely thin and crispy bread that is made from 2/3 hard flour and 1/3 regular flour, yeast, water and a bit of salt. After kneading the dough has to rise for six hours then slapped on the counter and kneaded again after which it is rolled out to a layer of 2 mm thickness. These layers of dough are put on plates with linen towels in between and set aside for three hours with a heavy weight on top. This kind of bread is best if it is baked in a traditional wood burning oven. After baking, these layers of bread are cut in two slices, put on top of each other until they are totally cooled and then baked again one by one. The shepherds and farmers used this method to keep the bread good for at least one month. In Sardinia people eat it with ripe tomatoes and pecorino cheese or make it into lasagna.

Casatiello, Casatello is Easter bread from Napoli, baked traditionally with a group of people. There is always one left over for an unexpected guest.

Ciabatta is a familiar Italian bread, original from the Como region in Northern Italy and literally means "slipper". The basic principle started with the old Egyptians who discovered that dough would rise better if it was sour. The Roman legions took small portions of natural dough to their battlefields and called it biga di piccolo madre (little mother). They would add flour to this dough and the formula for soft bread was created. Remaining dough was mixed with olive oil to soften it again. Ciabbatta needs a lot of work to enhance the real flavour. Dough has to proof for at least 16-24 hours, which makes it shiny and elastic, typical for this kind of bread. Today, ciabatta is one of the most well known breads outside Italy. This bread is made with 0-flour, so not the most refined, and gets its special texture from the long proofing time. Putting a small bowl of water in the oven or using a combisteamer creates a soft crust.

Colomba literally means "pigeon" and got its name for the sweet bread that originated in Lombardia. This sweet cake-like Easter bread with candied lemon and orange zests has the shape of a pigeon and is eaten at Easter as a sign of peace.

Cornetto, Chifel looks like a French croissant and has the shape of a cone. The dough is made of 00-flour and is made the same way as puff pastry. A variety is dough made with olive oil or butter and has a crumbly texture.

Crostini di Pane started by working with remaining dough. This Tuscan toasted bread has achieved real status and is often used as small snacks with different toppings.

Donzelle are rolled out bread squares from Prato, deep-fried in olive oil.

Farinata is unleavened bread made from all kinds of flour. The best known is from Piedmont and Liguria made with chickpea flour. The bread is eaten whole with fresh ground pepper. In Palermo one adds fennel seeds and chopped parsley. The bread is cooled, sliced in squares and baked in olive oil. Another variety is Castagnaccio made with chestnut flour and rosemary.

Fiandole was originally made for foresters and miners from Monte Amiata. The dough is prepared with chestnut flour and rosemary.

Focaccia is a flat bread, made with ordinary bread dough and olive oil and salt. Before baking, the dough is sprayed with olive oil, pressed with fingers on the baking sheet and sprinkled with sea salt. This bread has its origin from Genoa and the name is derived from the Latin word "focas" (fireplace). The old Etruscans baked their bread on a hot stone on top of small coals on a glowing fire. Varieties are made with buckwheat (**smacafam**) from Trentino, onions and sausage. The Calabrian **Pita** is baked in a ring form and often filled with parmesan cheese or **fitascetta** from Lombardia with stewed red onion, salt or sugar. A Ligurian specialty is **pizzalandrea** or **pissadella**, closely related to the French onion tart pissaladière.

Olive Ciabatta

Bococcino

Grissini

Quadrato toscane pomodoro

Quadrato naranja

The best known is probably the ***focaccia al formaggio*** from Camoglia. This is a kind of strudel made with two very thin layers of dough, generously filled with straccino cheese and sprinkled with olive oil. Focaccio exists in many regions under different names: ***pinza*** in Veneto, ***pitta*** in Calabria, ***pizza*** in Naples, ***pissalandrea*** in Genoa, ***schiacciata*** in Lombardia, ***sardenaria*** in Liguria and ***stiacciata*** in Tuscany.

Frisella, fresella, frisedda or ***pan biscotto*** are the names for twice baked bread, that originated out of need to create a fully dried bread that could not get moldy. It was made mainly with hard flour and yeast. After it has baked, it is cut in slices and then baked to dry.

Filone are small buns with a crisp crust made with unsalted dough from Tuscany.

Galetta is a kind of sea biscuit that was mostly baked for the army and the marine.

Grissini are thin long cheese sticks thoroughly baked but should not get too brown. Because of their long baking time they are easily digested. Its origin started at the palace in Turin, but is now popular all over Italy. The soup sticks we buy today come from these cheese sticks but are a far cry from the original grissini and don't have much flavour.

Guastedde is a Sicilian bun baked with sesame seed, and well known for its variety of fillings. These are available at the market of Vucceria in Palermo. This little bun is cut in the middle and filled with slices of spleen, first boiled and then fried in lard, sprinkled with bacon bits and Peccorino cheese.

Maritozzo is a sweet bread that is similar to a brioche. It originated in Rome and strangely enough was only eaten during lent (religious fast for the Catholics). The dough has to proof a long time before the eggs, sugar, olive oil and salt are added. It is baked like little round balls.

The region of Puglia is known for its bread traditions, so much so that the ***pane di Altamura*** has received the IGP status (Indicazione Geografica Protetta) and is sold everywhere in Italy. Altamura bread is from the region Apulia and very nutritious bread for its population.
It used to be common to knead the dough at home and then bring it to a public oven for baking. To recognize each owner's bread, initials were carved in the dough before it went in the oven. To meet the high demand of the market, the baking of Altamura bread has intensified, but is still baked on the floor of a wood fired oven. This is to honour the tradition. Those ovens reach a temperature of 300° / 575°. Pane di Altamura is a

White bread

Brown bread

Tramezzone

Pan stivale

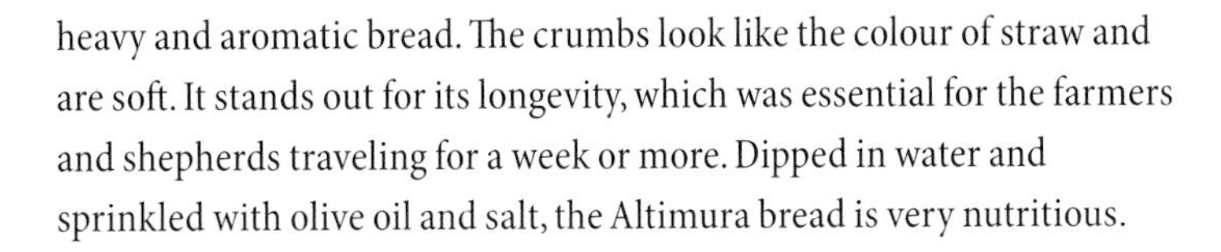

heavy and aromatic bread. The crumbs look like the colour of straw and are soft. It stands out for its longevity, which was essential for the farmers and shepherds traveling for a week or more. Dipped in water and sprinkled with olive oil and salt, the Altimura bread is very nutritious.

Pan di mei or ***pan meino*** is sweet soft bread from Lombardia, made with a mix of flour and cornmeal.

Pan di ramerini is a sweet Tuscan Easter bread with rosemary oil and sweet ingredients like raisins, sugar and butter.

Pan di San Guiseppe is a bread of different shapes that is offered on Saint Joseph Day to the Holy Family. It is often given to friends on the day that Salemi, high up a mountain near Trapani, Sicily, celebrates the legend of St. Joseph with a special meal. The legend claims that a poor fisherman and his wife lived in the village. The wife promised she would invite the whole village to an evening meal if her husband would return home safely. When the husband returned, his wife offered her guests the only thing she could afford: bread in the shape of foods that she would have liked to offer her guests.

Pandolce is a sweet bread from Genoa with rich ingredients like candied fruit, raisins, nuts, star anise and orange blossom water. It is made especially for Christmas and people start early as it takes a lot of preparation and proofing time.

Pandoro is gold bread from Verona and Venice that gets its colour from the many farm eggs used in the dough. It is a very light spongy Christmas bread that takes three days to make. Because of the time it takes it is hardly made at home anymore. The bread is in the form of a star and it is most delicious if it has a slice of butter on top and is browned under the grill.

Pane con grassetti is bread from Garfgnana with pieces of bacon in it. Can be baked as a baguette or little buns.

Pane a cassetta, pan carré is a square bread that got its name because it is baked in a square pan. Here we call it *casino*. Since the baking form has a lid on top, the dough cannot rise much and becomes a compact bread; it has a thin soft crust. It is mostly served as a *tartine* (a sandwich or canapé). It is also used cut and fried in olive oil for croutons.

Pane classico integrale is unsalted whole grain bread with a very crispy crust.

Pane con l'Uva is raisin bread from Milan, prepared with lots of butter, sugar, currents and raisins.

Pan di Granturco are small breads with a crunchy crust made from cornmeal.

Panettone is a rich fruit bread, filled with currants, raisins and finely chopped candied orange and lemon zest. This specialty originated in Milan and has a light texture and a tall round form. It is similar to the French brioche and is often sliced and eaten like a piece of cake. Christmas without panettone is unthinkable in Italy.

Passatelli is made with leftovers of bread. In Emilia-Romagna, the soft dough is made with breadcrumbs, one egg (whisked), Parmigiano-Reggiano Cheese, salt and pepper. The dough is pressed through a sieve above a pot of bouillon and cooked until it is done. Can be served with different sauces and cheese.

Piadina is unleavened bread from Emilia-Romagna that is very much like Turkish pita bread but has more flavour. There are as many recipes as there are bakers but it is always made with the same base of 0-flour, lard and salt. Can be baked in a cast iron pan on the stove.

Pan Pugliese is a large round bread from Puglia, measuring 40cm in diameter and 12-14 cm in height. Some hard flour is added and it has a thick hard crust.

Pan Aosta is prepared with rye flour only. The large round breads used to be baked four times a year in communal bakeries. Everyone carved their name in the bread to recognize it after it was baked, which gave this bread its character. While they were waiting the village people entertained themselves with village gossip. This bread could be kept almost indefinitely but got so hard that a special tool was developed to cut or slice it: the copapan. Today wheat flour is added which makes the bread lighter, but cannot be kept for long.

Puccia di pane is a small round bread with olives. After baking it is rolled in flour to symbolize the purity of the Virgin Mary.

Puddica is made with bread dough and mashed potatoes.

Parels are small buns from the Venosta valley. They are always baked in pairs to represent a married couple. If one had died, only one bun was baked. Traditionally flavoured with clover.

Tarali is made of flour, lard, olive oil, fennel seeds, fresh ground pepper and some salt. Baked to a crisp in the form of a wreath.

Tramezzino is the Italian name for sandwich which means "in the middle" that refers to the toppings between the slices of bread. The crust is removed from white bread, cut in triangles and traditionally topped with fish or meat mousse and arugula. Also with tuna, egg, ham and mozzarella. Often served with a cocktail pick and an olive.

Fillings and Toppings

Many breads are topped or filled with local ingredients and served as a small snack or antipasto to accompany a meal or a meal in itself. Tapas in Spain are the same as a panini, crostini or sandwich in Italy. All of these are a variation of bread and are eaten between meals. Depending on the imagination of the chef it can be as creative as possible. Some examples:

Tartine Salmone: small bun sometimes toasted, with salmon, butter and lemon juice.

Prosciutto cotto, formaggio e pomodori: bread filled with ham, cheese or ripe tomatoes.

Fiore di Zucca: zucchini flower stuffed with mozzarella and anchovies.

Parmigiana di melanzane, a royal dish from Southern Italy: deep fried eggplants baked with cheese and tomatoes.

Primavera; white bread cut in small diagonals topped with a bouquet of fresh greens.

Coffee?

In this chapter we will demonstrate some spectacular techniques with coffee. We usually choose instant coffee because it's easy to work with; you don't need much and it can easily be integrated in the recipes. These techniques don't require years of experience as a pâtissier and the result won't be any less. These techniques can be done mise en place and don't ask for a lot of work.

Caviar and coffee

Ingredients: **20 g basil seeds, 240 g water, 30 g sugar-water 1:1, 20 g instant coffee**

Mix seeds with water and let stand for 30 minutes. The seeds will swell up with water and look like real caviar. Add the sugar water and dissolve the coffee in it. Keep "caviar" in the fridge until serving time. Serve in a small glass with a little caviar spoon. If you serve this with small vanilla pancakes instead of blinis, and whipped cream instead of sour cream, you have flirted with real caviar!

Ultra light coffee cookies

The texture of these cookies is very light and airy. These cookies can be part of a coffee dessert or be filled.

Ingredients: **125 g water, 125 g pasteurized egg white, 7.5 g egg white powder, 25 g sugar, 5 g instant coffee.**

Mix all ingredients together in a bowl and stir. Beat 5 minutes and let rest for 2 minutes. Beat another 10 minutes until stiff peaks are formed, then spread one layer of one centimetre thick on silicon paper. Let dry in the oven for two hours at 100°C / 210°F. Cut the way you want it and keep in a tightly closed container with silica grains.

Ganache with coffee and chocolate

For filling of a bonbon or as part of a dessert or amuse.

Ingredients: **170 g unsweetened whipping cream, 20 g water, 12 g instant coffee, 180 g dark chocolate couverture.**

Heat whipping cream, water and coffee to 90°C / 195°F and make sure the coffee is totally dissolved. Add the couverture, let rest and then stir well. Cover with foil to avoid skin forming on the surface and cool.

Coffee-white chocolate sauce

Ingredients: **150 g milk (2% fat), 20 g glucose, 2 tbs instant coffee, 300 g white couverture, 500 g unsweetened whipping cream.**

Melt chocolate au bain-marie to 50°C / 120°F. Bring milk and glucose to a boil and mix with instant coffee. Add to the chocolate, stir well and blend with the non-whipped whipping cream. Cool until ready to use.

Paper thin coffee cookies

These ultra thin tuilles can be used as a delicate garnish with a coffee dessert. They can also be served as sweet chips with toffee sauce of coffee and Baileys.

Ingredients: **100 sugar, 75 g water, 10 g instant coffee, 125 g icing sugar, 125 g flour, 80 g pasteurized egg white.**

Bring water and sugar to a boil and cook for a few minutes. Let cool to 70°C / 160°F and dissolve the instant coffee in it. Let cool to room temperature and combine with sieved flour and icing sugar. Mix this with egg whites. Spread batter on a silpat and bake for 5 minutes in a pre-heated oven at 170°C / 340°F. Shape cookies while they are still warm. Place in a tight container with silica grains.

Toffee of coffee and Baileys

Ingredients: **150 sugar, 50 g water, 50 g espresso coffee, 150 g unsweetened whipping cream, 25 g Baileys.**

Mix water and sugar and caramelize. Add whipping cream and espresso, cook loosely, add Baileys and cool.

Pousse café granité

Ingredients: **300 ml espresso coffee, 80 g sugar water 1:1, coffee liqueur.**

Mix espresso with the liqueur and sugar water and put in the freezer. Stir regularly with a fork to create a fine granité.

Zeeland

a sweet portrait

Zeeland is a Dutch province that consists mainly of islands. Over the centuries, their constant fight against water has hardened the people from Zeeland. With the exception of the dunes, almost the entire province lies below sea level. Zeelanders are known for their character and aren't afraid to go into battle. The people from Zeeland have always been involved in building bridges and dikes in an effort to conquer their water problems. After a catastrophic flood in 1953 that destroyed the province overnight, they developed a delta plan built with the largest floodgates in the world. It is now a safe province where living has become very enjoyable. Zeeland is known for famous people from sea heroes to innovators. One of the most famous people from Zeeland was America's President Franklin Delano Roosevelt.

Super classic to ultra modern

Zeeland is not just the largest producer of mussels and oysters, it is also a province where you will find great classic pastry products, like the Zeeuwse Bolus, Zeeuwse speculaas and the Zeeuwse boterbabbelaar. The Dutch province is also very modern with top restaurants that have one, two and three Michelin stars. We will show you the classic and modern, both faces, in this article.

Zeeuwse speculaas

At first, Zeeuwse speculaas reminds you of a gingerbread cookie that is quite popular in Holland during the celebration of Sinterklaas around December 6. However, the taste is different and has little in common with the taste we have come to expect.

We visit Peter Arrebout, a real cookie baker and our teacher for this part of the article. "Zeeuwse speculaas can be compared with shortbread. However, there are differences like the spices in the dough. For flavour, mace, almond slices and a bit of lemon juice are added." Peter has just finished kneading the dough. We follow him. Because the dough has to be made the day before, it has to go in the cooler and we proceed with another dough that was made yesterday. It has to harden a bit first so it can easily be taken through the speculaas machine. The machine is simple but very effective. A large rubber roll with patterns pushes the cookies out of the dough. The cookies are placed on long narrow plates and are ready for the next step. The baking is done in a rotating oven at 145°C/295°F for 15 minutes. Immediately after baking sugar is sprinkled on the dough; since it is still soft it will absorb the sugar.
The result is a brittle and crispy cookie, and guaranteed to make you ask for more.

Ingredients: **100 g butter, 800 g icing sugar, 1300 g flour, 2 g mace, 40 g ground nutmeg, 8 g baking powder, 6 g ammonium bi-carbonate, 5 g salt, 35 g lemon juice, 120 g sliced almonds.**

Mix ingredients together and knead into a smooth dough. Divide in parts and let rest overnight. The next day, put dough through a special speculaas machine and bake cookies at 145°C/295°F for 15 minutes. You can also use your own speculaas molds. Sprinkle speculaas cookies with sugar after they are baked.

The Bolus

We visit Bliek Meesterbakkers in Middelburg. In 1930 he started a small bakery in the village of Veere. Peter Bliek is a third generation baker but he doesn't call himself a real baker because he started his career in banking. To keep it in the family he took over the business from his father. He learned by trial and error, as he didn't like going to school. "At school I was watching the teacher doing all kinds of things with his hands. I always wondered if there were no machines able to do what he did. I realized how important the basics are, but I think you have to think ahead." This is where Peter got his practice; the small bakery grew and grew.

The bolus has a lot of history; each version of the history doesn't necessarily make sense with the others. The most believable story has the bolus coming with the Portuguese Jews, also called Safardiem, who established themselves in Zeeland. The Portuguese word bolus means cookie. Originally the bolus was made with pieces of white bread dough. There is evidence that boluses were baked in Zeeland around 1680, but the eating habits have changed since. The bolus used to be a treat every Saturday morning, when it was lathered with creamy butter; now it is eaten every day.

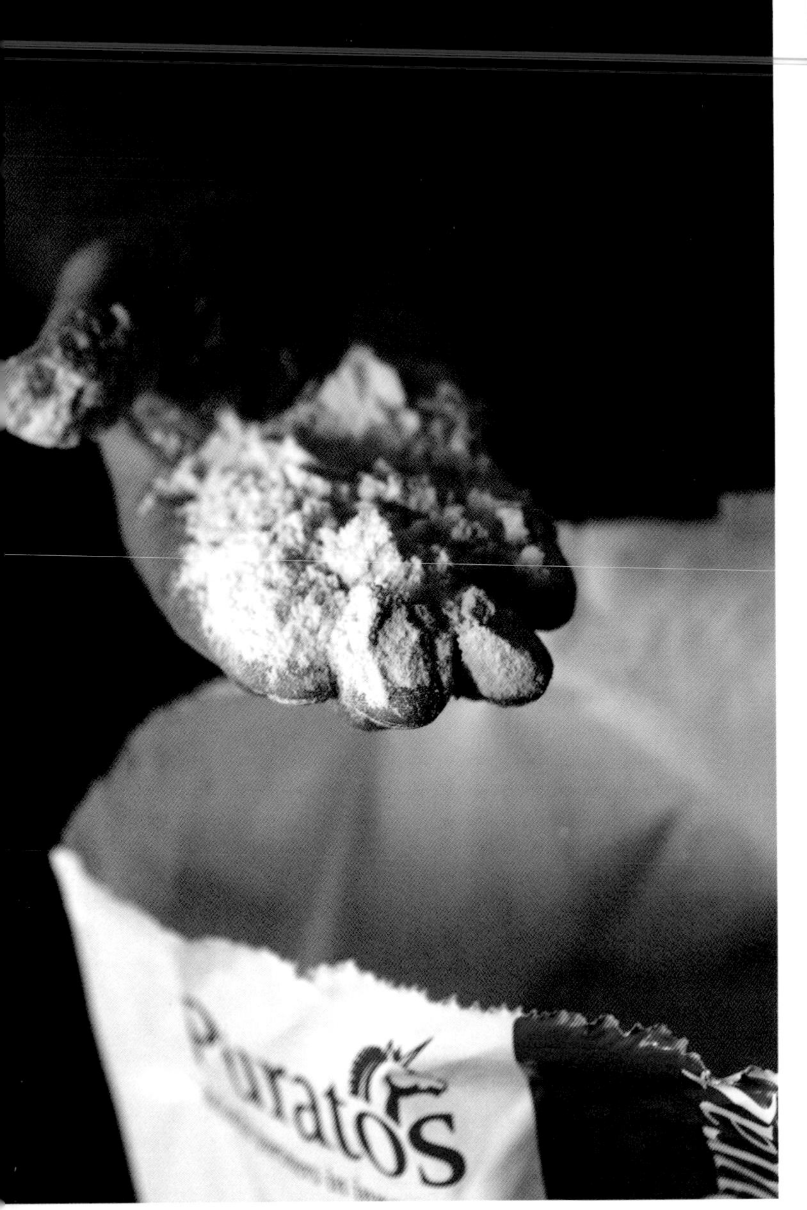

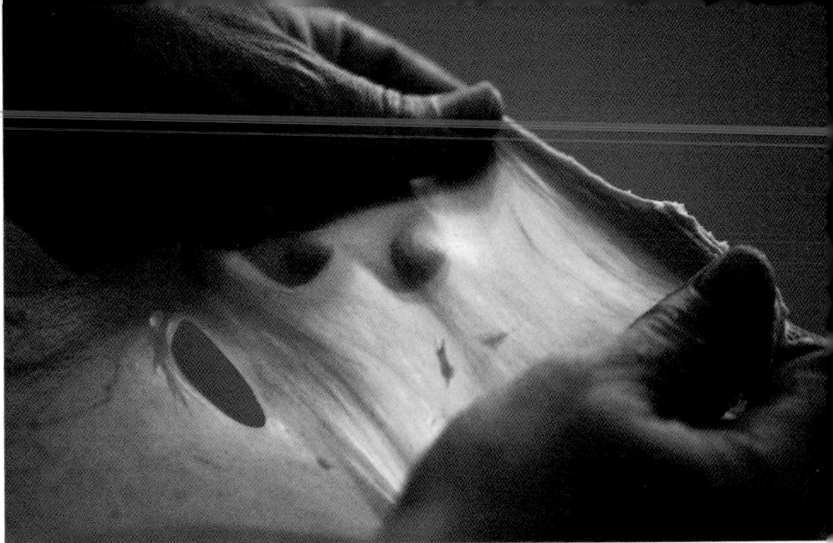

The Practice

At Bliek's bakery 30,000 boluses are made every day! Commercially produced? No, they are all done by hand. We took a lesson from Patrick who at one time became the champion in making the best bolus. It starts with a basic bread dough made with unsalted butter. White flour is used with a high content of protein, which enhances the gluten. The dry ingredients like milk powder and other enzymes are delivered to Bliek; they export a lot and want the keep the bolus the same quality at all times. They always use fresh yeast which, according to Patrick, is much more active than dry yeast. The kneading of exactly 12 minutes is very important. It starts with 2 minutes and then 4 minutes at a higher speed. After this the butter is added and the kneading repeated. Patrick: "Once the butter is added the dough becomes smooth. Ideal dough should be a bit poky and almost overworked." Almost overworked? "You should knead as much as possible to get the best gluten. However, if you go too far the gluten content diminishes. It is a fine line."

The dough can then be divided and rolled out. An ideal bolus weighs about 80 grams. They have now developed an ingenious machine, because rolling 30,000 rolls by hand is almost insane. Patrick showed us the authentic way. "The piece of dough is formed into a small ball and put in a mix of dark brown sugar and cinnamon; then rolled into a string of 30cm in length. Traditionally it should rest a few minutes, before it is rolled into shape." Three people do this all by hand. Although it seems simple, it is not easy. The string is rolled around a finger with the ends fastened in the centre (similar to a donut). Thirty are placed on a baking sheet and put in a proofing case. "This takes about 90 minutes. A proofing case has a humidity level of 50%, whereas normally it would be 85%. Why? Because otherwise it would dissolve the sugar and we like to keep the sugar crystals."

7 Minutes and 5 Seconds

Now it is time for the most important part: the baking. "The oven can make or break this. We have to find the ideal balance between temperature and time. The bolus has to be soft and smooth but should not taste like dough and should have a nice texture. Baked too long it will be hard and dry." We see a number of thermal oil ovens, somewhat like a hot water based CV boiler. Oil is heated and the temperature regulated by adding cold oil. The boluses are baked at 225°C/440°F in 7 minutes and 5 seconds. Yes, those 5 seconds will do the trick. Since he has been a bolus baking champion we don't want to argue with him. The colours play an important part and tell you where they are made. On one of the islands in Zeeland, Schouwen-Duivenland, you will find the darkest boluses, whereas you will find the lightest variety in Zeeuws-Vlaanderen, another island. After baking, the baking sheets are immediately turned upside down, so that the flat part of the bolus becomes the top part.
This is to get the caramelized sugar on top; otherwise it would become hard and difficult to remove from the sheet. In the past children would eat the caramelized pieces that were stuck on the baking sheet. After the boluses have cooled off they are ready for transport. Boluses are known for being sticky, soft and sweet. You always need a napkin!

The "Zeeuwse" Bolus

For 20 boluses: dark soft brown sugar, cinnamon to taste
The dough: 1000 g flour, 100 g milk powder, 30 g crystal sugar, 50 g egg, 20 g salt, 100 g fresh yeast, 530 g water, 50 g unsalted butter.

Mix all ingredients except the butter. Mix for 2 minutes at normal speed and then 4 minutes on high speed. Add the butter and mix again. Divide the dough in small balls of about 80 g each and let rest. Roll strings of 30 cm long in brown sugar and cinnamon and shape into a bolus.
Bake in the oven at 225°C/440°F for exactly 7 minutes and 5 seconds. The temperature can differ depending in which part of Zeeland you are. After baking immediately turn baking sheet upside down.

Boterbabbelaar

The real one

The province of Zeeland in the Netherlands has lots of specialties, one of which is a hard candy with a creamy taste. There is only one address left where they make this authentic candy and that is at Bas Christiaansen's bakery.

The sugar bakery Diesch is in Koudekerke and in this case you don't need a GPS, because when Bas is making his boterbabbelaars, the whole street smells like sweet caramel. This candy has been made for around 150 years; nobody knows who invented it, but some history was available from Bas' aunt, Mrs. De Witte. This lady has had a candy shop at the market in Middelburg for almost fifty years. "Boterbabbelaars have been around as long as I can remember. Years ago every city in Zeeland had a boterbabbelaar maker. The tradition started on the farms where the farm wives cooked the candies each Saturday as a treat with their coffee." Slowly more and more sugar bakers left Zeeland, but in 1892 the Swiss sugar baker Jan Diesch established himself at Middelburg, Zeeland. His shop got the name In den Zoeten Inval (meaning "a sweet welcome"), a name that was often used for candy shops. The logo represents a young boy jumping over a pot of honey. Diesch specialized in the boterbabbelaar. In 1925 his son took over the business but died quite young and had no children. Then Bas' father, Johannes Pieter Christiaansen took over the business and the recipe. In the Second World War the shop was

destroyed; fortunately the original logo was kept intact. Unfortunately, the gold medals that were awarded for the candy were lost. The candy was always made by hand. They used to be sold in pointed bags or bottles, but in 1925 cans became the norm for packaging. The Diesch cans have become a collectors' item that are worth a lot of money.

From sugar to salt

The workshop of Bas is still old fashioned. A small historic stove, an electric-driven roller, a pump and some small tools are the most important items. The recipe is simple, the preparation is everything. Bas: "This candy carries a lot of details, everything has to match or you won't have the desired result." The process starts with water and sugar. We understand that the recipe is highly secret, but Bas is willing to reveal a bit. "About 2/3 sugar is put in a kettle with a bit of water." The kettle has a 40 litre content with a hollow bottom so the flame can heat all around. Water and sugar are heated. A little bit of brown sugar is added, about 1/50 of the regular crystal sugar. "The real boterbabbelaar is made with 100% brown icing sugar." About 1/3 glucose is added that has been preheated and runny. The syrup is cooked to 114°R so 142°C/287°F. This is the temperature needed to get the so-called hard effect that happens with the sugar. An extension is placed on the copper kettle to prevent overflowing of the boiling sugar. Once the sugar has reached its temperature a lid containing a thermometer is put on top. During the whole process Bas keeps his kettles clean with a wet brush, to prevent graining. "Some people add vinegar to their recipe, also to prevent graining. I don't like it and believe in perfect cleaning, it works just as well." Once the syrup has reached the right temperature, the kettle is put in a special holder.

Today Bas works with his son Joost, because you never make boterbabbelaars on your own. Once the heavy kettle has been put in place and the syrup has cooled off, the butter is added, which is about 3% of the total mass. Needless to say that only unsalted butter is used. Then 1.5% salt is added for an extra touch. The whole mixture is stirred with a stick made of ash wood. This has a different acidity than the stirring stick, made of willow, used in the cooking process. You might think: do you taste this? But if Bas would use the same stick after the cooking process, chances are that crystals will form. This is one of the little touches that make boterbabbelaars so special.

Under pressure

Because the mixture has a lot of air, a pump is attached. This extracts air from the kettle and the mixture will be cooked under lower pressure. This is necessary to remove as much water as possible, because the moisture in the mass will attract even more moisture. The babbelaar mix is very hygroscopic. The suction is very heavy, we read almost 1 bar. It is a good thing that the kettle is well secured because the pressure makes the kettle almost dance. The cooking under pressure takes about 20 minutes. In the meantime another kettle is produced and the process continues. On a full day about twelve kettles of forty litres are processed. Knowing that one botterbabbelaar weighs only 2.5 grams, you can quickly figure out that 192,000 babbelaars are made each day. Bas says: "I have never counted them."
Back to the syrup. When it has reached its right consistency, it is poured on a stainless steel table. With help of son Joost the pot is totally emptied. "The table is so greasy, it will never rust. The sugar won't stick to it either. We only clean it with a dry brush. Soap would ruin the table instantly."

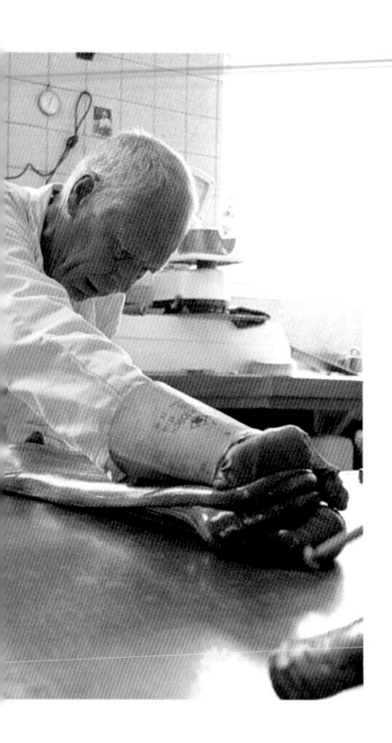

On the table, the syrup is just under 100°C/210°F. The syrup is collected with iron scrapers and divided in several parts so the mass stays warm. Now the glazing process can begin. The mixture is pulled to achieve the best structure and hardness. "My father always told me that I was working with gold. That wasn't a lie, it's just like gold and it's just as pure." Should glazing take too long, it can become grainy; you need skill to do this. The smell is very inviting. Suddenly the door opens and we see two school children. Bas knows what that means: "Do you guys want a boterbabbelaar? That's why the children are here." Bas pulls a piece of the mass. He enjoys their interlude, knowing that this has gone on for centuries and that these visits will be a memory forever. A kind "thank you" and they are off on their bikes. The babbelaar mix goes through a moulding machine with the initials of the first owner J.D. imprinted on it. On the other side of the machine de Zeeuwse boterbabbelaars appear. With an old vacuum cleaner that still has a blower attached to it, the strips are cooled and once they are 1½ metres long, Joost releases them and let the candies harden on a granite table. The cooled candies are loosened and a sieve is used to remove small pieces or half candies. These are not thrown out, but mixed with the new syrup that has just been poured. Recycling is important nowadays. The candies are transported in barrels and later packaged in cans. Bas has several buildings now where production, storage and delivery take place. He would prefer to have everything under one roof and make a museum of the production house. We feel that Diesch Boterbabbelaar deserves to get an official cultural heritage award. We should honour our real tradesmen.

In this province we meet two real craftsmen who belong to the top echelons: Edwin Vinke and Jannis Brevet. For this edition of Pastry in Europe, both gave us their vision on the pâtisserie of Zeeland.

De Kromme Watergang
Edwin Vinke

About fifteen years ago Edwin started building his Kromme Watergang in a very small hamlet close to the coast. Previously a kindergarten, Edwin transformed it slowly to a large ultra modern store, where ambiance and informality was top priority. This store would fit very well in London or New York. One can describe the kitchen as very subtle and innovative, where the beauty of the ocean plays a crucial role. This even shows in his desserts, like the little posts in the chocolate dessert that are symbolic to the breakwaters of the ocean.

Passion fruits

Combination of passion fruit, white chocolate and speculaas from Zeeland.

For 4 people: finely ground speculaas, freeze dried pieces of passion fruit, puffed rice, yellow calendula.
For the Turkish fruit: 500 g passion fruit coulis, 15 g pectin, 50 g icing sugar, 600 g crystal sugar, 4 g cream of tartar, 10 leaves of gelatin, extra crystal sugar, gold powder.
For the bavarois of white chocolate and passion fruit: 100 ml cream, 200 ml milk, 150 g white chocolate, 1 teaspoon speculaas spices, 2 + 1 leaves of gelatin, 100 ml passion fruit pulp.
For the small rolls of advocaat liqueur and passion fruit: 100 ml passion fruit coulis, 3 + 1 leaves of gelatin, 150 g advocaat, 50 g milk, 100 ml cream.
For the speculaas tuile: 125 g icing sugar, 45 g soft butter, 50 g flour, 10 g speculaas spices, 50 ml water.
For the ganache: 100 g white chocolate, 100 ml cream.

For the Turkish fruit, soak gelatin in cold water and in the meantime bring coulis and crystal sugar to a boil. Mix the pectin, crystal sugar and cream of tartar together, add to the hot mixture, stir well and bring again to a boil. Cook for 8 minutes, dissolve the soaked gelatin in it and pour in the desired forms. After it has hardened, remove from the forms and roll through a mixture of crystal sugar coloured with gold powder.
For the bavarois, heat part of the passion fruit pulp, dissolve 1 leaf of soaked gelatin in it and add the rest of the pulp. Pour in forms and let set. Heat milk and cream, add the speculaas spices and dissolve the chocolate and rest of the soaked gelatin in it. Cool slightly; pour on the thickened passion fruit and let set. For the small rolls, heat the passion fruit coulis and dissolve 1 leaf of gelatin in it. Pour a bit of this jelly in cylinders and let set. Mix milk, cream, and advocaat liqueur, heat slightly and add the rest of the soaked gelatin. Combine with the rest of the mixture and put

a second layer in the cylinders. Then add a thin layer of passion fruit and repeat the layers. For the tuile, mix all ingredients and set aside in the cooler for 30 minutes. Using a shablon (template) spread small triangles on a baking sheet and bake in the oven at 180°C/355°F for 5 minutes. For the ganache, heat the cream, pour over the chocolate and stir to a smooth consistency. Place bavarois with a small roll, the tuile and the Turkish fruit on a plate. Mix the freeze dried passion fruit, speculaas, and puffed rice together and serve with calendula. Finish dessert with drops of ganache.

Chocolate dessert and Zeeland's bolus

For 4 people: freshly picked small tips of dill.
For the caramel crumble: 150 g Zeeland's syrup, 50 g raw brown sugar, 100 ml water.
For the chocolate foam: 100 ml milk, 2 Tbs cocoa powder, 1 tsp lecithin
For the chocolate tuiles: 125 g icing sugar, 45 g soft butter, 35 g flour, 15 g cocoa powder, 50 ml cold coffee.
For the bolus parfait: 200 g meringue powder, 100 g water, 1 tsp cinnamon powder, 150 g brown icing sugar, 200 ml cream, 75 g salted butter, 5 g fleur de sel.
For the chocolate parfait: 150 g dark chocolate, piece of butter, 250 g whipped cream, 2 egg whites, 120 g sugar, 1 Tbs glucose syrup, 1 small cup of ristretto (espresso coffee).

For the crumble, bring all ingredients to a boil and caramelize at 145°C/295°F. Pour on parchment paper and let harden. Grind to a powder in a Thermomix. For the foam, heat milk with cocoa powder until completely dissolved. Take off the heat and cool to 40°C/104°F. Add the lecithin and create foam with the hand held blender.
For the tuile, mix all ingredients into a batter, rest in the cooler for 30 minutes and using a shablon spread small triangles on a baking sheet. Bake triangles in the oven at 180°C/355°F for 5 minutes. For the bolus parfait, caramelize the sugar, deglaze with cream and add the cinnamon powder, butter and salt. Set aside to cool. Whip meringue powder and water for about 10 minutes and blend carefully with the caramel until smooth. Fill 8 cylinders and freeze. As soon as they are frozen, take them out of the forms and finish by piping a mixture of 50% dark chocolate and 50% cocoa butter on top. For the chocolate parfait, melt chocolate au bain-marie with a piece of butter. Add the ristretto and mix with part of the whipped cream. In the meantime heat the sugar with glucose syrup and a drop of water to 120°C/250°F. Beat egg whites till stiff. Add the glucose syrup drop by drop to the egg whites and beat 5 minutes until cold. With a spatula blend chocolate mixture with egg white foam, fill the cylinders and freeze. Take from their forms and pipe with a mixture of 50% dark chocolate and 50% cocoa butter. Set cylinders in different heights on a plate and put tuiles in between. Sprinkle crumble on the side and finish with tips of dill and chocolate foam.

Inter Scaldes

Jannis Brevet

Inter Scaldes is synonymous for enjoying luxury and gastronomy at the highest level.
The large villa with thatched roof contains the restaurant and next to it is the hotel with luxurious suites. Jannis has been one of the top chefs in Holland for many years. His kitchen is refined, elegant and perfect and is known for its use of spices. Naturally he likes to be inspired by the abundance of products and special offers of Zeeland, where the ocean is king.

Tablette de chocolat fumé

For the chocolate biscuit: 55 g dark chocolate, 30 g butter, 50 g egg white, 30 g sugar, 8 g flour.
For the ganache: 25 g egg yolk, 65 ml milk, 65 ml cream, 120 g dark chocolate.
For the jelly of banana and passion fruit: 75 ml passion fruit coulis, 95 g sugar, 50 ml water, 200 g banana, 1.2 g agar-agar.
For the glaçage: 50 g dark chocolate, 70 ml cream, 70 ml water, 60 g sugar, 25 g cocoa powder.
For the praline parfait: 24 ml milk, 24 ml cream, 10 g egg yolk, 4 g sugar, 6 g glucose syrup, 30 g praline pasta, 20 ml passion fruit coulis, 50 ml cream, 400 g chocolate, 80 g cocoa butter.
For the chocolate mousse: 25 ml milk, 70 g dark chocolate, 50 ml lightly whipped cream.
For the mascarpone crème: 30 ml cream, 10 g egg yolk, 6 g sugar, 30 g mascarpone, 5 threads of saffron.

For the biscuit melt chocolate and butter au bain-marie. Beat egg whites and sugar and carefully combine with chocolate mixture. Add the sifted flour and spread on parchment paper. Bake in the oven at 170°C/340°F for 10 minutes. For the ganache, heat and stir egg yolk, milk and cream and heat to 85°C/185°F. Dissolve chocolate in it and process to a smooth batter. Put in cooler for 2 hours and roll out between two sheets of wax paper of 16 x 8 cm. For the jelly, heat coulis with sugar until sugar is totally dissolved. Add pieces of banana; puree and pour through a fine mesh sieve. Add agar-agar. Cook for a few minutes and pour on a shallow plate. For the glaçage, smoke chocolate for 1 ½ hours in a lukewarm smoker. Heat part of the cream, dissolve the chocolate in it and set aside. Heat the rest of the ingredients until sugar is dissolved. Take off the heat and mix with the chocolate. Slice biscuit in a rectangle of 16 x 8 cm, put ganache and jelly on top and cut in slices of 8 x 4 cm. Frost with the glaçage and set aside. For the parfait, heat milk, cream, egg yolk, sugar and glucose to 85°C/185°F and cool. Take a spatula and mix it with praline pasta and the coulis and lastly the lightly whipped cream. Pour on a flat surface of 1 cm high and freeze. Melt chocolate and cocoa butter, pour in chocolate gun and pipe for a velvety appearance. For the chocolate mousse bring milk to a boil, dissolve the chocolate and cool. Blend with the lightly whipped cream and pipe on the praline parfait. For the crème, heat the cream, egg yolk and sugar to 82°C/180°F, cool to 45°C/113°F, mix with the mascarpone and add the saffron. Arrange all pieces on a plate and garnish with a dried vanilla bean.

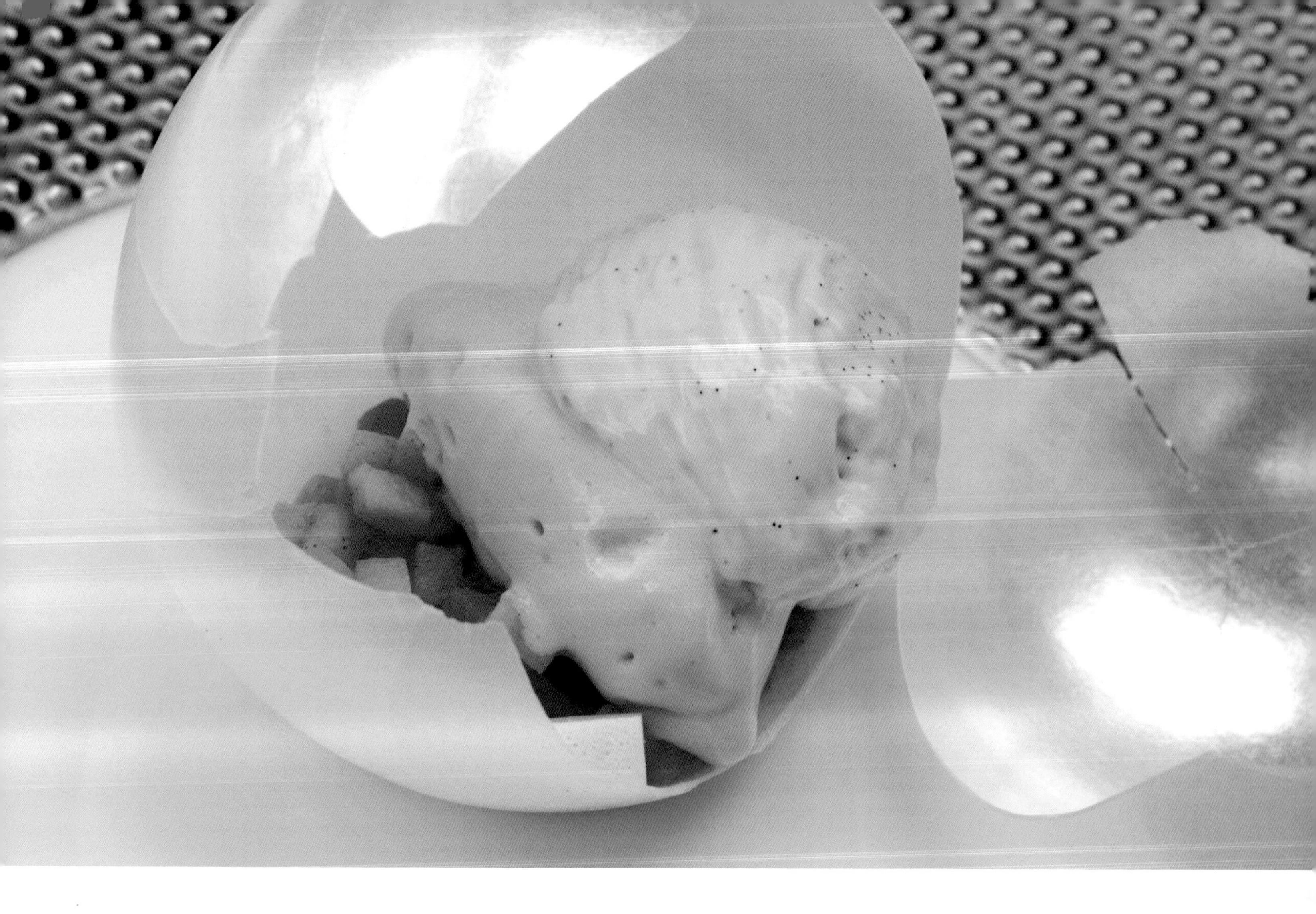

Bal Masqué

For the apple and pineapple compôte: 30 g apple, 30 g pineapples, 10 g butter, 1 Tbs honey, dash of cinnamon powder, 1 tsp vanilla butter.
For the jelly of tonka bean and milk: 100 ml milk, 1 tonka bean, 1.3 g agar-agar, 2 Tbs honey.
For the cardamom ice cream: 140 ml milk, 70 ml cream, a few drops of coffee cream, 32 g coffee beans, 5 cardamom beans, 40 g egg yolks, 30 g egg, 50 g sugar.
For the vanilla mousse: 1 vanilla bean, 15 ml sugar water (28°B), 100 ml double cream, 4 egg yolks, 4.5 leaves of gelatin, 100 g mascarpone.
For the sugar ball: 350 ml water, 1 kg sugar, 200 g clear syrup, 1 tsp lemon juice.

Cut apple and pineapple as brunoise, sauté in butter and flavour with honey, cinnamon powder and vanilla butter. For the jelly, heat the milk, add the tonka bean and simmer for at least 3 hours. Remove bean, add the agar-agar and honey and cook thoroughly for a few minutes. Pour in a shallow dish, let set and cut in squares. For the ice cream, heat milk, cream and coffee cream to 80°C/175°F, add coffee beans and roasted cardamom. Slowly simmer for 25 minutes and pour through a sieve. Mix egg yolk, egg and sugar, add to the cream mixture and heat to 78°C/172°F. Cool completely and spin in ice cream maker. For the mousse, slowly simmer sliced vanilla bean in sugar water. Heat cream, add the sugar water and then add the egg yolks. Stir and heat to 80°C/175°F and add the soaked gelatin. Mix with mascarpone and put in cooler. For the sugar ball, bring water and sugar to a boil and keep stirring; remove any residues with a spoon and clean sides with a small brush. Add the syrup and cook to 115°C/240°F, add lemon juice. Pour mass on a marble slab and fold with a stainless steel spatula. Cut a small ball; press it on an air pump and pump in air to desired size. Use your hands to mould it to a smooth ball. With heated scissors or heated knife cut ball away from pump and carefully expand the opening. Place the different items close together on a plate and cover those with the sugar ball. This ball is served at the dining table and broken in half with the tap of a knife.

Confitures

The love of beautiful fruits

When we are traveling the countryside of France, we notice a man climbing rocks to pick berries. We are interested so stop to have a chat with him and are fascinated by his story.

For Dja Zidoun it is quite normal to risk his life to find wild berries. He was born in Algeria but grew up in the French region of Lozère. There was no money at home so he was forced to go out to the forests hunting food for his family. This unfortunate necessity led him to join Articulture, a group of gardeners who cultivate forgotten vegetables and fruits. Dja is totally specialized in fruit. For him the year starts in the spring with different strawberries called mara des bois, garriguette and pajrao. Summer brings the raspberries, wild strawberries and blackberries. In September it is the egelantier (rose berry). His greatest love is searching for wild fruits like ash berries, hawthorn berries, medlars, and little wild grapes, all rare fruits. In our busy cities and even in the countryside we can only dream about these kinds of fruit. It is different in the heart of France. Dja would have a hard time selling these fruits, but there is one chef in the area who loves to work with these products. His name is Martial Paula of Restaurant L'Adonis in Florac, so we visit him.

An authentic product

Martial is also a child of this area. However, he didn't want to stay in the region all his life so traveled to broaden his horizons. Paris and London impressed him. He found a new love and returned with her to his place of birth in France. Since 1967, his parents ran a restaurant in Florac, a little village on the deep ravines of the river Tarn. Here it is quite common that children take over the business from their parents. This was no hardship for Martial, he loved it. He started off with the traditional cooking of his parents but slowly changed to a more haute

cuisine. Martial describes his region: "The diversity of products is enormous as well as the quality. The area is poor but fortunately more and more people enjoy gastronomy." For this reportage, Martial doesn't overwhelm us with rich and luxurious products but wants to share the secrets of his confitures. His confitures are now so well known that you can find them in local shops. Although health regulations have been tightened and require that all products have to be pasteurized or sterilized, he has his own principles and makes his products the way he thinks they should be made. He doesn't add any colour, aroma or flavour enhancers, or even pectin. "Sometimes the confitures are a little thinner than normal, but that is the unpredictability of nature, I don't want to change that."

The Process

His process is simple as long as you pay attention to details. First of all and most logical is to use only the best quality products, but that doesn't mean that the fruit has to look perfect. Martial only works with copper pots. Copper has a chemical reaction to fruit, sugar and the acids. The recipe is always one part fruit and one part sugar. All fruits have to be washed except raspberries and black berries, as they will hold too much water. The fruit is heated on a slow burner with a little bit of sugar. Too much sugar initially would create a caramelized taste rather than a real fruit taste. Half of the sugar is slowly added, stirring constantly to a temperature of 93°C / 200°F, or 60-63° Brix. Martial always uses a thermometer. When the confiture is partly done, the rest of the sugar is added and mixed with a hand held blender to avoid a layer of foam. The mixture is not boiled so as to keep the fresh colour and avoid extra foam in the jam. After the temperature of 93°C / 200°F has been reached, the jam is mixed again. The canning jars should be warm to avoid a drop in temperature. The jars are filled to the brim, closed and put upside down to get rid of any air. Martial uses the same recipes and the same temperature for all his confitures, except for peaches, pears and strawberries when he adds the juice of 3 lemons to a 9 kilogram mix to disturb the pectin a bit. Orange marmalade is a different game. The oranges are first put in hot water to remove the wax. Then they are sliced very thinly in a slicing machine and prepared the same as the confitures. As you can see, life doesn't have to be difficult as long as you use good quality.

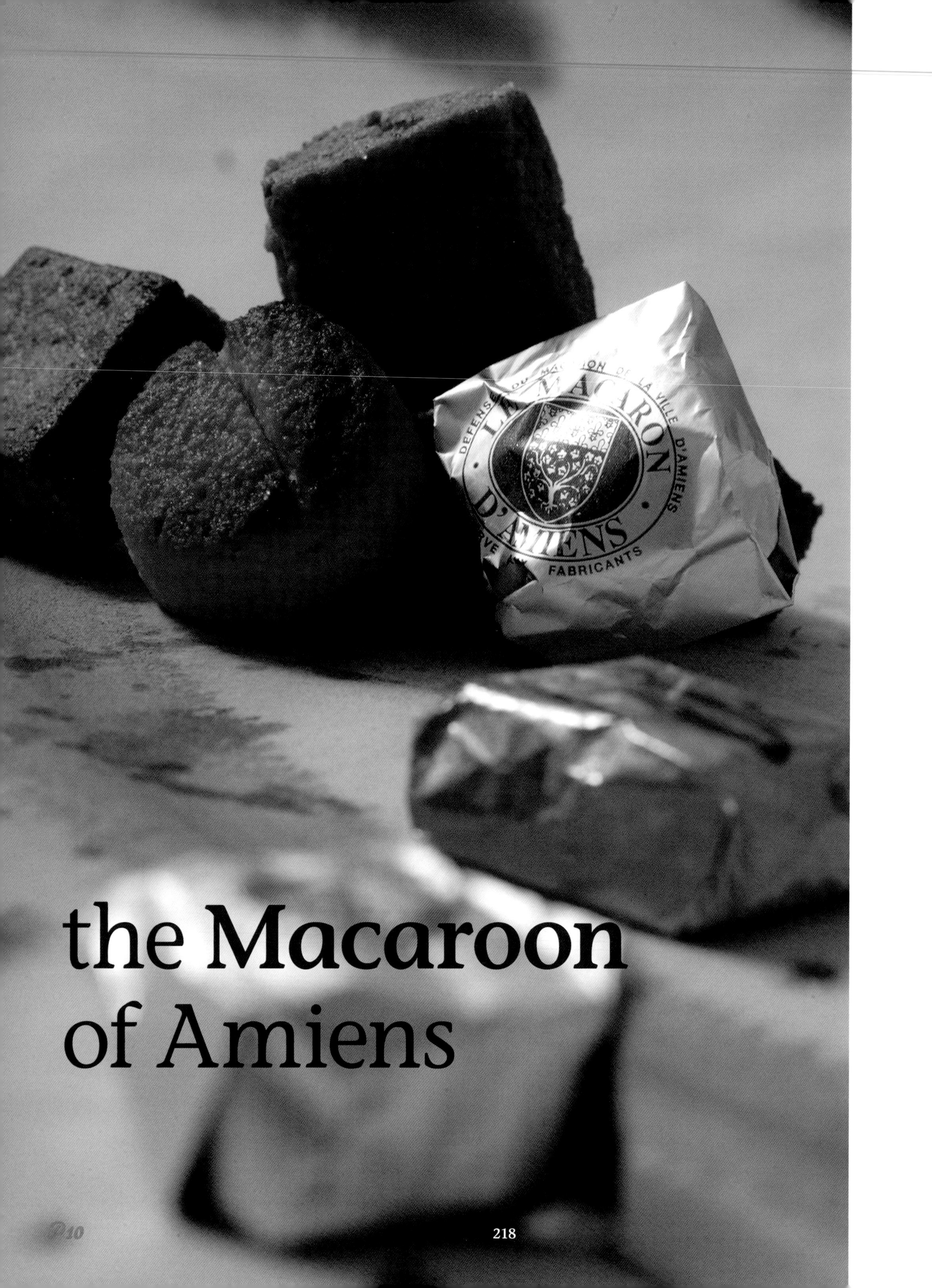

the **Macaroon** of Amiens

When you mention macaroons in France you know immediately what it means to be patriotic. Everyone has their own version and wants to prove that his or her macaroons belong to the history of their region. And yet the history is totally different.

This article could be the basis for a whole series because one can easily write a book just on the macaroon. Originally the macaroon was anything but French, as the dough originated in North Africa. At the time when we, in the north, still lived in the Stone Age, people there were already making refined pâtisserie of almonds. The pâtissiers of Catherine de Medici introduced the macaroon to France. According to the history books this happened in 1533 during the Renaissance. The Court and the Church approved the macaroon, which was important in those days. Soon everyone developed their own dough with its own mark. Nancy, Boulay, Lusignan, Poitiers, Montmorillon, Amiens, all these cities claimed to be the experts. In those days the recipes were top secret. A different kind is the one from Paris as it is smooth and filled with ganache. But this one was not known until the beginning of the 20th century, created by the well-known pâtissier Ladurée. For the authentic macaroon, we travel to Amiens in the North of France. This city declares that it has the most expertise.

Artisanal

Amiens, the capital of Picardië, is very impressive to visitors. The branches of the river Somme cut through the Quartier Saint Leu. The beautiful cathedral is quite comparable to the Notre Dame in Paris. We leave the city to go to a little village nearby: Corbie. There we meet with Allain Langlet who is supposed to be the largest macaroon specialist. A sign on the road tells us that we are going in the right direction. The family Langlet has been here since 1792 with a bakery and pâtisserie and Allain belongs to the fifth generation. In the atelier (workshop) we notice that the craftsmanship is skillfully exercised. When we see that Lubeca marzipan is used we know that quality is most

important. Allain is born in flour! He opened his own bakery in 1974, but returned home in 1996 when his father passed away.

The Macaroon

Allain: "We don't know much about the history of the macaroon in Amiens except that the recipe is very old. I think that the recipe was created in the monastery since that used to be the kitchen where everything happened. At the time of Karl the Great butter cookies were the specialty of our monastery." Together with his right hand man, Guilhain Pichon, Allain gives us a demonstration. "The secret is patience. The preparation takes three days. A good macaroon should be soft and almost raw inside whereas the crust has to be crunchy." He mixes almond powder with sugar, honey, apple compote and egg white. Once the mixture is homogeneous he puts it in the fridge for 24 hours. Then he uses an old machine that we recognize from butchers: a filler for sausages. "In the old days we used a spout pressing it against our belly while the other hand did the slicing. That was heavy duty." The macaroons are all cut the same size and laid on a baking sheet. Then they dry at room temperature for a whole day. Afterwards they are baked in the oven for 6 minutes at 250°C/480°F.

Variant

"Because of the addition of almonds I didn't find the macaroon really local. Therefore, I created a variety: the Pavé Picard." Allain remembers that his region used to be covered with hazelnut trees. His Pavé Picard is a macaroon, but prepared with hazelnut powder. It has a square shape (pavé is a brick) and Allain uses two kinds of hazelnut powder. But when we ask for the recipe Alain is almost annoyed: "This is top secret! It is almost the same composition as macaroons but you'll realize that there is a difference between the fat content of almonds and hazelnuts. That is the key." So not really a world secret, if you think about it. When we taste his pavé we understand immediately why he won the first prize at the Saveurs de Picardie. By the way he is a serious collector of first prizes just as his ancestor. He loves his profession and is an avid promoter of it. It's nauseating to him that there are bakeries selling their products via franchises. For this baker the profession is about art and skill without artificial agents. If you understand a bit of French, we recommend you go to his website where Allain shares several of his recipes.

The Macaroon of Amiens

Ingredients: **1 kg almond powder, 1 kg sugar, 250 g egg white, 100 g honey, 100 g apple compote.**

Mix all ingredients to a homogenous mixture and let rest for 24 hours in the fridge. Roll dough like a sausage and cut this in slices of 3 cm thick. Put slices on a baking sheet and let rest at room temperature for 24 hours. Bake for 6 minutes at 250°C/480°F.

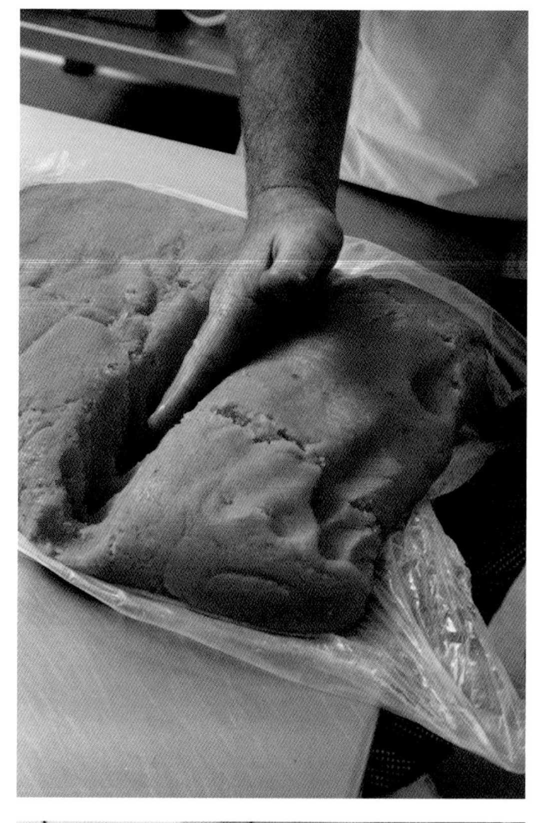

ROGHA na TUAITHE
An Rogha Nádúrtha
Country Choice
25
Delicatessen
Coffee Bar
25

The traditional Irish Christmas Pudding

It's a long way to Tipperary

If there is just one Irish and English specialty, it is the Christmas Pudding that involves the whole family and is sure to be on the table every Christmas Day. There are as many recipes as the puddings that are eaten. The list of ingredients changes from baker to baker. Our focus is on one of the Irish varieties.

We are making an extensive trip through Ireland; it's partly business and partly to enjoy the small winding farm roads, little stone walls and thousands of sheep. During a trip to Ireland you can be sure to meet all four seasons in one day: a pleasant morning changes suddenly in a short but heavy hail and thunderstorm, followed by heavy winds and one hour later you are back in full sunshine.

To learn more about Irish traditions and products we traveled to Tipperary. In this little village you will automatically meet one person: the very talkative Peter Ward of Country Choice. It is not easy to describe this self-made shop. It is a tea-salon, a bakery, a delicatessen, a distributor of farm produce and organizer of local gastronomic events. Peter Ward has made it his mission to educate the Irish on quality and to help small local farmers. He invites every farmer in his area to drop off their local products and Peter makes sure that these products are used for cakes, making jams, marmalades and more. One of his greatest specialties is the traditional Irish Christmas Pudding. Thousands are made each year and distributed all over the world. To make your own means turning your whole kitchen upside down with every bowl used to stir the batter. If you don't feel like making your own Christmas Pudding, go to www.countrychoice.ie to order one. He treats us to a large piece of pudding with fresh farm cream while we listen to Peter's fascinating stories.

Lots of traditions

Naturally the English claim that they invented this pudding, but the Welsh, the Scottish and the Irish make the same assertions. We at Pastry in Europe would never make a choice in this case and prefer to look at traditions and of course the recipe. The most important ingredients and the flavour enhancers are the dried fruits and the exotic spices. While these ingredients didn't originate on the British Isles, they are somewhat British in that they were first transported to Britain by ships that returned from exotic colonies. The oldest kept recipes date back to the 17th century when butter was not used as fat content but the much cheaper beef suet. The making of Christmas pudding is a real family tradition where everyone is involved and religion is part of it as well. Traditionally the pudding is decorated with a piece of holly that has a few berries left. These are supposed to protect against witchcraft. Because the berries grow only on male bushes, the branch is carried in by men. The bakers that sell thousands of these around Christmas time start their production in September. Traditionally, the pudding should be made the Sunday before Advent, as it needs a long time to mature. The Irish call this day Stir-up Sunday. Everyone in the home has to stir the heavy batter clockwise with a wooden spoon. One is supposed to make a wish while stirring. After the Christmas dinner the Christmas pudding comes on the table, is sprinkled with brandy and lit with a match. Although this has been a tradition for centuries, many Irish children are not interested, but they have found a solution for that. They put coins in the batter as a bit of cash or to bring luck to the person who finds it, providing he or she does not swallow it!

The traditional Irish Christmas pudding

***Ingredients:* 500 g beef suet cut in small pieces, 200 g self rising flour, 400 g bread crumbs, 8 large eggs, 1 tbsp salt, 4 tsp ground nutmeg, 4 tsp cinnamon, 2 tsp dried and ground ginger, 1 tsp ground cloves, 1 tsp allspice, 1 tsp ground mace, 1 tsp ground coriander, 500 g brown icing sugar, 200 g dried dates, 200 g dried plums, 100 g candied orange peel, 2 peeled and cut apples, 2 peeled and cut pears, zest of 3 lemons, 600 g currants, 500 g raisins, 100 g chopped almonds, 600 ml Guinness, 1 glass Irish whiskey.**

In a large bowl, mix suet, sifted flour, spices, salt, sugar and breadcrumbs. Mix well, clockwise, with a wooden spatula. At this point you should make your wish and hand the spatula over to the next family member. Add fruits, nuts and lemon juice and blend well. In a separate bowl beat eggs with whiskey and Guinness and add, if you want, the coins.
Add mixture to the first bowl and keep stirring clockwise, making your wish and then let other family members take over to stir. The batter should become deep brown in colour and should easily remove from the spatula when you lift it. If it is too thick, add some Guinness to get the right consistency. Press dough with your hands to remove air pockets. Let rest overnight so the fruit and breadcrumbs can absorb the liquid. Take pudding forms that hold about one litre, grease with suet or butter and dust with icing sugar. Fill forms to about 1 cm from the edge, cover with two layers of wax paper and tighten it with kitchen string.
Put forms on top of a grill in a large pot so the forms won't touch the bottom. Add boiling water; the forms should be about ¾ in the water and put on high heat. As soon as the water is boiling again, put lid on the pan and lower the heat. Steam for about 8 hours and check regularly so water doesn't evaporate. If necessary, add more boiling water. You can also steam the puddings in a modern steamer. Remove pudding from the pan, and replace the wax paper with clean wax paper. The pudding will keep for years in a cool place.
Steam again on Christmas day for two hours as described above.
Take out the pan, let steam escape and loosen cake from the form.
Put upside down on a plate, sprinkle with brandy and light immediately.
Serve flaming pudding with whipped cream, custard or whipped butter.
Be careful, don't swallow the coins!

SWIN
Four people und
by Dan Collins
and Mary Regan
FOUR people have undergone
specialist medical tests amid fears
that the deadly swine flu has

BAR

Jean-Luc Wahl

As a chef, Jean-Luc Wahl had a Michelin star, and now that he has opened his own restaurant, we think it won't be long before that will happen to him again. His Hostellerie de L'Illberg is in Hirtzbach, a picturesque little village in the Sundgau, located between the French Alsace and the Swiss border. Jean-Luc is an official French Master Chef.

Pastilla of chocolate with bieawaecka fruits and honey caramel

Prepare a classic ganache, not too runny. Cut dried prunes, dried apricots and candied figs in small cubes and mix these with bruised pistachio nuts and hazelnuts. Grease a non-stick pan, put two sheets of brick dough (comparable to phyllo dough) in it, place fruits and nuts in the centre and cover with ganache. Close dough tightly to make a pocket and bake carefully in the pan. Then put in the oven for another 5 minutes. Sprinkle with cinnamon and icing sugar. For the caramel, heat 250 g sugar with 1 tbsp of honey, caramelize and deglaze with 250 ml crème fraiche. Put pastilla on the plate, pour caramel over it and serve with sorbet made with quince.

Joachim Wissler

Vendôme

For years we have been thinking that the German kitchen would consist of mostly heavy and solid foods, supported by the classic French kitchen, but we have changed our minds since we met Joachim Wissler. Restaurant Vendôme in Bergisch Gladbach has changed the tradition of the German kitchen in very modern ways and the same holds true for their pâtisserie. The extremely luxurious restaurant with the perfect host has been recognized with three Michelin Stars. Chef Joachim has a lot of help from the Pâtissier of the Year, Andy Vorbush. Together they create miraculous desserts that are hard to be matched in taste and presentation.

Schwarzwälder Kirschtorte

For 4 people: icing sugar, 250 g chocolate shavings, 1 chocolate crepe, 4 hippenröllchen filled with whipped cream, schnapps or gin, 12 cherries.
For the chocolate ball: 50 g cream, 2 g licorice root, 30 g bitter chocolate, 50 g marzipan, 30 g icing sugar, 10 g almond powder.
For the batter: 50 g flour, 50 g starch, 65 g milk 50 g cocoa powder, 10 g icing sugar, 1 egg white.
For the cherry sorbet: 40 g sour cherry juice, 200 g cherry puree (no pits) 20 g sugar, marrow of 1 vanilla bean.
For the banana sorbet: 100 g peeled banana, 100 g mango pulp, 50 g banana or apple juice, 10 g lime juice, 10 g cane sugar, marrow of 1 vanilla bean, 5 g dark rum, 2 g pectin.
For the cherry compôte: 100 g pitted cherries, 15 g sugar, 20 g sour cherry juice, juice of half a lemon, 20 g red port, 500 ml cherry liqueur, 1 tsp cornstarch.
For the kaffir espuma: 100 g kaffir, 60 g quark, 75 g cream, 30 g honey, juice of half a lemon.
For the chocolate espuma: 125 g milk, 50 g cream, 60 g bitter chocolate (60%), 35 g cocoa liqueur, 2 leaves gelatin.

For the chocolate ball, heat cream, licorice root and chocolate. Pass through a sieve and put in the fridge. Form balls with the cold mixture and freeze. Mix marzipan, icing sugar and almond powder. Roll out to 2 cm thick; wrap it around the frozen chocolate ball. For the

batter, mix flour, starch and icing sugar to a smooth dough. Mix with slightly beaten egg white and cocoa powder and pour through a sieve. Let dough rest for 30 minutes. Using a toothpick, dip chocolate balls in the batter and deep fry at 170°C/340°F for 3 minutes. Sprinkle with icing sugar before serving.
For the cherry sorbet, mix all required ingredients in a blender and make a sorbet. Put sorbet in a long container but leave room for the banana sorbet. Make banana sorbet the same way with required ingredients and put a layer next to the cherry sorbet. For the compote, caramelize the sugar and deglaze with cherry juice, cherry liqueur and lemon juice. Mix the port with the starch and add to the hot caramel. Drain cherries from their juice, keep a few aside for decoration and cut the rest in pieces.
For the kaffir espuma, mix all ingredients and pass through a sieve. Pour in a siphon, attach a charger and put in the fridge. For the chocolate espuma, heat milk, cream and chocolate. Add the pre-soaked gelatin and liqueur. Mix well and pour in a siphon. Add a charger and cool. Pour compote in a glass, add espumas and garnish with chocolate shavings. Slice a strip of a chocolate crepe and fold. Lay a quenelle of cherry-banana sorbet on top. Create a little tart of the cherries, garnish with hippenröllchen sprinkled with schnapps. Serve with chocolate ball.

A walk through the forest

Four 4 people: **blackberries, reduced strawberry juice.**
For the goat quark ice cream: **125 g milk, 190 g goat quark, 190 g sour cream, 125 g sugar, 50 g glucose, 50 g reduced orange juice, marrow of 1 vanilla bean.**
For the caviar of fir needles: **250 g washed and chopped fir needles, 400 ml mineral water, 150 g vanilla sugar, juice and peels of 3 lemons, 120 g elderberry blossom, 40 sago pearls, ice water, lime juice and mineral water.**
For the herb salad: **mint, basil, chervil, chopped lemon thyme, lemon balm, fennel, coriander, tarragon, blackberries, candied orange zest, roasted hazelnuts, raspberry vinegar, apricot oil, lemon zest.**

For the ice cream, heat water and sugar and dissolve glucose in it. Mix with the rest of the ingredients and pass through a sieve. Pour in Paco or Frix beakers and freeze and spin to make ice cream. Bring 400 ml mineral water, vanilla sugar, lemon juice and peels to a boil to make a clear liquid. Add the elderberry blossom, and stop stirring. Let mixture sit in the fridge for 24 hours. Fill Paco or Frix beakers with fir needles and press tight. Pour blossom syrup through a sieve and add to the fir needles so they are just covered with syrup and freeze. Wash sago well and boil for 2 minutes on low heat with the rest of the syrup. Cool sago in a bowl of ice water and add lime juice to taste. Process fir needles to a

smooth consistency like a paste. Add the fir paste to the sago and add some more lime juice. If necessary, add some mineral water to make it thinner.
Make a salad of all the herbs, the zests, blackberries and hazelnuts. Sprinkle with vinegar, oil and lemon zest. Divide the caviar on a plate with salad, blackberries and sauce. Serve with a quenelle of quark ice cream.

Blood peaches of white chocolate-almond sorbet and raspberry sauce

For the almond sorbet: **500 ml water, 250 g white chocolate, juice and zest of 1 lemon, 50 g white chocolate liqueur, 16 g dissolved pectin, 50 g sugar, 50 g glucose, 50 g almond puree.**
For the peach preparation: **6 blood peaches, 250 g white peach puree, 60 g frozen raspberries, 5 sprigs of lemon thyme, marrow of 1 vanilla bean, 1 star anise, 15 coriander seeds ground in a mortar, 20 g blossom honey juice and zest of half a lemon, juice and sap of half an orange, 50 g peach liqueur, 100 ml mineral water, 50 g champagne, 3 g xanthan gum.**
For raspberry foam: **200 ml liquid from thawed and slightly mixed raspberries, 100 g peach puree, 50 g peach liqueur, 60 g vanilla sugar, juice of half a lemon, 180 g egg white, 20 g emulsifier.**
For the salad: **chervil, tarragon, basil cress, some lemon zests, blackberries, peach poaching liquid, olive oil.**

For the almond sorbet, bring water, lemon juice and zest, pectin, sugar and glucose to a boil. Dissolve herein the white chocolate. Add the rest of the ingredients, mix well, pass through a sieve and process for ice cream.
For the peach preparation bring all ingredients, except the peaches and thyme to a boil and simmer on low heat for 10 minutes. Add the thyme and let simmer for another 15 minutes. Pass through a fine mesh sieve and poach peaches in this liquid. Cool peaches in ice water and remove skin and pit. Return peaches to the hot liquid and let cool.
For the foam, mix required ingredients until smooth, pass through a sieve and beat to foam in a KitchenAid. Make a salad of the herbs and fruits and make a dressing with the olive oil and poached juice.
Put peaches in a tall and narrow glass and cover with ice cream. Spoon 15 mm foam on top of the ice cream. Dust with icing sugar and flambé. Pour some poaching liquid along the dessert and put some salad on the side.

Jacques Lameloise

Restaurant Lameloise

Jacques, established in the village of Chagny in Burgundy, is one of the biggest 3-star Michelin chefs in France. He shows what desserts mean in top gastronomy.

Shortbread with caramelized bananas, muscovado crisp and banana-passion fruit sorbet

For the shortbread: 80 g butter, 70 g sugar, zest of 1 lemon, 30 g almond powder, 20 g ground hazelnuts, 70 g egg yolks, 105 g flour, 5 g dry yeast.
For the crisp: 40 g butter, 50 g muscovado sugar, 45 g flour, ½ vanilla bean.
For the caramel: bananas, 40 g sugar, 10 g glucose, 85 g cream.
For the banana and passion fruit mousse: 50 g passion fruit puree, 100 g fresh bananas, 125 g cream, 8 g kremfix (whipping cream stabilizer), 25 g icing sugar.
For the sorbet ice cream: 270 g passion fruit coulis, 100 g mango puree, 500 g fresh cut bananas, 60 g orange juice, 300 g water, 200 g sugar, 50 g trimoline.
For the dried bananas: bananas and icing sugar.

For the shortbread beat butter and sugar until white in colour, add egg yolks and the rest of the ingredients, roll out to 3 mm thick and let rest overnight. Cut pieces of 3 x 9 cm and bake in the oven at 160°C / 320°F. For the crisp, soften the butter, add sugar and flour as well as the vanilla bean. Roll one layer between two sheets of parchment paper and put in the freezer. For the mousse put all ingredients in a Pacojet except the passion fruit puree. Spin once with the cutting blade and once with a chantilly blade. Pour in a glass and cover with passion fruit puree. Put in freezer. For sorbet ice cream, mix all ingredients, sieve and spin in ice cream machine. Slice bananas in a slicer, 2 mm thick, place on a silpat and sprinkle with icing sugar, bake in convection oven at 80°C / 175°F for 2.5 hours. For the caramel boil sugar and glucose and deglaze with cream. Add the pieces of bananas, sauté a little bit, place on shortbread and finish with the same size crisp. Bake in the oven at 180°C / 355°F. Caramelize 3 more pieces of banana and put this on top of the crisp. Garnish with the dried bananas. Add a quenelle of sorbet and a glass with mousse on the side.

Trilogy of pear with almond crumble and caramel sauce

Ingredients: pears, puff pastry, chopped almonds, syrup 15° Beaumé.
For the poaching liquid: 400 g water, 88 g sugar, 1 vanilla bean, pepper, lemon juice.
For the crumble cookie: 50 g brown sugar, 50 g golden brown sugar, 100 g almond powder, 100 g flour, 100 g butter.
For the sorbet ice cream: 1 litre pears in syrup, 200 g icing sugar, 50 g glucose, juice of 1 lemon.
For the caramel sauce: 100 g sugar, 25 g glucose, 210 g cream.

For the syrup heat all ingredients and in it cook the peeled pears until they are done, about 25 minutes. Let cool and then cook in a vacuum pouch for about 10 minutes at 80°C / 175°F. Mix all ingredients for the crumble. Press dough in rings and bake at180°C / 325°F in the oven. Set a bit of baked crumble aside and grind to a powder. Mix all ingredients for the sorbet ice cream and spin in turbo machine. For the caramel, heat caramel and sugar till dry and deglaze with cream. Re-heat again and cool. Make sacristains (twists) by rolling puff pastry to 1 mm thickness, coat with some egg yolk and sprinkle with chopped almonds. Cut in thin strips and twist them. Bake in the oven at 200°C / 390°F. Cut pears in slices of 1.5 mm thickness, dip these in the cold 15° Beaumé syrup, put on a silpat and let them dry in the oven at 82°C / 180°F.
Put cookie on a plate, dip pear in crumbled powder and place on the cookie. Add a quenelle of sorbet ice cream and pierce a slice of dried pear on top. Finish with a sacristain, caramel sauce and some crumbled powder.

Lameloise

Chicory

Chicory has played a major role as a foodstuff over the years; even in Egypt where people knew it as cichorium intibus and used it as a food staple. In the 19th century, in the time of Karl the Great, Flemish monks started to select seeds of chicory and created a sativum, the so called coffee chicory. But in the 17th century it was the Dutch who started to roast and grind chicory root as a substitute for coffee beans.
This discovery traveled quickly around the world, except in the south of France and Turkey, where the dried fig was used as a coffee substitute. When Napoleon decided to stop all coffee trade with England, no more coffee was imported. That was when this surrogate coffee really took off. Chicory has always been associated with wars and thus with poverty and food shortage.

Niche Product

The largest chicory cultures were mainly in the north of France. Soon after the Second World War, there were 3000 chicory growing farmers, 300 drying plants and 30 roasting plants. Today we only have 300 farmers, 2 drying plants and 2 roasting plants. Unfortunately the little field ovens with cute chimneys that used to be prominent in the landscape of the north of France have disappeared as well. Poverty was eliminated so people no longer buy substitutes.
This enormous decline in profit has now made chicory a rare niche product. It is nice to see it used in gastronomy in an interesting way. But how do we get the taste of a toasted bean from a root? We went to witness that at Vincent Luton, one of the last roasters in a small rural community, l'Etoile, close to Oye-Plage, at the most northern tip of the French coast. "Chicory is planted between April and May and harvested between September and November. The roots are washed, cut in slices and dried. The end result is called cossette. It used to be done in small factories, mostly by Belgians who did the hard work. Now we do it in warm tunnels." The cossettes are kept in hangars waiting to be processed. Once at the roaster they go into large kettles and are roasted for 2 hours at 200°C / 390°F. After a rest period of 30 minutes the batch is ground. There is also liquid chicory. This happens when the ground product is infused in water of 80°C / 175°F, filtered, dried and steamed.

Many possibilities

Vincent considers chicory a perfect flavour component for all kinds of preparations, sweet or salty. "Don't see it just as a flavour but also as an enhancer of other flavours. In some dishes chicory can be present

without taste." It is also a natural colouring agent, a natural flavour enhancer and a natural emulsifier. Bakers use chicory flour to diminish salt content or fat content. In the north of France chicory is still deeply revered in the hearts of its people. Some add chicory to their dried sausages, others to their cheeses. We met a baker, Mr. Fasquel, who bakes every weekend with chicory, from bread to brioche, from pâtisserie to sugar bread. He lives in the village of Vieille-Église.

We also visited another specialist to get his opinion: Alexandre Gauthier. This young chef, who is the driving force in the kitchen of Auberge de la Grenouillère in La Madeleine-sous-Montreuil, just saw the Michelin star returned that had once been owned by his father Roland.
Alexandre grew up in the north so chicory has no secrets for him.
He uses it as a spice in his cold and hot dishes. We are convinced that you will understand, after reading the recipes, that chicory has a promising gastronomic future.

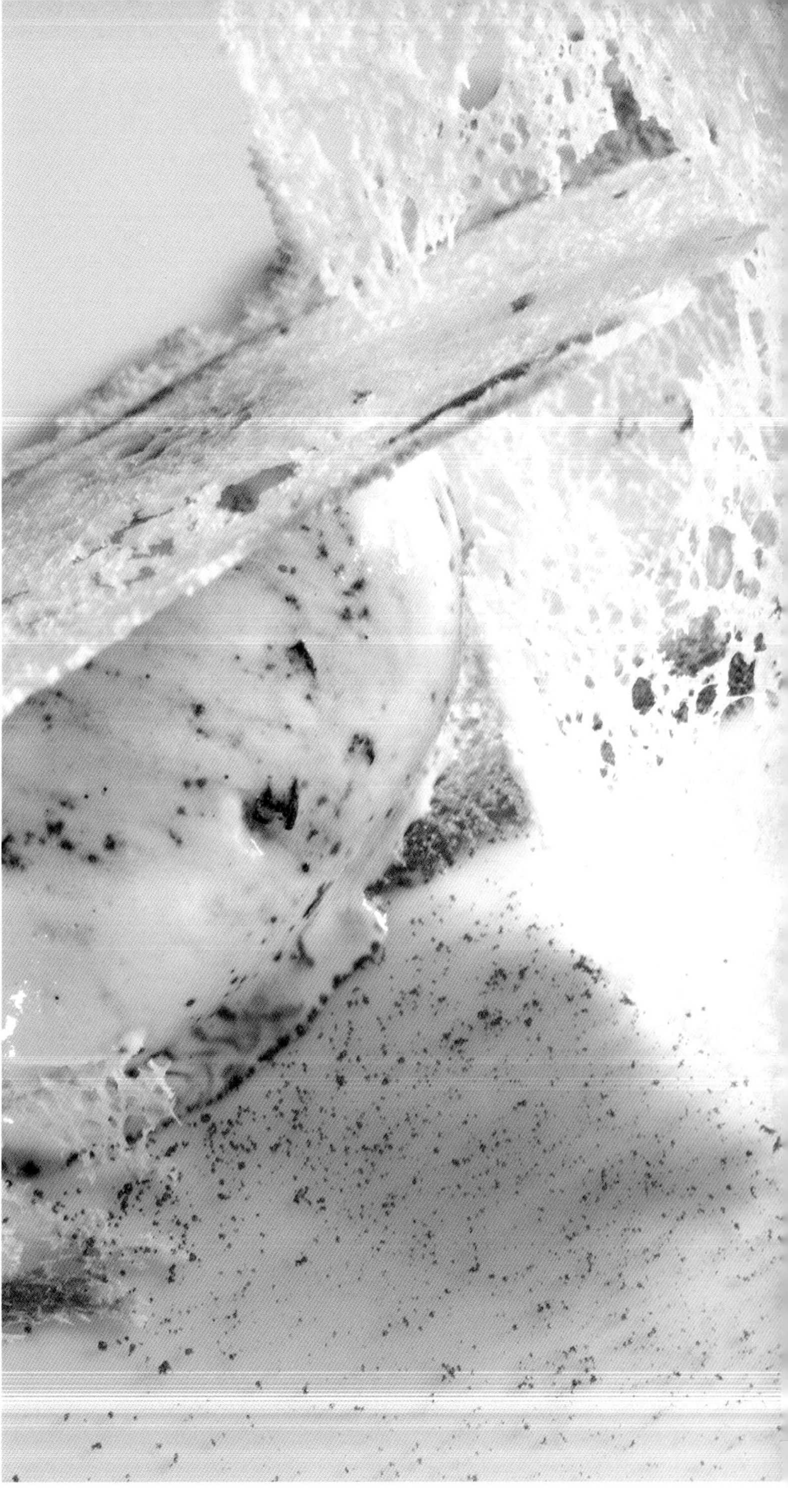

Brioche, yeast and chicory

Ingredients: **brioche bread, ground chicory, chicory powder, honey.**
For the yeast ice cream: **40 g yeast, 1 litre milk, 200 g sugar, 10 egg yolks.**

Heat milk with yeast, beat egg yolks with sugar. Pour warm milk on egg yolk mix and boil until it thickens. Pass through a sieve and pour in Frix beakers. Before spinning add some chicory granules and powder. Slice brioche in thin slices and dry in a drying cupboard. Place a slice of the brioche on a plate. Put a quenelle of ice cream on top and sprinkle with some chicory powder. Put another slice of brioche on top and garnish with honey.

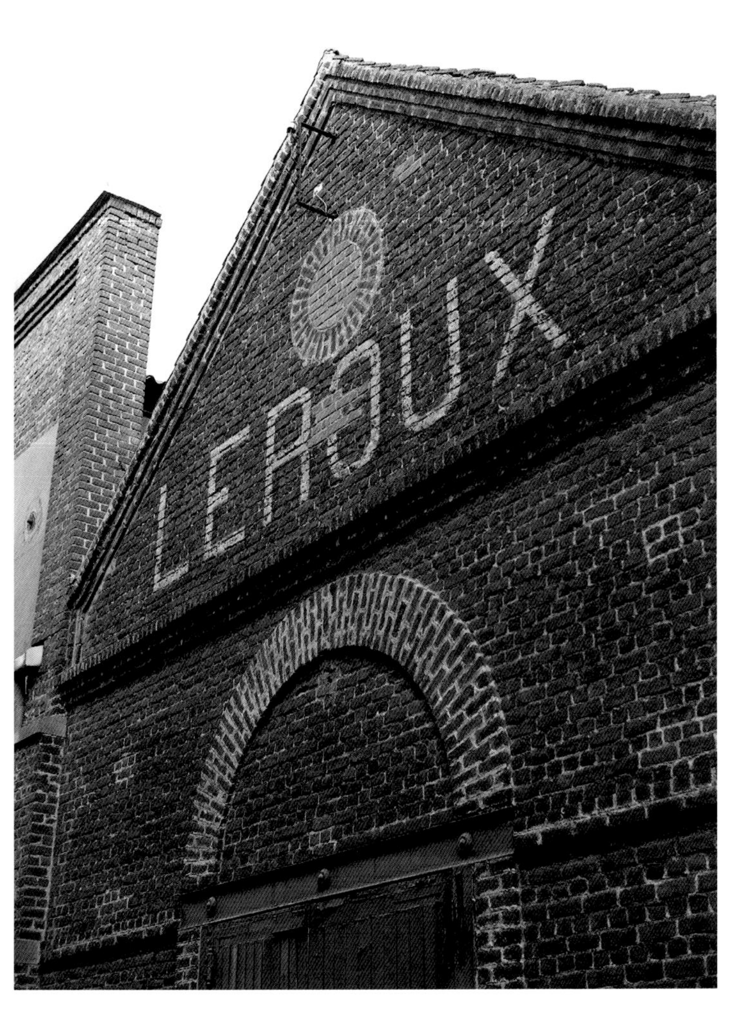

Sugarbell, chocolate and chicory

Ingredients: **isomalt, water, yogurt, chicory granules.**
For the chocolate-chicory mousse: **100 g egg yolk, 50 g eggs, 85 g sugar, 40 g water, 50 g chocolate 99%, melted, 250 g whipped cream, 30 g liquid chicory.**

Cook sugar and water to 121°C / 250°F. Pour on egg yolk and eggs and keep beating until it is completely cold. Then add the chicory, the melted chocolate and the whipped cream. Pour in a siphon and insert the charger. Heat some isomalt with water to 170°C / 340°F and pour into four forms. Reduce temperature to 80°C / 175°F and blow bubbles using a little pump. Pour a bubble bell on a plate. Pierce a little hole in the bell and fill with the mousse. Put some yogurt next to it. Fill a pepper mill with chicory granules and grind on the dessert to taste.

Vin de Paille

When we visit this region, preparations are under way for La Fête de la Percée. This is an annual celebration when the barrels of the Vin Jaune are opened after six years and three months. We are in the Jura on the French-Swiss border, a terroir where many kinds of wine are produced. During our visit we focus on a very special nectar that has been created with lots of patience.

The vineyard of the Jura is 2000 hectares. That is nothing compared to the 20,000 hectares that existed before the phylloxera (an aphid related pest) and the World Wars. Fortunately it didn't influence the diversity of the wines. Here you can find the Vin Jaune, the Macvin and the Crémant du Jura. For us the most beautiful product is the Vin de Paille. Literally it means "straw wine", it's obtained by drying grapes of different varietals, which makes it into a liqueur wine. Vin de Paille used to be made in other regions as well such as the Alsace, the Tourraine and even Hermitage. Rumours have it that they are starting this production again. The method used is called passerillage and is meant to dry the grapes in a way that increases the natural concentration of sugar. In the old days one would put the grapes on carpets of straw (paille), but the wine growers changed this to wooden or plastic crates to avoid infection and rotting. This is not at all related to the vendange tardive (wines made from late-picked grapes with higher sugar levels) or the German method of Trockenbeerenauslese or ice wine, where the ripe grapes must freeze on the vine before they are harvested. For Vin de Paille the grape has to be ripe and healthy, something that needs all the attention of the wine grower.

No recipe

The Jura has five kinds of grapes: Savagnin, Trousseau, Poulsard, Chardonnay and Pinot Noir. The Savagnin is the prominent grapevine of the Jura because it gets a lot of expression from the Jura soil. It is a derivation of the Traminer varietal and related to the Klevener, its origin as obscure as that of its relation to Heilingenstein. The Poulsard or Plousard is a red grapevine, typical for the Jura. The village of Pupillin, a few kilometers from Arbois, claims to be the world capital of this grapevine and calls it the Plousard. The Trousseau is a red grapevine, the Chardonnay doesn't need any introduction and the Pinot Noir is not used for the Vin de Paille. The most important part of producing a Vin de Paille is the harvest. Only a few selected wine growers supply the grapes

Vin de Paille
CHATEAU CHALO

for the Vin de Paille. The grape must be ripe and healthy with a firm skin. Each parcel is picked separately, with the right balance of different grapes. The picking is slow and demands much knowledge and experience, mostly because the ripening on the vine is different for each cépage. The basic harvest of 20 hectolitres per hectare has to be taken seriously and respected. Each wine grower has his own method and that depends mainly on the terroir of his vineyard. As soon as the grapes are harvested and put in crates, they can slowly dry and mature further. Officially this should be done within six weeks, but often it takes four to six months in a ventilated space with no heat. At some spots in Jura, where moisture and bugs are considered real enemies, the bunches of grapes are hung up to dry. When the desired sugar content has been reached, the grapes are pressed. Naturally this is done with a lot of care. After fermentation the juice gives an alcohol percentage of 14.5 to 17° and is kept in oak barrels for a minimum of three years to further age.

Vin de Paille is famous for its aromas of candied fruit (especially orange) and dried plums, caramel and honey. During a sinful tasting we have a chance to discover all of these aromas. We move to Château Bethanie, the wine cooperative of Arbois with 120 wine growers. The Director, Laurent Hagnere, explains some of the work, while we view the hundreds of crates that are waiting to be pressed. The harvest or rather the picking is done by September 20th and will be pressed on February 28th, which means that the important selected grapes of the Plousard, Savagnin and Chardonnay have had a chance to ripen for another five months. This year they are of the same quantities but this can differ from year to year. In contrast to the grapes for botrytis-liqueur wines, there are no different triages; here we have only one harvest. Making Vin de Paille in the Jura is seen as an obligation, even though it doesn't give much income. Vin de Paille is mainly sold in the top French gastronomy. There is hardly any export.

Granité

Today's kitchen is full of new preparation techniques. But it's sometimes nice to go back to the most primitive way of making ice cream; simple and easy but more than delicious.

The consumption of ice cream goes far back into history, even to old China. The ice cream man then did exactly the same as what Indians in the Andes do today: get ice from the mountains, shave it and mix it with fruit puree and/or honey. The old Romans did the same, creating the myth of Italian ice cream preparation. The name granité comes from the Italian word grana meaning grainy.

SORBET OR GRANITÉ

On first sight sorbet and granité look the same. However there is one huge difference: the structure. A sorbet is made in an ice cream machine; a granité is frozen as a solid mass. A regular granité contains less sugar than a sorbet with a ratio of one part sugar and four parts liquid. The liquid is often a combination of water and fruit puree, coffee or tea. Liquid containing alcohol is used as well, although alcohol freezes at lower temperature and that should be taken in consideration. The watery mass is poured in a bowl or on a plate, frozen and scraped off regularly.

SUGAR

The function of sugar is very important in a granité. The more sugar, the longer the freezing time. Too much sugar and the granité would not freeze; too little sugar and it will be hard to scrape off. Most of the time a sugar content of 8 to 11° Baumé is the target but sorbets have a 17 to 20° Baumé and that's why there is a difference in structure. Instead of sugar, honey or syrup can be used.

FRUITS

For a granité based on fruit, syrup is mixed with a puree and brought to the right Baumé concentration. It is also possible to have fruit juice, peel or other parts of the fruit cook in the syrup. Besides alcohol or fruits, one can also use other ingredients. Herbs and spices can be added to the syrup as well, as long as the Baumé density is respected.

FREEZING OF ALCOHOL

The rule of thumb is that every degree of alcohol needs one degree Celsius to freeze. A granité is especially suited for working with alcohol, but don't forget the rule of thumb as above.

AOC MONBAZILLAC

Sweet bliss from the Périgord

Sauternes is a world-renowned sweet wine. It is also very expensive. Fortunately, there are a few other wines that are comparable to Sauternes, and they are not quite so expensive. In the shadow of a majestic castle, near Bergerac, one of these wines is produced.

The wines that are comparable to the Sauternes have one important thing in common: rot. A rot so valuable it is called Noble Rot. In the fall, morning fog in the vineyards leaves much humidity, but in the afternoon there is lots of sunshine. This is an ideal situation for the mould Botrytis Cinerea to grow. This fungus attacks the grapes and they shrivel up.
It may sound silly, but the winegrowers love it. Because all sugar stays in the grapes, the sugar content gets higher and higher. The shrinking doesn't happen simultaneously. While one grape may already look like a raisin, the one next to it has not yet been affected. In Monbazillac they might do seven separate pickings, and every single grape is picked by hand. With this amount of labour involved, you can understand why this wine is never cheap. As well, there is the risk factor. In order for the mould to have an effect the harvest might have to wait for a long time. But during the wait, if there is a heavy rain, the mould will be washed away and the harvest will have lost its value.

The Vineyard

The area of Monbazillac is the largest and the oldest region in the world for liqueur wines. The vineyard, a few kilometres south of Bergerac on the bank of the river Dordogne, is about 3,600 hectares. 75% is designated to the famous AOC Monbazillac. The elevation goes from 50 to 180 metres and the soil is a combination of lime and clay. This area can be divided into the flat river valley of St. Laurent-des-Vignes, the foothills of Colombier and the villages of Monbazillac, Pomport and Rouffignac. The saying goes that a good vineyard should overlook the river of the Dordogne, which means that the grapevines will be facing north. The climate is a bit more subtle and delays the ripening process. There are three varieties of grapes grown: Sémillon, Sauvignon and Muscadelle. A Monbazillac wine is a combination of all three.

Medium Priced Dessert Wines

The rules and regulations of the AOC (the French appellation laws) are very strict. To call a wine Monbazillac, it is important that one litre of wine contains a minimum of 246 grams of natural sugar. As a pâtissier you will find that is a lot. The harvest has to be done by hand, appropriate rotting is a must, and the wine should contain 12.5% alcohol, minimum 45 grams residual sugar per litre and have been resting in oak barrels for at least 18 months. The result of these rules is a fantastic wine.
A young Monbazillac pairs well with foie gras and light pâtisserie since it is a wonderful light dessert wine. When the wine is a bit older, the taste is more distinct and can be served with heavier desserts. The same quality is known in Sauternes, but... Sauternes cost a few thousand euros per bottle! A Monbazillac has a friendlier price; a top wine costs about 20 euros.

Château de Monbazillac

At the top of the hill overlooking the entire area, sits a heavily fortified grand castle, build in 1550. The castle, with a wine museum inside, now belongs to the local wine cooperative. Twenty-two hectares are planted around the castle. Madame Annette Goulard, president of the

cooperative, gave us a tour. The 100 farmers who, with their 1000 hectares, are connected to the cooperative, must be pleased with the facility. The tens of thousands of visitors who visit the castle every year have to exit through an enormous degustation (tasting) area where they can also buy. No tourist leaves without some bottles of wine. We have to add that the degustation area is incredibly organized. There are several counters staffed by sommeliers who welcome the visitors. All châteaux wines can be tasted with the help of experts offering multilingual advice. If you are a really good customer they might even open a can of foie gras to enjoy with the wines. The Château de Monbazillac is of course centre stage but that has a lot to do with the marketing aspect. There are also other good wines. The one we tasted is the Château La Sabatière, located next to the airport on 22 hectares. The best wine for us was the Château Versant du Haut Poulvère 2000, a well-defined wine with essence of ripe apricot. It gives fullness in the mouth, integrated with ripe fruit. It has a pleasant heart warming aftertaste. Yes, we would love to have one with our dessert!

The Count and His Wine

It is afternoon and we are having lunch at La tour des Vents, one of the better restaurants in the area. There we start talking to a wine grower sitting at a nearby table. We begin with small talk, but slowly the discussion becomes more fascinating and philosophical. We don't think that this is your average wine grower with callused hands and a casual sweater. And we are right. It is Count Laurent de Bosredon. After our meal, the noble man takes us to his house, a castle on top of the hill: Château Bélingard. Laurent explains that the name of the castle is Celtic and literally means the garden of the Gods. The old Celtics owned more of these holy places where the Druids ruled the laws, gods were worshipped and offerings were sacrificed. A few years ago, a heavy storm brought down a tree next to the castle and suddenly a religious sanctuary was revealed: a stone sculpture of a Druid chair.

You shouldn't be surprised that many bottles of Château Bélingard were shared that afternoon. Maybe you are also not surprised that we think the very best Monbazillac is the one from the Count!

Pastry in europe

Anthony Delhasse
Belgium

Nobuyuki Matsuhisa
United States

Jorge Bandeira
Brasil

Teruaki Tamura
Japan

Ferran Adriá
Spain

Joël Robuchon
France

Hervé This
France

Grant Achatz
United States

around the world

Juan-Mari Arzak
Spain

Bruno Menard
Japan

Eric and Tistan Martin
Belgium

Thierry Baldinger
France

Myrtle Allen
Ireland

Heston Blumenthal
Great-Britain

Yoshihiro Murata
Japan

Magnus Ek
Sweden

01
02
03
04
05
06
07
08
09
10
11
12
13
14
15
16
17
18
19
20
21
22
23
24
25
26
27
28
29
30
31
32
33
34
35
36
P10

europe

01. Iceland
◉ Reykjavik

02. Norway
◉ Oslo

03. Sweden
◉ Stockholm

04. Finland
◉ Helsinki

05. Estonia
◉ Tallinn

06. Latvia
◉ Riga

07. Lithuania
◉ Vilnius

08. Ireland
◉ Dublin

09. United Kingdom
◉ London

10. Denmark
◉ Copenhagen

11. Belarus
◉ Minsk

12. Netherlands
◉ Amsterdam

13. Belgium
◉ Brussels

14. Luxembourg
◉ Luxembourg City

15. Germany
◉ Berlin

16. Poland
◉ Warsaw

17. Ukraine
◉ Kiev

18. Czechia
◉ Prague

19. Slovakia
◉ Bratislava

20. France
◉ Paris

21. Switzerland
◉ Berne

22. Austria
◉ Vienna

23. Hungary
◉ Budapest

24. Romania
◉ Bucharest

25. Slovenia
◉ Ljubljana

26. Croatia
◉ Zagreb

27. Bosnia
◉ Sarajevo

28. Serbia
◉ Belgrade

29. Bulgaria
◉ Sofia

30. Portugal
◉ Lisbon

31. Spain
◉ Madrid

32. Italy
◉ Rome

33. Macedonia
◉ Skopje

34. Albania
◉ Tirana

35. Greece
◉ Athens

36. Russia
◉ Moscow

[◉ = capital]